POWELL RIVER
100
THE LARGEST SINGLE SITE NEWSPRINT MANUFACTURER IN THE WORLD
Barbara Ann Lambert, Editor

1945 Powell River Company mill and Townsite
Alice Johnson (Dice) on rock. Photo: Jack Dice
1995 Powell River Townsite declared
National Historic District of Canada

Front Cover: Rodmay Hotel 1910-2010, Powell River Townsite   Photo: B.A. Lambert 2009

Back Cover: Old Lambert Farm (from 1923), Paradise Valley   Painting: Joanne Clark 2008

Order this book online at www.trafford.com
or email orders@trafford.com

Most Trafford titles are also available at major online book retailers.

Note for Librarians: A cataloguing record for this book is available from
Library and Archives Canada at www.collectionscanada.ca/amicus/index-e.html

ISBN: 978-1-4269-0547-6 (sc)
ISBN: 978-1-4269-0548-3 (e-book)

We at Trafford believe that it is the responsibility of us all, as both individuals and corporations, to make choices that are environmentally and socially sound. You, in turn, are supporting this responsible conduct each time you purchase a Trafford book, or make use of our publishing services. To find out how you are helping, please visit www.trafford.com/responsiblepublishing.html

Our mission is to efficiently provide the world's finest, most comprehensive book publishing service, enabling every author to experience success. To find out how to publish your book, your way, and have it available worldwide, visit us online at www.trafford.com

Trafford rev. 9/16/2009

www.trafford.com

North America & international
toll-free: 1 888 232 4444 (USA & Canada)
phone: 250 383 6864   fax: 812 355 4082

Mayor Stewart Alsgard and Elder Elsie Paul. Spirit Pole tour – North American Indigenous Games, Willingdon Beach, Powell River, B.C. May 6, 2008.   Photo B.A. Lambert

May 9, 1971 Queen Elizabeth II, Prince Phillip, and Princess Anne attended a service at St. John's Westview United Church, Powell River. Rev. Roy Rogers led the ecumenical service.
Photo: Private collection

Tla'Amin First Nations 1918 Easter Sunday after a fire had swept through their village.
(L to R) #2 Johnson Johnny/#3 Bill Williams/#5 Basil Nicholson (teacher & government agent)/
#9 Joe Galligos/#12 Father Brabander of Sechelt/#13 Captain Timothy
Photographer: Rod LeMay   Photo: Courtesy of the Powell River Museum

Display of cedar baskets of the Tla'Amin (Sliammon) First Nations at Spirit Pole tour –
North American Indigenous Games May 6, 2008, Willingdon Beach, Powell River, B.C.
Photo: B.A. Lambert

A Tribute to Tla'Amin (Sliammon) First Nations

For thousands of years Tla'Amin First Nations have lived in the Powell River area. Their traditional territory included: the coast of Malaspina Strait, Okeover Inlet, Desolation Sound, the Powell River Townsite, and a number of islands (including Harwood and Myrtle Rocks). There were summer camps along the coast: Grief Point, Westview, Myrtle Rocks, Palm Beach, and others. A large winter village, Tees Kwat (Big River) was located in the present Townsite, near the mouth of the river; here was the best fishing. Powell Lake was used by First Nations to reach Jervis Inlet for fishing and hunting. First, they travelled by canoe to the Head of the Lake, then they portaged the rest of the way.

Canada World Youth Student – Heather (2001)

"Long before anyone heard of Mr. Isaac Powell, the Sliammon people inhabited the land which is now home to the Townsite residents. It was also a winter home for the Homalco and Klanoose tribes.

The Sliammon had used the entire Powell River area. Travelling in different types of dugout canoes, the Sliammon explored the immediate areas around Powell River. Their knowledge of the country was crucial in the acquisition of foods and sustaining their way of life."

Prior to the colonization of Canada by the British Empire, **First Nations had their own economic system which had supported them for over 10,000 years. They were skilled traders, hunters, and fisherman – successfully living off the land and sea. First Nations had sophisticated cultures and well-established territories.**

On initial contact with Europeans, half of the First Nations population died of disease. The newcomers imposed their own laws and traditions. In the 1880s, First Nations were confined on small Indian Reserves – losing vital traditional territory which supplied food from the ocean, foreshore, and land.

The laws and policies of the Federal Government of Canada created the Residential School system. This system was designed to destroy the rich culture and traditions of First Nations. Children were forced to speak English and punished for speaking their own language.

Sliammon children (Grades 1-7), from the early 1900s, were taught at a one-room school in Sliammon by Mr. Basil Nicholson, who was born in England and had served overseas in WWI with the Canadian Expeditionary Forces. Basil and Norah Nicholson lived at the teacherage, on the reserve, with their three sons: Felix, Basil, and Wilfred. Mr. Nicholson was the Government Agent and Mrs. Nicholson (a field nurse in WWI) looked after the reserve infirmary.

Sliammon Secondary students attended St. Augustine's residential school in Sechelt. St. Augustine's was demolished in 1975.

In 1960 the Sliammon School was closed. From this date, students at Sliammon were either bussed locally to Assumption Catholic School in Westview or James Thomson Elementary in Wildwood. Secondary students attended Brooks and Max Cameron schools. In 1974 Sliammon Chi-Chuy preschool and kindergarten were opened. The school programme taught the importance of traditional values and the Coast Salish language, Kla ah men.

Bessie Banham (Miller), Wildwood (1960)

"The Sliammon branch of the Coast Salish First Nations held exclusive hunting and food gathering rights in the Cranberry Lake area. The lush berries, which gave the lake its name, grew in profusion on the low, marshy flats bordering the lake, and were eagerly gathered by the women. To preserve them for winter food, they were mashed and boiled, then dried in the shallow cedar trays in the sun. Served with salmon oil, after soaking the sheets in water, they made a delectable dish."

Mary Masales (Powell), Southview (2002)

"The men at Sliammon used dugout canoes and brought in large quantities of salmon. Clams were collected in large gunny sacks. Rakes were used to get the cockles under the sand.

We used to see the women searching, by the washed out areas of Sliammon Creek, for the fine, long cedar roots. Some were peeled and dyed with berry juice. The roots were made into baskets.

We walked down the beach trail (from Southview) to visit with the Nicholson family at Sliammon. Mrs. Nicholson was the nurse at Sliammon."

Tla'Amin First Nations are presently negotiating a final treaty with both levels of government (Federal and Provincial).

In 2003 an Accord between the City of Powell River and Tla'Amin First Nations was signed.

**This book is dedicated to my late husband Stuart Lambert,
my daughter Ann Bonkowski,
and my sister Joyce Stapleton.**

Tom & Gertie Lambert *with Stuart and baby Russell.*
Cortez Island 1920   Photo: Gertie Lambert collection
Pioneer West Coast Family: Cortez Island (1907-1916)
Powell River Townsite (1916-1918), Cortez Island (1918-1923),
Paradise Valley, Powell River (from 1923)

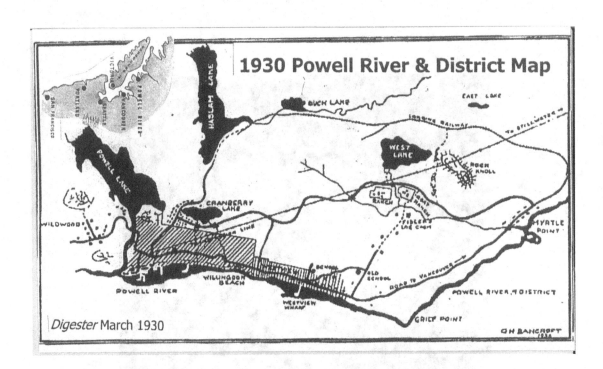

Digester March 1930

Acknowledgements

My thanks to: Frank Haslam, Roy Leibenschel, Ina Lloyd, and all the old-timers for sharing their memories and photographs.

My thanks to: Teedie Kagume at the Powell River Museum for her patience, support, and good humour. My appreciation goes to the Powell River Museum & Archives Association for the use of their archives, photographs, and taped recordings of old-timers.

My thanks to: Glacier Ventures for permission to publish items from the *Powell River News* and *Town Crier*.

My thanks to: my daughter, Ann Bonkowski, for her support and technical assistance.

My thanks to Joyce Stapleton for help in proofreading.

POWELL RIVER MILL 1910-2010

1910-1959 Powell River Company built the mill and created the company Townsite.

- 1912 #1 and #2 paper machines in production – **first newsprint in Canada, west of Ontario.**
- 1930 – 1,300 mill employees, 680 working on construction - mill payroll - $2,256,437.00
- 1947 – 1,700 mill employees - $5 million payroll
- 1948 - #8 machine in production
- 1955 - Powell River Company sold off the Townsite.
- 1955 – Corporation of the District of Powell River formed from the Townsite, Cranberry & Westview Villages, and Wildwood District.
- **1957 - #9 paper machine in production - Powell River mill largest single unit producer of newsprint in the world.**

- 1959 - Powell River Company merged with MacMillan Bloedel – known as **MacMillan Bloedel & Powell River Ltd.**

- 1964 – Company known as **MacMillan Bloedel Ltd.**
- 1969 - #10 machine in production.
- 1971 - #1 and #2 machines shut down.
- **1973 – 2,500 employees – mill at its peak.**
- 1976 - #3 and #4 machines shut down.
- 1981 - #11 machine in production.

- 1981 – **Noranda of Toronto** acquired controlling interest in MacMillan Bloedel Ltd.
- 1982-93 - #5-#8 machines shut down – job losses of 700 employees
- 1993 – 1,300 mill employees

- 1998 – **Pacifica Papers Inc.** purchased **MB Paper Ltd.** (this transaction included the Powell River and Port Alberni paper mills from MacMillan Bloedel Ltd.)

- 2001 – **Norske Skog Canada Ltd.** acquired Pacifica Papers Ltd., name changed to **Norske Canada**.

- 2005 – name change to **Catalyst Paper**.
- 2009 – reduction of 127 positions at the Powell River Division, loss of $12 million in wages to the community.
- 2010 – mill employees 350 – three machines in operation.

Contents

REFLECTIONS

Editor's Note: The majority of old-time stories are from interviews by Barbara Ann Lambert from 1998-2009. These stories are copyrighted.

* Stories contributed
** Material researched from the Powell River Museum and Archives

Stella Saunders with the Potter family, celebrating her birthday (93) with a visit to the Patricia Theatre, Townsite,
Powell River in 2007. Going to the show at the Patricia Theatre was the #1 choice of family entertainment for the
Townsite and villages before television came to Powell River in the 1950s.
Photo: Stella Saunders collection

From 1934, 120 Ocean View, Powell River Townsite, was rented by William and Elizabeth Graham. The Powell
River Company town was designed on the English Garden City concept. Today this building is the Granada
restaurant.   Photo: Ena McKenzie (Graham) 1935

Provincial building (1939-1980) Powell River Townsite. All provincial government services were located here (including the government agent, courtroom and jail cells) until 1980 when they were transferred to Westview, the fastest-growing area in the Municipality of Powell River.
Photo: Ann Bonkowski 2008

The Postmaster's house (opposite the Patricia Theatre) built in the Craftsman style in 1912 and rented by the first two postmasters, Reginald Lane and Robert Banham. Photo: B.A. Lambert 2008

The Powell River pulp and paper mill – The Economic Hub of a Company Town, surrounding villages and districts (from 1910)

Barbara Ann Lambert

In 1955 the Townsite, Cranberry Village, Westview Village, and Wildwood District were incorporated into the Corporation of Powell River. The same year, the Powell River Company went out of "the Townsite business", selling off the company houses and lots to their employees.

THE POWELL RIVER TOWNSITE 1910-1955

It was **Dr. Dwight F. Brooks** and **Michael J. Scanlon** who planned the development of the area near Powell Lake as the first pulp and newsprint mill to be built west of the Great Lakes. With hydro-electricity from the lake, the potential for the site was far-reaching.

The Powell River Company was formed in 1910. In 1911 the pulp mill was under construction; in 1912 #1 and #2 machines were in operation. Three decades later, in 1941, when **Russell Cooper** was appointed General Superintendent **the Powell River Company paper mill was the largest single unit pulp and paper mill in the world**. In 1947 there were 1,700 employees in the Powell River mill with a $5 million payroll and a plant area of 800 acres.

Powell River's First Fifty Years 1910-1960:

Powell River... from its inception had been mainly **the story of the beginning and the expansion of a one single-industrial enterprise upon which the economic fortunes of the area have depended**.
 The lack, for many years, of road connection with the giant city (Vancouver) 70 miles away, has had its advantages.
 Particularly in sports did Powell River obtain pre-eminence, producing from a centre of 3-4000 people, championship track-and-field athletes, and football, baseball and lacrosse teams which defeated the best that the heavily populated centres could produce.
 Music and drama had their triumphal days too, and the Powell River Pipe Band became provincially, then nationally, and internationally famous.

Harry Taylor

The Powell River Company created the Townsite: Craftsman style houses, schools, and recreational facilities in an isolated area north of Vancouver on the British Columbia coast. It was built on the philosophy of the English **Garden City Movement**

– creating a town with all the amenities which gave the workforce a pleasant place in which to live: the magnificent Dwight Hall to host community events – plays, concerts, dances, etc.; the Patricia Theatre for the latest films; the Powell River hotel for meals and drinks in the pub; a "modern" hospital; and three churches (United, Anglican and Catholic). Recreational facilities included: the Rodmay sports ground (for baseball games), golf course, bowling green, tennis courts, and parks. Everything was designed to be in walking distance of the home and mill.

Frontier towns, with single men, were known to be wild with drinking, gambling, brawls, and "loose" women! The Powell River Company wanted none of that!

The Company designed a **model community**: in 1910 the construction crew (mainly Italians) with shovels, pick forks, and hammers started putting together the "nuts and bolts" of a frontier town. In those early years of construction **Powell River (the Townsite) was a tent city**. **Rod LeMay**, an outstanding photographer was here – also living in a tent. Amazing panoramic shots of an emerging Townsite are his legacy for Powell River.

From 1919-26 **Jack Cossarin**, an Italian with an interest in photography, worked with the construction crew and lived in **Riverside**. He photographed everyday life in Riverside. His photographs are a unique record of Powell River's Italian-Canadian community – a community that put down roots and enriched the town's heritage, a community in 2010 celebrating 100 years of cultural heritage in Powell River.

Frank Haslam (age 104) (09/2008)
"I remember coming to the Townsite (1911) with my family from Bolton, England when I was only 7 years old. I soon lost my Lancashire accent as the town was mainly made up of Americans. There were English and Scottish families living there too. Italians lived at Riverside.
Baseball was the big game in town. I was the best player at that time – I could have gone professional if I'd agreed to leave Powell River. We played against teams from Sliammon: Joe, Alec, Willy, and Peter Galligos from Sliammon were great players."

Housing

Large attractive homes, with ocean view, were constructed for mill management – known as "Bosses' Row"; one of these big houses was the Company guest house.

Graeme Cooper (2002) - Russell Cooper (father) was General Superintendent 1941-47, resident General Manager and Vice-President of Operations 1947-62.

"A large house was provided by the Powell River Company in 1941 when the Coopers moved to the West Coast. **Powell River was a model community of**

company-owned residences. The General Manager's family occupied a home overlooking the mill, and situated very near the company guest house, whose staff consisted of a cook and his wife, reported to the manager's wife. The manager's house was also equipped with servant's quarters.

Professionals resided in a specific area, merchants in another, and everyone in town rented from the Powell River Company. The houses were maintained by a permanent paint crew, electricians, masons, and carpenters, all company employees. Those who chose not to rent but preferred, instead, to be homeowners, built or bought in Westview, Cranberry, or Wildwood."

The size and location of other homes reflected the status of employees in the mill. Mainly American, English, Scottish, and Canadian-born Caucasians lived in the main area of the Townsite, while European Nationals lived across the river in Riverside. A move to a senior position in the mill resulted in a corresponding move to a bigger house, and a better location in the Townsite.

The building program started in 1911 with 21 houses; the first house to be built was that of **Dr. Andrew Henderson** (2008 – purchased by the Townsite Historical Society). The Haslam family were the third family to arrive in the Townsite and they lived on Maple Avenue.

In 1925 there was a big plant expansion, with it came a large building program; 114 new houses were built on Maple Avenue and Ocean View. The majority of Townsite houses were built by 1930; in 1937 there were 401 houses in the Townsite and 2 apartment blocks with 32 suites; while in 1941 Townsite houses increased to 450. In 1955 there were 500+ Townsite houses to be sold off by the company.

Bev Falconer (Carrick) 2002 (from 1937 Townsite resident)
"Almost everyone who worked in the mill wanted to live in one of the well-maintained Townsite houses – and the price was right; the monthly rent was $4-$5 per room plus $2 if you had a view. However, newcomers like us, had to put their names on a waiting list."

During the Great Depression the Powell River Company pro-rated rents to the shortened work week of three or four days.

After WWII the Powell River Company generously gave 10 acres of orchard land (near Cranberry fire hall) for the site of veterans' homes – to be built by the Veteran's Association and purchased by the vets. The Company built rental accommodation – duplexes on Willow Avenue in the Townsite for returning servicemen. It soon became known as Storks' Alley with the arrival of the baby boomers!

Riverside 1912-1955

In 1912, 11 houses were built at Riverside. They were lived in by groups of single men who "batched" on their own. In 1914 Riverside was known as **Balkan Village**. It was occupied by European Nationals – mainly Russian Cossacks.

According to Arthur C. Dunn in "An Old-Timer Looks Back", *First Fifty Year Book*, the Russians were...

"big men and wonderful workers. We had them on the wharf much of the time to load ships. They left one Sunday night on the old *Charmer*, en route to Russia to take their places in the army. As the boat pulled out they sang songs in their own language as a farewell to Powell River. None of them ever came back, as far as I know."

Construction workers and families (mainly Europeans) were placed in bunkhouses and houses at Riverside. Riverside was by the side of the river and was reached by a bridge. It was close to the dam. **Riverside became "home" to the early Italian community** (known as the first wave – the second wave came to Powell River after WWII).

Fides Prissinotti (Brandolini) 2007

Fides came directly to the Powell River Townsite from Italy, with her parents **Ottavio and Erminea Brandolini** in 1920 at the age of 4. Fides' aunt and uncle, **Mina and Fortunato Bressenutti**, pioneer Townsite residents, arrived in 1910; they lived on Maple Avenue.

"Lots of bachelors here (1920s) – they were all out here without their wives. Lots went back in the early 1930s. Lots brought wives and girlfriends over here, on the boat, and got married over here. Some left permanently. **Some families lived in Riverside, some lived in Wildwood, not very many Cranberry, and, of course, Westview wasn't here yet!**
We had an icebox at **Riverside**. We moved into one of the new houses (1920s) – no insulation – just heated with the woodstove in the kitchen. We had electricity and an indoor toilet.
We started the **Italian Club (1924)**. We had lots of dances in Dwight Hall (from 1928). We depended on each other for entertainment – what we did didn't cost us any money. There were few weddings – I can't remember any – not many girls."

In the late 1920s, 80 **Hungarians** – mainly bachelors who were hired as casual labour for the installation of #7 machine, lived in **Riverside**. The majority left after the job was completed but a few stayed, including **Lazlo (Leon) Kovacs** and **Joseph**

Kolezar. In 1929, before moving to Cranberry in 1930, **Leon and Suzanna Kovacs** lived at **Riverside**, sharing a house with other immigrants.

From 1935-42 the **Silvestrini family** lived in Riverside. Jim Silvestrini recalls the house as being very damp; every time the dam gates were opened to lower the lake level, a thick cold mist permeated over the area.

Martin Rossander – 2008 (born 1917 Broadacres, Saskatchewan)
"I came to Powell River in 1948 on the *Gulf Wing*, my fare was paid by the Powell River Company. First I lived in the bunkhouses at the east side of **Riverside**. They were cold, drafty, and uninspiring.
I was at the bottom of the social structure, living at **Riverside and working in the labour gang. Within the mill itself was a social structure.**"

Mildred Ross (Dice) – 2007
Mildred was born in the Townsite in 1922. Her father, **Sam Dice** came to work as an electrician for the Powell River Company in 1918. Her mother **Eva Dice (Small)** came to work as a waitress at the Rodmay Hotel in 1919. The Dice family rented a house on Marine Avenue, next to the staff quarters (opposite present-day Granada restaurant). In 1946 Mildred married **Alec Ross**. First they rented a house in Westview at $18 a month, then they rented a company house at **Riverside** from 1949-51 at $12 a month.

"**The Riverside, Powell River Company houses**, were built near the river (Powell river); they were accessed by a bridge across the river. **Italians lived in Riverside, but there were also a few Quebecers.** The houses had no insulation, and the winter of 1950 was very cold. On the dam side of the houses, icicles formed, hanging off the roofs. We had an oil stove going in the kitchen and one going in the living room all winter. Some residents at Riverside closed off the bedrooms and lived by the stoves in the main rooms."

In 1955 the Riverside Oval was permanently closed.

In 1957 the Forest Faculty of Sopron University of Hungary, after the Hungarian uprising, brought its entire faculty to live in temporary housing at **Riverside**.

In 1957 the Riverside houses were sold off for lumber. The Municipality refused to have the houses moved to the villages, as "they were old and depreciated". The Riverside bunkhouses were moved to Timberlane.

Rainbow Lodge – Powell Lake

Company guests were taken up to Rainbow Lodge on Powell Lake by **Jack Wilson** in his boat, *Erin Go Brau*. Guests fished and hunted. The Company made business deals in the relaxing environment of Rainbow Lodge.

> *"Today Rainbow Lodge is known to hundreds of publishers and their friends in many widely extended areas of the world."*
>
> The Powell River Digester (September-October 1954)

Agnes Silvester – 2002

"Rainbow Lodge was a busy place and guests of the company either flew to Powell River from Vancouver or came up to Powell River on the *Princess Mary*. Food was flown in from Vancouver, and sometimes, even the cook! In later years, guests came in by helicopter."

The Company Store

The Company store is at the heart of a company town. Remember the 1960s song, "I owe my soul to the company store?" In a company town there is no commercial competition – there is only one place to shop – the company store. Purchases were either paid in cash or made through coupon books, and debited against mill pay cheques. Prices at a company store were always higher than other retail outlets. Powell River Company built its own company store in 1911; the lower floor was the store, with a dance hall and offices on the second floor. All the store employees were paid by the company. In 1919 the Head Grocery clerk and the butcher were paid $125 a month while Grocery Clerk #4 earned $40 a month.

Frank Haslam – 2006

"My sister Minnie worked in the company store. She worked her way up from shop assistant, to taking delivery orders, to work in the office. At the counter each assistant put the cash in a cup, and this went by cable to the office. The money was taken out and the change sent back to the assistant."

In 1923 the Powell River Company bought out the **Sing Lee building** and renamed it the Brooklon Building (a combination of Brooks and Scanlon). They put in their own dry goods department and rented out the remainder of the space.

George Goddard was pharmacist at the Company Store from 1926-65. He had girls to work for him in the pharmacy who were bilingual, speaking Italian and English.

The Powell River Company expected their employees to show their loyalty by shopping at the company store. Jack Pearson, an employee of the company living in

Edgehill, received a letter from the Powell River Company encouraging **all** employees to shop at the company store.

Merve Wilkinson – 2002 – (worked for the Powell River Company in the early 1930s)
"I saw one man's cheque for two weeks of work. He only got 20 cents; the rest of his pay had been taken to clear his slate at the company store.
Everything was expensive at the company store – about 30-40% over Woodward's and Eaton's. The company could not prevent any employee from buying through the catalogues, as the goods came in at the government wharf as opposed to the company wharf. The company used a tactical way of getting employees to shop exclusively at the company store; those who were regular shoppers (and spenders) were given promotions in the mill!"

Ingrid Cowie (Andersen) 2002 Wildwood resident
"The goods at the company store were far more expensive than the same goods available from the catalogue. One time a big shot was up from Vancouver and he was surprised to see a mountain of goods on the dock. He said to the company manager, "What's the meaning of this?" "Well," replied the manager, "the families seem to think they can get cheaper goods from Vancouver." "It's up to you to see they don't!" was the terse reply. After that, the Company store lowered its prices and changed to Cash-and-Carry (this cut down on staff)."

Patricia Theatre

Everyone went to the movie theatre – this included folks living in the villages and those living north and south of town, at Lund and Stillwater. **It was the place of entertainment for an entire community.** The first movies were shown in a tent, while the first theatre was built in 1913 where the present cenotaph is located. It was named in a contest by Mrs. A. Oliver, in honour of the daughter of the Governor General of Canada, the Duke of Connaught. Her prize was 100 theatre passes! Silent movies were shown here until 1928; the building was then demolished. In November of 1928 the present Patricia Theatre was opened.

Al Hamerton's father, **Ernie Hamerton**, started working as a part-time projectionist in the first Patricia Theatre. The movies were black-and-white and were silent, with Stan Meade, and later Glen Hayden, playing the piano. Children sat at the front of the theatre and adults at the back. **Frank Haslam,** as a young boy, worked in the theatre cleaning the floor after the patrons left. His pay was a free pass to all the movies. As a baby, Al Hamerton was wheeled into the Patricia Theatre, in a perambulator, by his mother **Lucy Hamerton (Donkersley)**. Ernie became a full-time projectionist at the new Patricia Theatre. The first talkies came in 1930 – the first talkie was *Chasing Rainbows*.

Victor Poole came to Powell River as a child in 1922 and lived for a year in a tent at Willingdon Beach. Victor went at least once a week to the first Patricia Theatre. According to Victor the building of the second Patricia Theatre was "a marvel of the age and time".

From 1928 until the early 1970s, First Nations attending the Patricia Theatre were designated to sit in the balcony:

Graeme Cooper (2002)
"First Nations from Sliammon were forbidden to sit in the orchestra section of the Patricia Theatre and instead, were directed to the upstairs balcony where they were able to see the film."

On the 14th of March, 1932 the Patricia Theatre safe was blown by the notorious criminals **Bagley and Fawcett**. The story rivalled that of any movie shown.

Old-timers remember **Josie Mitchell** working in the sweet shop at the theatre during WWII. Coupons were required for the scarce delivery of chocolate bars.

Bessie Banham was at the theatre when, on a rare occasion, the famous **Billy-Goat Smith** attended. Everyone stood up and clapped!

Dwight Hall

Imposing Dwight Hall was built in 1927, near the mill, at company expense of $125,000. It was the largest recreation hall on the West Coast. It was here that plays, musicals, presentations, and balls were held. The Company was generous to those who missed a shift (while they participated in various cultural activities); they paid their wages.

The celebration of New Year, a Scottish tradition, became the main major event in the Townsite because the majority of employees (single men) left Powell River to enjoy Christmas in Vancouver.

The Company's Social Committee organized two outstanding Yuletide events: the Kiddie's Christmas Tree (before Christmas), and the Papermakers' Ball which was held on New Year's Eve.

All the children, under the age of 9, in the Townsite and surrounding areas were invited to the Christmas Tree event. Old-timers such as Frank Haslam (Townsite), Stuart Lambert (Paradise Valley), and Ina Lloyd (Stillwater) remember receiving gifts. This practice stopped in 1932 with the Great Depression.

In 1928, the New Year's Eve Papermakers' Ball was held in the newly-built Dwight Hall (1911-1927 – this event had been held in Central Hall). Electric lights were used, for the first time, to decorate the spacious hall. Chinese lanterns were strung around the walls with clusters of coloured lights. A large orchestra, of mainly local talent, played until 5 a.m.

It was not unusual for the Company, at its own expense, to bring in an orchestra from Vancouver. The magnificent bands and the expertise of the dancers drew many out-of-town guests. The Company's pipe band (formed in 1931) made their first public appearance at the 1939 Papermakers' New Year's Eve Ball; they looked splendid in their new MacGregor tartans.

A core of Old Time Dancers, under the tuition of Mrs. Alexander, led the Scottish dances. In 1933 the Old Time Dance Club had 170 members, in the 1940s it grew to 270. Old time dancing was the rage in the Townsite.

The Papermakers, professionals in the Townsite (doctors and teachers), and Company guests attended this magnificent affair. Ladies were dressed in the latest fashion – wives and daughters of mill management bought expensive dresses at Madame Loukes 5th Avenue Dress Shop in Westview. **The Papermakers' Ball was the highlight of the social year in the Powell River Company Townsite.**

The Powell River Hotel (the Rodmay)

Andrew and Barbara McKinney were the owners of the first Powell River hotel. Andrew McKinney was a distant relative of the Brooks family and had been invited to build a hotel near the mill site. It was in 1910 that Andrew McKinney was given a 100-year lease of a site close to the mill. He started to build the Powell River hotel that year, and in 1911 it was in operation. Chinese cooks and staff worked at that hotel and lived in the basement. Off duty, they gambled, played mah-jong and poker; it was rumoured one cook was killed in a poker fight. Today, his ghost haunts the present Rodmay Hotel!

Gertie Lambert (Mundigel), niece of the McKinneys, recalled the tales of opening night when drinks were on the house and construction workers danced in hob-nailed boots on the brand new billiard tables. Gertie was bridesmaid to her cousin Catherine McKinney. It was the first wedding to be held in the first Catholic Church in the Townsite.

In 1917 the McKinneys sold the lease to **Rod and May MacIntyre**. Andrew McKinney sold the hotel, at this time, as he was concerned the profits would go down during prohibition. It was Battleman MacIntyre that suggested his parents should call the hotel, "**The Rodmay**". Elisa Silvestrini worked at the Rodmay as head housekeeper in the late 1930s and 40s. In 1957 Al Mantoani bought the hotel.

Townsite Schools

In 1911, the Townsite was a tent city and the first one-room school was held for five months in the poolroom! The company designated a lot for a school building (present site of the Anglican Church); the school was quickly built and was ready for opening on September 1, 1911. Two teachers enrolled 53 students in the 1911-12 school year in the growing Townsite.

Frank Haslam (2000)

"I attended the second school in the Townsite with my sister Minnie. I remember a room upstairs for the bigger children and a basement for the smaller children. Mr. Buckton was the principal.

I transferred with all the other children to the first Henderson school (now a playground) when it opened in 1913. Children from Wildwood also attended Henderson School. They had to cross the river in rowboats until a bridge was built in 1916. In 1923 they transferred to a new school in Wildwood.

Tommy Alsworth was principal at the first Henderson school, until he joined up to fight in WWI. Miss Stevens became principal and, when he came back from France, he married her!

The games we played were Anti-Anti-I-Over (throwing a ball over the roof of the school house), marbles, nobbies (like lacrosse), and "scrub" football."

Henderson School was named after **Dr. Henderson, School Trustee**. Rapid expansion continued at the "old" Henderson school, opening with three classrooms in 1913 to an eight-room standard building in 1922.

In 1926 **Brooks Elementary** (named after **Dr. Dwight Brooks – first President of the Powell River Company**) was opened to cope with the overcrowding at the "old" Henderson school. It was constructed with eight classrooms and was built as a "model of excellence and beauty in school architecture".

In 1930, single grade senior high school classes were enrolled in Brooks. Thus, Brooks enrolled students from elementary level to high school level in one building. In 1930, a three-year technical course for male students was started. The Powell River Company and the educational authorities designed the course to fill the Company's requirement for skilled employees. Stuart Lambert graduated from the technical program in 1933; however, he was refused work at the Powell River mill. He was blacklisted because his father was a founder member of the CCF in Powell River.

In September 1936 **Brooks was designated a senior high school for Powell River and District**. The old system of one teacher teaching all subjects to a single grade was abolished. In 1950 a brand new gymnasium was built for Brooks.

In 1936 "old" Henderson school was designated as an elementary school for all Townsite students. In 1957 it was closed and demolished; the vacant lot became a playground. "New" Henderson was opened in 1957, nearer to Brooks school.

In 1937 Lang Bay School united with Annie Bay and Kelly Creek School into **Stillwater United School**. Amalgamating three one-room schools into a two-room school, in a new location, was a "revolutionary idea". **The Powell River Company donated the land for the building and provided electricity and running water.** Stillwater United was designated as a Superior school by the Department of Education, in order that rural students would be able to graduate from their own area.

A high school education was available to all students living in the Townsite and surrounding rural areas. New immigrants (including Italians) encouraged their children to make the most of this opportunity; many second generation and third generation Powell River students became professionals, business owners, or obtained managerial positions in the mill.

Townsite Churches

Churches were a cornerstone of a planned community. They brought stability in a frontier town and upheld moral values – as opposed to wild frontier towns with saloons and brothels. Some company towns had no church, some only one (designated by the owner); while in the Townsite there were three churches.

In 1911 the first church to be built was a low flat-roofed building for those of the **Roman Catholic** faith. In 1916 this building, not big enough for its congregation, was razed and St. Joseph's Catholic Church built on the same site. Since 1900 there had been a Roman Catholic Church at Sliammon.

In 1913 **St. John's Protestant Church** was built for those of the Protestant faith. In 1920 the **Anglicans** left St. John's and had their own church building. St. John's became known as St. John's Union Church (Canada's first "United" church). Churches of other denominations sprang up in the villages.

Dr. Henderson – Tent Hospital

Dr. Andrew Henderson from St. Paul, Minnesota, came in 1909 to check out the area. He came back again in 1910 as doctor for the Powell River Company; his job, at that time, was looking after construction workers. He set up a tent hospital (present site of the old Provincial Building) which consisted of a ward that could accommodate 11 patients, operating facilities, nursing quarters, a kitchen, and storehouse. On September 11, 1913 St. Luke's Hospital was opened; 10 years later, a big addition was made onto the original hospital. The first medical plan in B.C. was devised by Dr. Henderson.

During serious epidemics, patients were sent to the **Pest hospital**, a small house situated in the Company orchard on Lot 450 (near the Fire Hall, Cranberry). Ma and Pa Buttery looked after the patients.

Looking Back! 1916 Powell River Company Wage Schedule

From Chambermaids to Pipefitters:
The Powell River Company paid wages for all employees in the Townsite.

The Powell River Company created not only a mill, but a town. Everyone worked for the company. According to the 1916 Powell River Company Limited comparative wage schedule, employees included: the dock crew, ground wood mill, sulphite mill, paper mill, steam plant, electrical department, repair department, lumber yard, tram line, barn, boarding house, and departmental store. The entire town was on the company payroll.

Mill employees worked six days a week from 8 a.m. Monday to 8 a.m. Sunday.

"Employees not required or permitted to do any unnecessary work from 8 a.m. Sunday to 8 a.m. Monday. Time and one-half paid for necessary work done on Sundays."

The rates for papermakers were based on the following five mills: Spanish River Pulp and Paper Company, Great Northern Paper Company, Minnesota and Ontario Power Company, Ontario Paper Company, and St. Croix Paper Company.

1916 Agreement

Paper Mill Employees:
Boss Machine Tender: $175.00 a month
Machine Tender   48 cents an hour, $3.84 for 8-hour shift
Oilers   34 cents an hour, $2.72 for 8-hour shift
Cleaner   25 cents an hour, $2.50 for a 10-hour shift

Steam plant:
Engineers $120.00 a month

Electrical Department:
Head Operator $3.80 for 8-hour shift
Electricians   35 cents an hour, $3.50 for 10-hour shift

Repair Department:
Foreman Machinist 50 cents an hour, $5.00 for 10-hour shift
Blacksmith   40 cents an hour, $4.00 for 10-hour shift

Pipe Fitter	40 cents an hour, $4.00 for 10-hour shift
Millwright	40 cents an hour, $4.00 for 10-hour shift

Construction Department:

Carpenter Foreman	52 cents an hour, $5.20 for 10-hour shift
Tinsmith	37 cents an hour, $3.75 for 10-hour shift
Painters	30 cents an hour, $3.00 for 10-hour shift
Powder Man	25 cents an hour, $2.50 for 10-hour shift

Barn:

Foreman	$80.00 a month
Teamsters	25 cents an hour, $2.50 for 10-hour shift

Tramline:

Engineer	40 cents an hour, $4.00 for 10-hour shift
Signalman	35 cents an hour, $3.50 for 10-hour shift
Switchman	30 cents an hour, $3.00 for 10-hour shift

Watchmen:	25 cents an hour, $3.00 for 12-hour shift
Janitor	$75.00 a month
Gardener	$80.00 a month

1919 Agreement Monthly Men – General

Orchard Man	$115.00 a month
Fire Chief	$150.00 a month
Fire Hall truck driver	$130.00 a month

Boarding House:

Manager	$190.00 a month
Cook	$125.00 a month
Kitchen Help	$100.00 a month
Waitresses	$80.00 a month
Chambermaid	$75.00 a month

Department Store:

Head Grocery Clerk	$125.00 a month
Grocery Clerk #4	$40.00 a month
Furnishings	$150.00 a month
Dry Goods	$70.00 a month
Butcher	$125.00 a month

Causes for discharge:

Bringing intoxicants onto mill premises – smoking – sleeping on duty – incompetence – inefficiency – taking bribes to retain or procure a position – destruction or removal of company property – seditious utterances – neglect of duty – immoral or improper behaviour.

ECONOMIC GROWTH IN THE VILLAGES OF CRANBERRY, WESTVIEW, AND WILDWOOD DISTRICT

Powell River's First Fifty Years:
"With each enlargement of the mill, the Townsite branched out with more streets of closely-ranked dwellings; homes reared above the debris in Wildwood, Cranberry, and Westview; roads replaced tortuous trails to knit the four settlements; wharf and harbour development came; business centres grew apace as light, water, telephone, and paving brought comforts to all (1942 Westview and Cranberry achieved village status).

To complete the metamorphosis, the settlements became villages, and then unified to form a Council-ruled Municipality ranking second-to-none in services, roads, and planning."

Limited Townsite rental accommodation results in village growth:

As the mill expanded into world markets, so the Townsite grew. The Powell River Company added more Townsite houses. Houses that were well-built with the best of materials, houses that were built with modern amenities – running water, electricity, sewers. Houses with reasonable rents for the employees – **houses which could never keep up with the demand for rental accommodation from an ever-growing workforce.**

The turnover of Townsite rentals was low – no wonder, as many Townsite families stayed in their comfortable, attractive homes with reasonable rents for decades. **New employee families were on the Townsite accommodation list for years.** Housing was especially critical with the addition of new paper machines – even more so with the boom years of WWII, and the postwar boom in the late 1940s and 50s.

The economic growth of the villages and districts, surrounding the Townsite, was directly connected to the economic growth of the Powell River Company mill. The main reason being, the lack of available rental accommodation in the company town. This forced desperate families to put up tarpaper shacks in areas where there were no services, and only bush trails connecting their district to other areas. Many housewives thought they were living at "the end of the world".

Some folks just wanted to own their **own stump farms** – raise pigs, chickens, cows, gardens, and fruit trees. The Powell River Company did not allow the raising of stock in the Townsite – the only exception being in WWII when each household was allowed to keep 10 chickens; however, no roosters! The best land was in Wildwood; however, there were farms in all other areas.

The majority of male home owners in the outlying villages and districts (including stump farmers) worked for the Powell River Company.

As the villages grew, so did the school population. Elementary schools sprang up to serve their areas. They became the focal point of village community life. Churches sprang up in the villages. They, too, became the centre of village life. Teachers and preachers brought their families to the villages – all adding to population growth in the areas surrounding the Townsite.

Retirees from the Powell River Company also added to the growth of the villages. Retiring from the Powell River Company meant leaving your comfortable Townsite rental accommodation and buying a lot in the surrounding area. Some retirees left the area for the big city of Vancouver, or other points of destination. The majority stayed in the area with a pleasant climate, outstanding recreational beauty – pristine beaches and lakes. They stayed because their children, grandchildren, and great-grandchildren had good paying, steady long-term jobs in the Powell River pulp and paper mill. Powell River has a greater percentage of long-stay residents when compared to other towns in B.C.

The majority of workers in the villages and districts worked in the Powell River mill; however, although encouraged to shop at the Company Store, many shopped in the local village shops and/or ordered through the catalogue from Woodward's in Vancouver. It was more economical to shop at village shops as goods at the Company store were 30-40% higher. Bosa in Cranberry posted the Vancouver ads in his shop and sold goods at the same price.

Villages and Districts became self-contained mini communities. Mainly Italians lived in Wildwood in 1964, building their own hall. Everyone, from all areas walked along the trails from the outlying areas to the movie theatre in the Townsite. In 1935 the Roxy Theatre opened in Westview. However, the magnificent Patricia Theatre, with organ, was the theatre of choice. Students walked – some were bussed to the Townsite – to attend Brooks High School. Brooks High School gave generations of village children an excellent high school education in an isolated area of the province.

Population Growth- rapid growth in the Villages from 1920s

As the populations in the Villages and Districts grew they started to match, then overtake, the Company Town. The Townsite figures remained essentially the same as its growth was limited by Lot 450 (company-owned land) and the limited number of houses (500+) the company was prepared to build and service. The Powell River mill remained the economic hub of the area, providing good paying jobs to the male population in the area; however, the commercial areas grew faster in the villages and eventually dominated the business sector.

Government services, which started in the Townsite, gradually moved into Westview which had the biggest population growth of the villages and districts. Small businesses in Cranberry and the Townsite gradually moved into Westview.

Population Growth in the Townsite, Villages & District

	1921	1931	1961	1971
Townsite	1,657	2,152	1,833	1,705
Cranberry Lake	150	916	2,263	2,320
Westview (Michigan Heights)	47	1,111	5,504	8,355
*Michigan Landing	73			
Wildwood	212	546	1,130	1,345

Statistics Canada, Census of Canada figures from
An Economic Base Study of the Powell River Region by Karen R. Boyer

*Michigan Landing (Willingdon Beach) families lived year-round in tents and cabins on Company-leased land. In 1926 the Powell River Company terminated the leases. Some owners moved their cabins to other areas of Westview.

Farming in the Townsite, Villages, and Districts

In the early Townsite years, Joe Errico, an Italian, leased land (where the present-day tennis courts are located) from the Powell River Company for market gardening. Joe, with the help of a young **Frank Haslam**, sold vegetables door-to-door to Townsite residents. He kept two cows and became the first dairy farmer.

Later on, the **Powell River Company ran a company orchard and chicken farm on Lot 450** (near the present-day Cranberry Fire Hall). The orchard man, Bill (Pa) Buttery, was on the company payroll; in 1919 he earned $115 a month. In 1925, due to the heavy overheads running the orchard and chicken runs, the company leased the management of the farm to Frank Radford for $30 a month. The orchard produced a variety of fruits, frying chickens and eggs – these products went to the Company Store.

Looking back, it is hard to believe, **in 1938, there were 22 dairies in the Powell River area:**

Westview Dairy, DeGroot's Dairy, Erickson's Dairy, Skinner's Dairy, Melville's Dairy, Jean Pitton's Dairy, Springbrook Dairy, Adey's Dairy,

McMahon's Dairy, McIntosh Dairy, Culos Dairy, Beattie's Dairy, and 10 others known as "1 cow dairies".

In 1946 Joe Dorval's Tip Top Dairy had a pasteurization plant and central distribution system on Marine Avenue (near the present-day View Point).

The villages and districts produced enough fruit, vegetables, and dairy products to sustain the growing population of the area until the 1950s. At that time, the high price of importing feed and hay, the subdivision of farms (principally in the Westview, Grief Point, and Edgehill districts), and the advent of supermarkets with refrigerated supply trucks from Vancouver (from 1954 road – ferry connection from Saltery Bay), resulted in a **decline of the local agricultural economy** and the end of the local dairy farms.

Areas north and south of town were the outer rings of economic growth associated with the Powell River mill.

In the early decades of the last century, some folks had large pre-emptions in, what is today, the Regional District. **John Lambert** owned one of the last pre-emptions in the area, Westview Lot 3696, consisting of 50 acres. His son **Tom Lambert** bought another 50 acres from the government. From 1926-36 the Lambert family ran a dairy, with 80 milking goats, in **Paradise Valley**; it was the biggest goat dairy in the Dominion of Canada.

In 1930 the **Powell River Company** constructed the dam and powerhouse at **Stillwater**. Over 400 construction workers lived in the area in any shack they could find. Tom Lang worked on both projects.

In 1910 **John (Giovanni) D'Angio** worked on the construction crew for the Powell River Company. In 1914 he took up a 65-acre pre-emption with 700 feet of waterfront at **Okeover**. John married Catherine O'Callaghan in 1918. In the 1920s with seven children to feed, John was back working for the Powell River Company. At weekends he walked the six-hour journey, back and forth on the trail, through Southview to the Townsite. During the week he slept overnight on the mill floor! During WWII **Nancy Crowther** (Cougar Queen of Okeover Arm), worked for the Powell River Company and batched in the Townsite. At weekends, she walked the long trail home to Okeover.

In 1916 **Joe (Giuseppe) deVito** brought his family to a five-acre pre-emption at **Lund**. In 1917 Joe obtained a job with the Powell River Company; for two years he walked the 15 miles, along rough trails, from Lund to the Townsite. In 1919 Joe quit his job at the mill and went logging for five years; he ended up working for the Department of Highways – improving the road to Lund!

Bill Black was Powell River Forest Ranger in the early decades of the Townsite. In 1952 **Allen Roberts** and his wife Marjorie Roberts (Black) moved into the original forest station at **Myrtle Rocks**. Allen Roberts worked in the Powell River mill for 47 years. He served as Director of Area B, Regional District for 18 years and helped to establish the Myrtle Rocks Regional Park.

In the late 1940s, **Wilfred and Phyllis Gobbee** bought the old abandoned Woolridge homestead in **Paradise Valley**. They established the Blue Mountain Poultry Farm. At the peak of production it processed 3-4,000 eggs a day, 365 days a year. They were sold all over town, including the hospital. The farm was sold in 1960. It became the **Blue Mountain Trailer Park**.

1930s NO DEPRESSION IN POWELL RIVER AND VILLAGES

There was a steady economic growth in Powell River and Villages during the Great Depression. The Powell River Company was in operation three days a week through the "Dirty Thirties". The average monthly earnings for its employees was $54 a month. This was a small fortune during "hard times" when farm workers, on the Prairies, were lucky to get $5 a month and their keep. Thousands of families across Canada were fortunate if they received $25 a month on relief. Hundreds of young men were criss-crossing Canada "riding the rods" looking for non-existent work and relying on "hand outs" to keep alive. The Federal Government warehoused hundreds of single, unemployed men in relief camps. There was a relief camp at Duck Lake from 1932-36; the men received 20 cents a day. In 1937 the program was changed to a work-for-wages camp; the same site became a forestry camp and the men received $5 a month and their keep.

The second biggest employer in the area, after the Powell River Company, was the **shingle bolt industry** located at the Shingle Mill near Powell Lake, and at Stillwater. The shingle bolt industry employed 175 Japanese, 140 Chinese, some First Nations, and 50 Caucasians. The third largest employer in the area was the limestone quarries on Texada Island; there the workforce was 75-100 Chinese and 50 Caucasians. Stuart and Russell Lambert logged in the late 1930s for Doc Jameson's's shingle mill company.

Japanese and Chinese workers were paid $28.80 a month while non-Asians were paid $60 a month. These wages were for working 24 days a month while mill workers earned, on average, $54 a month for 12 days of work. **In 1930, 1,300 men worked in the Powell River mill and another 680 on construction. The company payroll for the mill was $2,256,437. The payroll for the company logging camps was $1,000,000.**

According to **Mildred Ross (Dice)** the rents for the Townsite homes were prorated to the number of days worked. The Company charged $2 a month for unlimited electricity.

During the Depression years, the company purchased cordwood for hog fuel. The income from cutting cordwood kept many families off the relief rolls. According to old-timer **Charlie Parsons** the Company paid $4 a cord; $2 for the trucker and $2 for the cutter.

New schools were built during the Depression years. The District payroll in 1937 was $36,000; teachers earned from $75-$100 a month. In 1937 there were 13 school divisions enrolled in the Townsite, 3 in Wildwood, 4 in Cranberry, 6 in Westview, 2 in Stillwater, 2 on Texada Island, and 1 in Lund. On the Prairies, teachers were as poor as their pupils. They received their board, and a "prayer and a promise" that they would receive their pay when times were better.

Over 40 small businesses were established in the villages of Cranberry and Westview and Wildwood District during the 1930s. The sound of the hammer rang out throughout the 1930s, as mill employees bought building lots for $100 from **William Joyce** to be paid off at $5 a month. The Lakeview Lumber Company at Haywire Bay run by **Andy and Clara Anderson** expanded their operation in 1938 in order to meet the demand for lumber.

First Nations harvested the sea for their own use, and also sold freshly caught salmon, door-to-door in the Townsite and villages. Cedar baskets were traded and sold for cash, produce and/or clothes.

Families on relief lived off the land and the sea. They survived by planting a garden, and keeping a few chickens and a goat. Salmon from the ocean and trout from the lakes were in abundance. Wood was free, and there was a never-ending supply on the B.C. coast. The climate was mild compared to the Prairies' "icebox".

The Powell River area, in its isolation, was living an economic miracle during one of the worst depressions in Canada.

A Political purge (1933-37) by the Powell River Company results in village and district growth

Company towns were generally anti-union. The Company set the wages and conditions of work. In order to "stamp out" new ideas and political allegiance, companies across Canada fired and blacklisted employees suspected of voting CCF. After the election of one Ernest Bakewell, an engineer at Ocean Falls, as the CCF member for the Mackenzie riding (of which Powell River was part), the Powell River Company fired and blacklisted company employees suspected of being CCF. The company also discharged those termed "foreigners" – a number of Italians were fired at this time. **Fides Prissinotti** recalls how her father, **Ottavio Brandolini** was fired; he left for Vancouver, never to return to Powell River. **Domenico (Benny) Silvestrini** was fired in 1933. He returned to Italy; however, he came back to Powell River in 1935 and was rehired.

Bill Jones (fired by the Powell River Company in 1932):
"After the 1933 election of Bakewell (CCF) the mill management panicked and literally fired dozens of people. It was the management, not the Powell River Company itself, but the local management and one or two people outside. But the town itself was desperate then; it wasn't a good place to be in."

Men who were fired from the mill were blacklisted from being hired anywhere else in Canada. They lost their company houses with their jobs, and **many ended up staying in the villages – some became independent businessmen**; others waited it out, with help from friends and family, until they were hired back in 1937 when the union was certified. There was simply nowhere else for anyone to go in the Great Depression. **Robert Taylor** (DCM MM - WWI) was fired and blacklisted; in desperation he left Canada for work in New Zealand. He never returned. Walter Patrick was fired; he moved with his family to Westview Village.

Merve Wilkinson (Powell River Company employee 1933-37)
"There was a great deal of fear in the mill during the time I worked there. There were Pinkerton agents in every department. Men were afraid of losing their jobs and being blacklisted during hard times. I was on the Flying Squad which organized for a union in 1937. It was a landslide vote for the union with 80% voting for certification."

Jack Dice -2002 (born in the Townsite 1923)
"Altogether 350 men were fired before the union was certified in 1937. There were no jobs in Canada for the CCF."

WORLD WAR II 1939-45

During WWII (1939-45) the Powell River Company returned to working a seven-day week after working half-time during the Great Depression. The Company donated $1 million to the war loan.

Out of a population of 8,000 people – 1,000 men and women (55) became members of the Canadian Armed Forces.

Women and children in the community enthusiastically collected tin foil, knitted socks, and made jam for Britain. "Mr. and Mrs. Powell River" dug gardens for Victory, and listened daily to news about the war on their radios.

At the outbreak of WWII, Italian families had lived in the area for 20-30 years, their children were bilingual, speaking English at school and in the workplace, and Italian at home. Some had married English, Scots, and other nationalities.

In 1939 Powell River was an integrated community with its citizens loyal to Canada.

On June 10, 1940 after Italy's Declaration of War and alliance with Germany, Canada's Italian population became subject to the War Measures Act; they were declared "enemy aliens". Camps (men only) were set up in Kananaskis near Banff, Alberta, and at Camp Petawawa in Ontario for those persons deemed sympathetic to Mussolini and/or Hitler.

The Powell River Company manager interceded with the Canadian government to keep its Italian workforce. Italians who came to Canada after 1922 (when Mussolini came to power) and those without Canadian citizenship (children "born on the boat" or in Italy) had to register with the RCMP. After Italy surrendered in 1943 these restrictions were lifted.

Many young men of Italian heritage, from Powell River, joined the Canadian Armed Forces: including the Mitchell brothers, Albert and Marino, and the Bortolussi brothers, Gino and Aldo. Aldo, an air tail gunner, paid the ultimate price for his country; he was shot down over Germany.

After the December 7, 1941 attack by the Japanese on Pearl Harbour, Canada and the U.S. declared war on Japan. In B.C. 24,000 "enemy aliens" were removed from the coast, this included the Japanese who were employed in the shingle bolt industry at Powell Lake and Stillwater.

Almer McNair – 2002 (from Stillwater)
"In 1941, after Pearl Harbour, the RCMP asked my father Nat McNair to bring out the Japanese on the coast. My father was pretty much in tears at having to do this, as he was on good terms with his employees. Many of the Japanese were third and fourth generation Canadians. About 250 Japanese (men, women, and children) were escorted to Vancouver and later placed in camps, in the interior of B.C. for the duration of the war."

Bob Astrophe – 2006 Powell River
"All the Japanese at the Shingle Mill (Powell Lake) were taken out in 1942. This was a big loss for Jameson to lose experienced workers who knew how to cut shingle bolts. After the loss of the Japanese, more Chinese were brought in and there were Chinese shingle bolt camps up the lake."

From 1940-42 a conscientious objector's camp was located south of Powell River between Nanton and Lewis Lakes. The men, mainly Doukhobours and Mennonites worked on tree planting, receiving $5 a month.

Women in the Mill – WWII – the Economy depended on them!

For the first time in its history, the Powell River Company employed women in the mill during WWII. On June 26, 1940 a mass migration of Powell River Company employees (all male) left town on the *Princess Mary*, and volunteered to enlist. The Powell River Company had no alternative but to hire women to do, what had been strictly been men's work. These women worked for the duration of the war; they worked hard and gained the respect of their male supervisors. Women (Rina Dalla-Pria and others) of the Italian community contributed to the war effort by working in the mill.

From November 1, 1943 to November 1, 1944 **Boeing of Canada** operated Subassembly Plant #185 in #3 Warehouse on the mill site. Twelve squads were formed from 121 women and 32 men, their job was to assemble parts of the PBY, a patrol and rescue plane. During the contract time, 16-25 aircraft were completed per month. Trainees made 47 cents an hour, fourth class workers 54 cents, and first class workers 70 cents an hour.

Eddie Needham – 2008
"My mother, Ina Needham, worked for Boeing for one year and then in the beater room until the war was over – then it was back to being a housewife!"

Stella Saunders (Hall/Hewson) 2007
"I worked in the Boeing Sub-Assembly plant on the Powell River Company mill site. I was a fitter and I learned to handle a drill."

Freda Stutt (Bauman) 2002
"I was able to get work at the mill; my sisters Lilly and Ruby also found work with the Powell River Company. We belonged to the Union and were paid the same wages as men. From 1943-44 I worked for Boeing which subcontracted parts for the PBY. All the girls were given a 10-day training course. We wore white coveralls and kept our hair back with a hair net. My job was to assemble the pilot's enclosure in the aircraft."

Nancy Crowther (Cougar Queen of Okeover Arm) 1987
"I was working in the mill capping and sheet laying. I worked for three years and three months in the mill. I lived in Powell River, but bicycled home at the weekends. At first, I walked home; it took 6 hours each way. Yes, I worked in the mill during the war, until the boys came home – and out I went!"

1943 "Invasion" of Powell River (training exercise)
1945 – May 7th Germany capitulated. August 14th Japan surrenders.

Post-war Powell River 1946-1950s

Powell River lost 55 of "our boys".
After the war the Powell River Company gave returning servicemen their jobs back. The widows of men lost in action were given jobs in the mill offices.
1947 – Veteran's village built on the old Company orchard in Cranberry.
1,700 mill workers. Annual payroll of $5 million.
100 war brides made Powell River home.
Post war immigration to Powell River: immigrants came from around the world, including: England, Scotland, Malta, Italy, Holland and Scandinavian countries.
A second wave of Italian immigrants. Italians "caught out" in Italy and unable to return to Canada to work during the 1930s and WWII were given a "once only" chance to obtain Canadian citizenship.

Due to the shortage of housing in **Holland**, the Dutch government sponsored families willing to emigrate: the Mayenburg, de Jong and other Dutch families came to Powell River.

Ted Mayenburg recalls coming to Powell River in 1951, at age 20, with his parents, four brothers and five sisters:

"We rented at the **Shingle Mill** with the prospect of work with the Powell River Company in the Townsite. My sisters, Mary and Martha, worked at the Sing Lee store. Martha married **George Samsin**, owner of the store. The store sold groceries, shoes, candy, etc. and had a post office."

Frank and Johanna de Jong, with their eight children, came to Powell River in 1952. They were sponsored by a relative, Cor Scheurs, who worked for the Powell River Company. They lived at the **Shingle Mill** for a few years before Frank bought one of the Riverside houses which came up for sale in 1955. He dismantled it and reassembled it in Westview. Two additional children were born in Powell River, Cathy and Frank Junior. Frank Senior found work with the Powell River Company.

WOMEN IN A PAPER TOWN

In the early years of construction there were hardly any women in the Townsite. A few married women or sweethearts came to join their husbands, as some men on construction saw the opportunity of long-term employment with the Powell River Company. They travelled great distances, across oceans and countries, often with very young children, in order to reunite with husbands and to make Powell River their permanent home.

In 1910 **Emily Fishleigh** left England with two young children and a baby, in order to join her husband, Bill Fishleigh in Ucluelet on Vancouver Island. In 1915 the Fishleigh family came to Westview – Emily was determined to find a place to live where her children (4) could go to school.

Emily Fishleigh
> "We squatted in Westview. We couldn't go into Powell River (Townsite) as we had no money. We were on a timber limit.
> They had to build a school (1916) for my children because they had no school there until the Courtes came. They attended the first Westview school."

Cornelia Viertelhousen, after discovering her husband had a secret mistress and a second family, left a comfortable middle-class life in Rotterdam, Holland in 1908 with her two daughters, **Julia** and **Jacoba** for a new life in Canada.

After a brief stay in Quebec they joined Cornelia's son, **Joe Viertelhousen**, in Powell River in 1910. Joe had found work with the Powell River Company. Jacoba also found employment with the Powell River Company as post mistress in the Company Townsite. In 1912 she married a young Englishman, **Reginald Victor Stuart**, a scaler and bookkeeper for the Canadian Puget Sound Lumber Company at Powell Lake. The family lived in tents at Haslam Lake.

With incredible courage, speaking little or no English, Italian wives and sweethearts made the long journey to Powell River from Italy. **Anna Piccoli (Zorzi)** made the journey from Italy to Powell River in 1913 with her two children, Gagliano and Mafalda, in order to join her husband Giuseppe Piccoli. Giuseppe came to work on construction in the Townsite in 1911.

Dora Buse (Piccoli) 1987
> "Mother came out in 1913. Can you imagine a woman, who didn't speak the language, had hardly any money with two little kids, to come all the way from Italy to go to Powell River? All on their own, with no house to live in. They lived in a tent when they first came here, down by the old cemetery (old golf course)."

Ida Scarpolini (Toigo) made the journey, on her own, from Italy via the U.S. to Canada. This story was retold in the 1924 Powell River Company *Digester*:

> "Don't stop me. You needn't puzzle over your immigrant quota, for I am merely passing through the United States. This country means only 3,000 miles of my 7,000 mile journey to get married.

I know this sounds strange, and people would think it a very unconventional thing for a girl to go running like mad around the world to marry a man. But the world is changing. Girls are doing things today that would have shocked their mothers. I would go to the end of the earth to be his (Louis Scarpolini) wife, for life holds nothing bright when he is away and wants me."

Ida Toigo married Luigi Scarpolini on her arrival in Powell River.

There were many Italian bachelors working on construction. **The few married Italian women, who came out to Canada to join their husbands in Powell River, played an important economic role in the town by taking in boarders.**

Discovery Royal B.C. Museum (November '98)
"Italians in B.C.: A Short History" by Lorne Hammond

"Italian women played a crucial role in defining these early communities. The mechanism was running boarding houses, which acted as a gateway into the community. Here, new immigrants received credit, help finding a job and advice, learned a new language, kept their ties with Italy and entered the life of their new home. By operating the boarding houses, women subsidized the living costs of working men and made it possible for them to accumulate savings on their wages."

Dora Buse (Piccoli) 1987
"Mother (Anna Piccoli) told me how she used to cook for the Italians in one tent because as soon as they (bachelors) knew an Italian lady was there, they wanted Italian food. We slept in another tent, and she served in another. We had three tents. She had 16 boarders.
My dad had the first bank because he used to keep all the Italians' money. He made a little safety box with a combination lock and he had all their money in envelopes. They didn't know where to put their paycheques."

Fides Prissinotti (Brandolini) 2008
"We all stayed in that big, long bunkhouse (Townsite). She (Ermina Brandolini) had about five or six boarders. When we moved to Riverside – five or six boarders would be sleeping upstairs. My mother worked hard – everything was done by hand. Mother cooked from scratch – all these Italian dishes. I'm sure she cooked a lot of spaghetti. She'd cook stews and roasts. The men always got a glass of wine with their meals. My dad made wine, beer, and root beer."

Children delivered lunches to the Italians in the grinder room:
"We had a wicker basket with a lid. We'd put everything in there – the dish, fork and knife, and a glass (for the wine) – just like they were eating at home. We had to get down there fast – so it was hot!"

Successful Business Women

Madame Loukes ran the profitable 5th Avenue Dress Shop on Marine Avenue, Westview, supplying dresses to professionals and wives and daughters of mill management. (See Westview section.)

A different **Madam** operated the Cat House (House of Ill-Repute) in Wildwood during the 1930s and 40s. A well-kept secret for decades was that Madame Loukes also supplied gowns for the ladies in the Cat House! (See Wildwood section.)

From 1919 **Francis Rowe** was a well-known nurse and midwife in the Townsite. Her daughter, **Faith Rowe** owned Rowe's Junior Style Dress Shop (1955-73).

Olive Devaud, property owner, gave the old Westview log house to the Unitarians. She also gave land for the Olive Devaud nursing home.

Eva Mosely was a successful business owner in Cranberry (page 119 & 145).

Company Wives – Social Events and Responsibilities

Wives of company managers had various responsibilities:

Graeme Cooper (2002) Douglas Bay:
"Being the manager's wife precipitated many demands. Elora (Cooper) was expected to convene a steady procession of community events, from music festivals to charity teas. Her most challenging role was to manage the guest house. How Yen Doy and his wife, Mrs. How, lived in and attended food preparation and house cleaning under Elora's supervision. The house had to be in perpetual readiness. Elora was, far often then not, expected to entertain out-of-town guests in the guest house, and often the Cooper children were included for meals."

First Nations Women

First Nations women went door-to-door, in the villages and Townsite, selling fresh salmon and cedar baskets from the 1920s to 1940s.

Elsie Paul "Elder in Residence" – Vancouver Island University
(10/08 Powell River Museum Presentation)

"My grandmother gathered materials for basket weaving. I watched her weave baskets. She would go into Powell River (from Sliammon) to sell her baskets – I'd help her pack them in. She traded for part – cash, food, blankets, men's clothing, etc. There were times when she sold a basket for $5. Today they are worth thousands! Sometimes my grandparents would walk to Wildwood, and they'd trade fresh salmon for meat, chickens, and beef at a farm there."

Women in a mill town – WWII – see WWII section

LOOKING BACK AT THE POWELL RIVER COMPANY

In 1959 the Powell River Company merged with MacMillan Bloedel and became known as MacMillan Bloedel and Powell River Limited. In 1964 the new company became known as MacMillan Bloedel. The "good old days" of a Company Town were over.

Old-Timer, Douglas Bay (2008)
"Without the mill there would be no Powell River."

Frank Haslam (age 104) (12/2008) (Townsite resident from 1911)
"The Powell River Company was a d--- good company!"

Josie Mitchell (1912-1991) – Josie's father, Pietro Michelus (Peter Mitchell), an Italian, came to Powell River in 1910. He worked on the construction of the mill and the Townsite. Her mother Teresa came out in 1911, at first she refused to unpack her trunk because she was not staying in Powell River's tent city!

"I was born in a tent (Townsite). We moved from a tent to a bunkhouse and then when the house was built, we moved to Cedar Street. We were the first occupants. When you grow up in a town you don't realize all the changes. **There was no Westview.**
The Townsite today (1987) is so sad. It was so beautiful; all the streets were lined with trees. It was so busy. Everything was centralized. Of course, there was shift work. You'd see the men coming off shift with their buckets and the men going on. **The Powell River Company was very good – marvellous."**

Fides Prissinotti (Brandolini) 2007 (Riverside, Townsite 1920s)
"The Powell River Company, at that time, did a lot of nice things for their workers. They made all those nice homes. We were allowed to use the heaters to keep the houses warm in winter – and not pay the electricity!"

Jim Silvestrini – 2008 (born 1923 Townsite):
"Yes, looking back, the Powell River Company was good to its employees. They built Dwight Hall and Brooks school. They provided a ball park, a bowling green, tennis court, and a golf course. All the employees could use these facilities. They provided land for churches and the fire hall in Cranberry on Lot 450. **We didn't realize how good we had it back then."**

Almer McNair – 2009 – Stillwater pioneer

"The Powell River Company employees had to be a certain height and weight because the mill was labour intensive and the jobs required physical strength!"

Mildred Ross (Dice) (born 1922 Townsite):

"Looking back, apart from the difficult years in the early 1930s (before the mill became unionized in 1937), **I think the Powell River Company was good to its employees**. The Company houses were well built. In 1955 the Company gave their employees the opportunity to buy the houses they lived in. The prices ranged from $5,000 to $8,000 depending on the size and location of the house."

Bill Jones (fired from the Powell River Company – 1932)

"**Powell River was a real Company Town. Everything was run by the Company.** There were some restrictions – you couldn't have a battery radio without the permission of the chief electrician!"

Martin Rossander (born 1917 – Broadacres, Saskatchewan)

"After two days of indoctrination (1948) by a Powell River Company supervisor, I was assigned to the labour gang. During the indoctrination I was told once you were employed by the Powell River Company you are secure for life.
In the two years I worked for the Powell River Company – it was the most mind-stifling thing I ever encountered."

Bev Falconer (Carrick) 2008 – Townsite resident from 1937

"When I grew up here, it was not called the Townsite – it was **Powell River, and it was the hub of the universe.**
The Townsite has kept within its boundaries; the last of the original houses were completed around 1930. In 1946, a row of duplex houses were built on Willow Avenue for the returning service men – as the baby boomers arrived thick and fast, it became known as Stork's Alley!
The Townsite Gang, a division of the mill consisting of all tradesmen required (35 in total), kept houses painted; sidewalks, roofs, and fences in good repair.
In the early days, people came from other districts to shop in the modern company store – a big department store on three levels.
The Townsite really was a big model community."

Norma Smith (Flett) 2008 – Townsite resident 1930s & 40s

"After the **Powell River Company sold out** and subsequent owners did not support the pipe band and community events, the world got out,

"Father Christmas has left town!"

Sam and Eva Dice 1920 Donkey House, Powell River Company mill. Photo: Jack Dice

Diane Carew (Wilcox) and Bev Falconer (Carrick) 1938 "dressing up" – walking the boardwalk near the backyard of 950 Maple Avenue, Powell River Townsite. Photo: Bev Falconer

Looking Back with George Orchiston
Vice President Local 76

A History of the Powell River Pulp & Paper
(A presentation given in 1999 at the Western Canada Forestry Conference attended by Union delegates from the pulp & paper mills west of Manitoba)

Powell River Mill

- The events prior to construction of the mill.
- The building of the mill.
- And the constant change the Powell River site has gone through from 1912 to 2001.

This history does not and could not begin to describe what would obviously be a rich human story, when people with a pioneering spirit invested their lives and some, their capital, to build out of the wilderness a community and what became, at one point, the largest single unit producer of newsprint in the world.

Long before Europeans arrived on this part of the B.C. coast, **First Nations** had lived here for thousands of years. In fact, the present mill site and the Municipality of Powell River are located in the traditional territory of the **Sliammon People** who today live just three miles to the north of the mill site.

June 25, 1791

- It was 208 years ago, on June 26, 1791 when **Captain George Vancouver** explored this part of the coast and while anchored off the east shore of Harwood Island, he recorded in his journal, his observations of the river (directly across from his anchorage) on the mainland which eventually became known as Powell River.

1880

- In 1880, 32 years before paper was made at this location, both the river and the lake behind what was to become the mill site, was named after a **Dr. Israel Wood Powell**. It is noted that it was Dr. Powell, at a public meeting on March 18, 1867, who moved the main resolution that B.C. join the Confederation of Canada. A few years later, B.C. became the sixth province of Canada. Dr. Powell was also instrumental in the planning of Vancouver and streets in both Vancouver and Victoria bear his name.

- The Powell River area entered the forest industry in the early 1880s when the **Moodyville Saw Company** established two small logging camps in the area and there was no turning back.

1902-1909

- The development of papermaking at Powell River can be formally traced to the **"PULP LEASES"** of 1902 which were created by the provincial government of the day in an effort to encourage the development of a permanent large scale pulp and paper industry in British Columbia.

- Those leases granted timber and power licenses, of a tenure of 21 years with renewal provisions for successive similar periods, to the applicants in return for their investment in pulp and paper manufacturing.

- The original terms required the lessors, by November 1, 1909, to spend at least $500,000 on a pulp mill with a daily capacity of at least 100 tonnes or a 50 tonne per day paper mill.

- One such **PULP LEASE** was granted in 1902 to the Canadian Industrial Company and was comprised of 134,551 acres of timber land in the Powell River area.

- For whatever reason the **WATER RIGHTS** at Powell River were not included in the CIC's lease but were awarded to another company called the Pacific Coast Power Company.

- The Canadian Industrial Company and the Pacific Coast Power Company were unable to reach an agreement with each other prior to the Government's November 1, 1909 deadline.

1908

- In 1908 the **Brooks-Scanlon Lumber Company**, which was one of the largest logging and sawmilling companies in North America, established logging operations at Stillwater, 12 miles south of Powell River and they soon recognized the potential for the production of pulp and paper in this area.

1909

- On October 21, 1909 the Brooks-Scanlon Lumber Company purchased the **timber** and **water** rights for the Powell River site for $1.8 million.

- Brooks-Scanlon formed the Powell River Paper Company and with a working capital of $1 million set out to build a paper mill.

- Problems plagued the new company. The **Michigan and Puget Sound Logging Company's railroad** ran right through the new paper mill site and they refused to move it. Finally, with the intervention of the Premier of the province, an agreement was reached allowing construction of the mill to proceed.

1910
- By 1910, the new company's money was running low; however, it was decided that the planned two paper machine mill would not be economically viable and that for the new mill to be successful, its capacity would have to be doubled.

- The company was reorganized as the **Powell River Company**, as the Brooks-Scanlon Company invested a further $1.5 million dollars. Construction of the mill continued.

- Homesteaders and squatters who lived around the shores of Powell Lake were refusing to vacate their land which was soon to be flooded with the completion of the dam. A shotgun battle was narrowly averted before a settlement was reached.

- The Powell River Hotel (Rodmay) was built adjacent to the mill site and many a worker, throughout the years, satisfied his/her thirst at lunchtime or after day shift of 4-12. Although it still stands today, business is down, reflecting the commercial shift to Westview and downsizing at the mill.

1911
- A portable sawmill was set up at the Mill site and construction of the Powell River Townsite began.

- After completion of the dam, disaster struck when one of the wood stave penstocks burst, washing out the hillside and filling the basement of the newly-completed paper machine room with sand and rocks. A short time later, the end of the concrete canal that supplied water from the dam to the penstocks broke, causing further damage. At this point, Brooks and Scanlon seriously considered abandoning the project. With great uneasiness, they decided to carry on. New steel penstocks were ordered and other paper companies were contracted to fill paper orders.

1912

- **#1 and #2 Paper Machines were started up, producing the first newsprint paper in Canada to be made west of Ontario.** At 660 feet per minute, these were the fastest in the world. – Now it should be said that the first paper mill in B.C. used rags imported from Britain and operated at Port Alberni from 1894 to 1986, and that it was not until 1909 that wood pulp was made at a small 20 tonnes per day mill at Howe Sound.

- The *Vancouver Province*, calling it a collector's item, used for the first time the paper produced at Powell River. This was a big step in the development of B.C.'s Pulp and Paper Industry.

- The basic wage rate at the Powell River mill was 22.5 cents per hour.

- Workers operating the Paper Machines were organized by the International Brotherhood of Paper Makers and became **Local 142**. A key objective was to reduce the working day from 13 to 8 hours per day.

1913

- The Powell River Company **started up its #3 and #4 Paper Machines**, thereby increasing the capacity of the Mill to 39,900 tonnes. These two machines were designed to run at speeds up to 1000 feet per minute.

- Management resisted **Local 142's** efforts to obtain an 8-hour day and locked the Union out.

- The original Patricia Theatre was built. It is said to be the oldest operating theatre in B.C.

1918

- **Local 142** which represented the paper makers, disbanded.

- Workers, other than paper makers were organized by the International Brotherhood of Pulp, Sulfite and Paper Mill Workers Union and became **Local 76**. Its goal at the time was better wages and a Union shop.

1919

- The Company signed its first Union Collective Agreement, providing wage parity with Eastern Canadian mills.

1920

- The use of work horses for various hauling needs was ended and trucks were employed.

- The Powell River Company installed 200 (rotary) dial telephones in their main buildings. These were the first dial-type telephones to be used in B.C.

1921

- **Since start up in 1912, over the next nine years, the mill produced 476,000 tonnes of paper, an amount that can be produced annually today with the remaining three paper machines.**

- With the paper business having tougher times, Local 76 was pressing for better wages. The Company responded by refusing to deal with the Union and reduced the wages 16%. A strike ensued and the Company brought in strike breakers from eastern Canada. Many employees were dismissed because they were considered disloyal.

1922

- Local 76 disbanded.

1923

- The total population of Powell River was 2,139.

1926

- A program of expansion began. Projects included: raising the Powell Lake dam 12 feet, a fourth penstock, a hydro-electric generator, new grinder room, new steam plant, two paper machines, new docks, and expansion of the sulfite pulp mill.

- With the **start up of #5 and #6 machines** the mill's annual production capacity increased to 155,000 tonnes.

- The basic wage rate at Powell River was 48 cents per hour.

1927-31

- The Powell River Company was looking to expand again, however, without more electrical power it could not proceed. Enough electrical power for at least two new machines, increased ground wood capacity and sulfite pulp expansion would be required. It looked to the Lois River watershed 12 miles south of Powell River and was granted those water rights by the B.C. Government.

- The Stock Market crashed in 1929 and the Great Depression began.

- The first stage of the Lois River project was completed. This included: construction of a temporary log crib dam, a temporary wood stave penstock which ran 2,700 feet from the temporary dam to the site of the proposed permanent concrete dam, excavation of a 5,800 foot tunnel through solid rock, a further 2,700 feet of permanent steel penstock from the tunnel to the new power house, a 312 foot tall surge tower, and installation of one 18 Mva generator. Work on the tunnel was started from both ends, meeting in the middle. When work crews met at the middle of the tunnel, it is said that they were less than half an inch out of line.

- The Powell River Company built and **started up #7 Paper Machine**, which could produce 150 tonnes per day, increasing the mill's annual production capacity to 200,000 tonnes. This machine was designed for speeds up to 1,400 feet per minute, a speed not attained by any in the world. At the time #7 was called "the final word in paper machines".

1932

- Said to be the worst year of the Depression, the Powell River mill operated for 236 days, almost full-time, when one considers the mill was not running seven days a week at that time. Apparently, the Company even made a profit during this period.

- Workers, whose wages were lower than normal, had their rents for the Company Townsite housing reduced.

1933

- During the Depression years, labour relations deteriorated and got even worse when, with the support of Powell River workers, a Mr. Ernest Bakewell (engineer at Ocean Falls) was elected as a CCF member for this Mackenzie riding. In retaliation, the Powell River mill manager dismissed all mill workers he considered were "left wingers".

- The conditions of this period in time encouraged workers to again seriously consider reorganizing a union.

1935

- **The Provincial Government passed the B.C. Industrial Conciliation and Arbitration Act which helped Unions to be formed.**

- Dockworkers at Powell River organized and affiliated with the Independent Vancouver Longshoremen's Union. The Powell River Company refused to negotiate with them and blacklisted any Union member. The Union struck the mill and the mill manager ordered a lockout. Workers in Vancouver and other ports refused to hand the "hot" products from Powell River. This led to a violent four-month-long strike.

1937

- A Mr. D.A. Evans was hired by the Powell River Company as mill manager. He was said to be experienced in dealing with unions. D.A. Evans was mill manager from 1937-47.

- This same year, Local 142, the Paper Makers Local was reborn with the assistance of Mr. Harvey White, an organizer with the International Brotherhood of Paper Makers.

- Workers at the Ocean Falls mill, which was built during WWI, were also organized and a joint Wage Conference was held in Vancouver with Crown Zellerbach and the Powell River Company.

- These first multi-employer negotiations concluded successfully, giving birth to what became the B.C. Standard Labour Agreement (BCSLA).

- The Powell River Company began to export excess unbleached sulfite pulp.

1940

- **The first Credit Union Charter in B.C. was granted to the Powell River Credit Union**.

- The population of Powell River was 8,000.

1941

- The second stage of the Lois River Hydro-Electric Project was completed with the construction of the Scanlon dam.

1947

- **The Powell River Company had 1,700 employees and an annual payroll of $5 million.**

1948

- The third stage of the Lois Lake Hydro Electric Project was completed after the dam height was raised 20 feet, and a second 18 Mva turbo generator was installed in the Lois power house.

- **#8 Paper Machine was started up** raising the mill's annual production capacity to 226,000 tonnes per year.

- Ground wood pulp production was also increased.

1952

- The mill whistle, whose sound summoned workers to and from work for many years, was donated to the Powell River Company. This steam whistle served the ship *Princess Mary* for over 20 years and was used daily by the mill until the late sixties. Since then, the whistle is blown only at 11:00 a.m. on each Remembrance Day.

1953

- **The Powell River mill with the agreement of its Unions *began a seven-day operation*. This change resulted in an increase in annual production in 1954 to 318,000 tonnes and in 1955 to 352,800 tonnes, an increase of approximately 50,000 tonnes per year.**

1954

- The first road and ferry link to Gibsons and Vancouver went into service.

1955

- The Powell River Company became the first Canadian company to use self-dumping log barges, which it used to transport logs from the Queen Charlotte Islands to Powell River.

- 1,600 people in a local hall (CBC channel 2) watched the community's first commercial television reception.

- **The Powell River Company went out of the Townsite Business after 44 years of constructing, maintaining, and servicing the many homes and public buildings in the Townsite.**

- **The Corporation of the District of Powell River was formed with a population of 10,000. There were also another 5,000 persons living in the Regional District, which stretches from Saltery Bay in the south to Lund in the north.**

1957

- With Powell River and Lois Lakes already developed to their maximum electrical generating capacity, further expansion would require an alternate source of electrical power. To facilitate this need, the B.C. Electric Company built a 70-mile transmission line from the Lower Mainland to Powell River.

- **The Powell River Company started up #9 Paper Machine, increasing the mill production capacity to 450,000 tonnes and became the largest single unit producer of newsprint in the world.**

- At 2,500 feet per minute, #9 Paper Machine was the fastest in the world.

- An industry-wide strike lasted for 12 weeks from November 14, 1957 until February 4, 1958. The unions accepted a 7.5% wage increase and the companies were said to be pleased with the agreement because they didn't give in to the union's demand of a 12% wage increase

1959
- In spite of the controversy and concern over increased corporate concentration in the forest sector, - the largest merger of two B.C. companies occurred when the Powell River Company merged with MacMillan Bloedel to become **MacMillan Bloedel and Powell River Ltd.** with assets such as the mills at Powell River, Island Paper Mill in Vancouver, Port Alberni, Harmac (Nanaimo).

1964
- **The company became known as MacMillan Bloedel and began a modernization programme at the Powell River Division, costing $110 million by the end of 1969**.

- The Union Hall Society completed construction and officially opened the Union Hall.

1967
- The Kraft Pulp Mill began producing sulphate pulp.

1968
- The sulfite pulp plant was shut down.

1969
- By the end of 1969, the modernization had included a new Kraft pulp mill, a new wood room, **#10 Paper Machine**, and a modernized #6 Paper Machine.

1970
- The modernization and rationalization of the Powell River mill continued.

1971
- **#1 and #2 Paper Machines were shut down permanently.** They were 59 years old.

1973
- The basic wage rate at Powell River was $4.45 per hour.

- There were almost 2,600 employees at Powell River of which 2,233 were unionized workers.

1974

- Local 142 became Local #1 and both Locals 76 and 1 joined the Canadian Paper Workers Union.

1975

- Canada's first high yielding thermo-mechanical pulp machine (TMP) was installed.

1976

- **#3 and #4 Paper Machines were permanently shut down**. They were 63 years old.

Mid 1970s

- The Powell River mill began producing less newsprint and larger quantities of specialty ground wood printing papers called Hi-brite papers for use in advertising flyers and catalogues. Lighter-weight newsprint was also produced for catalogues, flyers, and telephone directory paper. By the late 1970s, about 40% of Powell River's production was in these grades.

1977

- Locals 1 and 76 celebrated their 40th anniversaries.

- The Union Hall Society celebrated as Past President Murray Mouat and National Representative Reno Biasutti burned the mortgage.

1978

- Under increasing pressure to improve environmental standards, a primary treatment plant was built to treat effluent to the ocean. Up to 150 tonnes per day of fibre were recovered and burned.

1981

- **#11 Paper Machine and related TMP facilities were started up**. This paper machine set the world standard for productivity at the time with a capacity of 180,000 tonnes per year and a start up speed of 3,500 feet per minute.

- **MacMillan Bloedel Ltd. was taken over by Noranda of Toronto.**

Early 1980s

- A corporate decision was made to transfer and concentrate telephone directory paper production from Powell River to Port Alberni on Vancouver Island. One reason for this decision was that this type of paper is very lightweight, requiring less wood fibre and Port Alberni's timber supply was apparently of good quality but dwindling.

1982

- **#5 and #8 Paper Machines were shut down**. #5 Paper Machine was 56 years old.

1984

- **Between 1980 and the end of 1984, approximately 450 jobs were lost and employment declined to 1,863.**

1985

- In order to maintain specialty grade production, #9 Paper Machine was converted to produce these grades.

1987

- By 1987 five lines of CTMP were in service, significantly reducing the need for the labour intensive ground wood pulp. Only one of four ground wood pulping lines remained in operation.

- The basic wage rate at Powell River was $14.087 per hour.

1988

- Paper markets were booming and #8 Paper Machine was restarted temporarily and closed again in 1989. Employment at the mill did increase during this period.

1989

- **#8 Paper Machine was permanently shutdown after 41 years of service.**

- Members of Local 76 struck the mill for 10 days over the company's use of contractors to overhaul #9 ground wood pulp grinder. An arbitrator determined the strike was illegal and awarded the company $4.2 million in damages.

1992

- **#7 Paper Machine was shut down after 62 years of service.**

- Between December of 1989 and December of this year, employment dropped from 1,966 to 1,497 employees, a loss of approximately 500 jobs.

- Locals 1 and 76 joined the Communications, Energy and Paper Workers Union of Canada.

1993

- On Christmas Eve of this year, 67 years after it was originally built, **#6 Paper Machine was shut down with an announced loss of almost 200 jobs**. There are now just three paper machines in operation - #9, #10 and #11.

- The mill basic wage rate is $18.17 per hour.

Early 1990s

- A secondary treatment plant, costing approximately $100 million was started up to treat all mill effluent prior to its discharge to the ocean.

1997

- A new single fluidized bubbling bed hog fuel boiler, costing $120 million was started up, replacing all of #1 Steam Plant which contained three hog fuel boilers. This resulted in a loss of 42 positions, 20 operating and 22 trades' people.

1998

- Lumber manufacturing ceased, resulting in a loss of 85 jobs.

- The employer paid the local Union $430,000 as settlement of the Union's grievance that the employer had contracted the jobs of laid-off Local 76 members.

- **Pacifica Papers Inc. purchased MB Paper, which included the paper mills at both Powell River and Port Alberni for $850 million from MacMillan Bloedel Limited**.

2000

- **On December 14th, the employer eliminated 104 positions, most of which (74) were from the Wood Mill, and contracted out the work.** The Union claimed through the grievance arbitration procedure that the employer's conduct was a wilful violation of the parties' collective agreement.

2001

- **On March 25th, Norske Skog Canada Limited announced its acquisition of Pacifica Papers Inc.**

Summary

From 1971-1999, employees have witnessed the closure of 7 of this paper mill's 10 paper machines, while the Saw Mill Complex has been reduced to a chipping plant. Today the Powell River mill produces approximately 240,000 tonnes of newsprint, 224,000 tonnes of specialty ground wood papers with 3 paper machines and also produces various amounts of Kraft market pulp, all with less than 1,000 employees. Compare that with 1913 when, with 4 paper machines running, we produced 40,000 tonnes per year with 500 to 600 employees. Yes, things have changed.

Bibliography

Alsgard, A.H. *Powell River's First 50 Years*. Powell River, B.C.: 1960.

75th Anniversary Book of the Powell River Mill.

Hayter, Roger and John Holmes. *Booms and Busts in the Canadian Paper Industry: The Case of the Powell River Paper Mill Discussion*. (Paper No. 27) Simon Fraser University (Hayter) & Queen's University (Holmes). November 1993.

Hayter, Roger and John Holmes. *Recession and Restructuring at Powell River 1980-84. Employment and Employment Relations in Transition*. Simon Fraser University (Hayter) and Queen's University (Holmes). November 1993.

Kennedy, Dorothy and Randy Bouchard. *Sliammon Life, Sliammon Lands*. 1983.

Postscript – Additional Information 2009

Four major events have occurred since 1999:

1) Pacifica Papers and Great Lakes Energy from back east formed PREI (Powell River Energy Inc.) Pacifica sold all its hydro-electricity facilities at Lois and Powell Lakes to PREI for $110 million and 50.1% of the PREI shares. Great Lakes Energy holds the other 49.9%.

2) Several months after Norske Canada purchased Pacifica Papers, the Powell River Kraft pulp mill was shut down.

3) Third Avenue Management from the U.S. purchased a 38% share in Catalyst Paper.

4) Job losses continue.

Powell River Co. Townsite

HOTEL RODMAY Ltd.

ROOMS WITH OR WITHOUT PRIVATE BATH

"Fully Licensed"   PHONE 2226

1910-2010 Rodmay Hotel, Powell River Townsite – originally called the Powell River Hotel, owned by Andrew & Barbara McKinney. Sold to Rod & May MacIntyre in 1917 – renamed the Rodmay Hotel. Purchased by Al Mantoani 1957. Insert left: Barbara McKinney 1900
Photo: Gertie Lambert collection

China Town, Powell River Townsite, B.C. 1911 photographer Rod LeMay
Courtesy Powell River Museum

Sing Lee Co. General store (1912-1923), Sing Lee Bock, Townsite. 1923 - bought out by the Powell River Company; company renamed the Brooklon Block (later called Upper Company store). 1940 - demolished, 1941 - new Powell Stores built on the same site. 1955-61 Hudson Bay Company.
Photographer: Rod LeMay (insert)   Photos: Frank Haslam collection

1930 Sam Sing & family, Pioneer merchants in the Powell River Townsite, Shingle Mill, and Westview village 1907-1987. Back row standing: Peter (left) George (right)
Front row sitting: (L to R) – Arline/Tom/May/ Sam Sing/Mrs. Sing/Henry and Paul
Private collection

Dr. Andrew Henderson's house (left), the first house to be finished in the Townsite – presently being restored by the Townsite Heritage Society. In 1910 Dr. Henderson started the first medical plan in B.C. (right) St. Luke's Hospital built 1913.. Centre: Tent hospital – Walter Patrick (Junior) born here Dec. 25, 1912. Photos: Powell River Museum

Golden Wedding 1951 – Walter & Hannah Patrick, Townsite.
Walter Patrick came to the Townsite in 1911. The family lived on Cedar Street.
Back Row: Walter Patrick (Junior)/Don McQuarrie/Syd Patrick
Front: Dan Patrick/Nora Patrick (McQuarrie)/Laura Patrick (Johnson)/Walter Patrick (Senior)/
Hannah Patrick (Parks)/ Heather Patrick/Madge Patrick (MacGillivray)/Larry McQuarrie
Photo: Laura Johnson

*1880 HMS Rocket/(far left standing) Lieutenant Scott Gray/(centre seated) Lieutenant-Commander Bernard Orlebar
R.N./(centre back row – in bowler hat) A.C. Anderson, Inspector of Fisheries/
(far-right standing) Dr. Israel Powell, Superintendent of Indian Affairs.
Captain Orlebar saw a river tumbling over a rocky ravine, after consulting his chart and finding the river had not
been named, he named it **Powell River** after his old friend **Dr. Powell.** Digester photo*

*Athletic ground, Powell River Townsite. Powell River Hotel (Rodmay) overlooking sports ground left of hotel
Central building – far right – first Patricia Theatre. Photographer: Rod LeMay 1916.
Courtesy of the Powell River Museum*

Tom Lambert and his Powell River Company horse. Tom worked on the company dock from 1916-18 loading rolls of paper. Tom & Gertie Lambert and infant son Stuart lived in a shack behind the Rodmay Hotel – location of the present cenotaph..   Courtesy of the Powell River Museum

Roy Bergot with Powell River Company truck 1930s.   Photo: Sylvia Alexander (Bergot)

Photo of George William Urquhart (a.k.a. Jim Springer) with his six sons (1930s), three sons named Springer and three Urquhart. Jim Springer seated centre, front row.
Insert photo: 1908 Jim Springer feeding deer in the future Townsite area.
Photos: Richard (Rip) Maslin collection

Saw room, Powell River Company mill 1915. Two figures far right: Mary and Tom Higgins.
In the early years 1912-1920s women and children were allowed in the mill to deliver homemade hot meals. There was no security fence around the mill until WWII. Photo: Brian Crilly collection

Looking Back with Jim Springer (George William Urquhart)
(1862-1945)

Logging the Townsite and Westview (from 1883)

Every time I walk through the streets of this modern community of Powell River (1932) with its well-ordered, immaculate-looking Townsite, modern stores and great buildings, housing ever-greater and more marvellous machinery, the urge to kick myself is almost overpowering.

Once I could have bought the entire site for something less than a song!

I caught my first glimpse of Powell River in January 1883. At that time, the focal point of civilization in the district revolved around two small logging camps, owned and operated by the Moodyville Saw Company. One camp, Dickenson's Camp, was located on the site of the present car shop; the other, Dineen's Camp, was set up just behind Willingdon Beach. The entire country was a virgin forest; and if anyone had prophesied that some day a district containing over 8,000 permanent residents and including in its boundaries one of the largest paper mills on the continent would grace the site, we would have sent him down on the next boat.

Each camp worked about 15 men; and each utilized the services of 12 oxen to drag the logs through the hastily-built skid roads. The timber had, as yet, been scarcely touched; endless vistas of forest stretched away for miles from the shoreline. Game was plentiful and close at hand; the wolves used to raid our pigpen nightly, and their fighting and growling over the meat bones, thrown aside by the cook, caused us many a sleepless night. In the end, it usually meant climbing out of the bunks and chasing them away.

On Harwood Island, across from Powell River, the late Timothy Moody maintained quite a large herd of cattle and sold beef to the camps. A Chinese man used to keep a trading sloop by which he visited the camps and the Indian settlements. To my knowledge, there was no life or activity on Texada Island in 1883, although we did hear that one party had a small sheep ranch on the lower end – a rumour we were never able to prove or disprove.

In the winter of 1884, Dickenson's Camp shut down and Dineen's Camp at Willingdon Beach was moved to Myrtle Point. Our complete outfit was transferred by scow, and on our first trip the scow ran ashore in a heavy storm off Grief Point. We cut a trail through the woods to Myrtle Point over which we moved the ox teams, and the old skid road now used as a government road, which we built in 1884 was the first piece of highway construction undertaken in the district.

In 1884 I left Powell River and did not drift back until 1900, when logging was started off the Wildwood district. From 1902-04 I worked with the B.C. Mills Timber & Trading Company, during which period logging was completed in the Wildwood area. On completion of this job, I went north, but found myself back in Powell River in May of 1907, engaged by J. Sayward of Victoria, B.C., who had started logging operations. We landed with the tug *Hope* and two scows, loaded with camp outfit and complete equipment for a logging railroad. There was no wharf – not even a float – and as our disembarkation took place at 3 o'clock in the morning, we had plenty of fun getting ashore.

We logged the Powell River area for the next two years, and it was during this time that we heard rumours of the possible building of a pulp mill. One or two wise lads bought lots, and we laughed at them for being poor "saps".

And thus, opportunity passed us by. I wouldn't have paid a hundred cents for the whole site of the present plant buildings. But that's the way it goes.

Issued in the *Digester* January 1932/September 1941/January 1949

Obituary June 18, 1945

Funeral services were held in Center & Hanna's chapel, Powell River for **George William Urquhart** aged 82 years, better known as **Jim Springer**.

George Urquhart, who was better known along the coast as "Jim Springer", was one of the earliest pioneers in the Powell River District. Born in Nova Scotia in 1862, he came to Powell River in 1883 at a time when the only settlements consisted of two small logging camps owned and operated by **Moodyville Sawmill Company**. Jim Springer helped clear the Townsite for the **Powell River Company**.

George Urquhart (Jim Springer) is survived by his sons, George William of Powell River, Charles of Vancouver, James and Robert of Seattle. A daughter, Mrs. William Mitchell, also resides in Seattle. Mrs. A Bell of Westview is a sister.

Editor's Note: Springer was a name given to early loggers using spring boards in their work. Possibly, George Urquhart was known in the bush as Jim Springer – he liked the name and chose to use it in his daily life.

Looking Back! Sam Sing & Family

Pioneer Merchants in Powell River: Townsite, Shingle Mill & Westview 1907-87

Sam Sing was in the area, we know as the Townsite, prior to the arrival of the Powell River Company in 1910. He started a laundry on Waterfront Street (location of #7 Machine Room) for the **Michigan Puget Sound Lumber Company** in 1907.

Townsite

Sam Sing was the first independent merchant in the community; in 1910 he built the Sing Lee block. Here he operated a general store, the upstairs quarters being used to board several hundred men for the Powell River Company during early construction days. The men boarded under contract with the Company, their numbers at time being so great that three sittings in the dining room were necessary. Jack Harper's men's furnishings, a jewellery business owned by Mr. Somerton Senior, and a drugstore and ice cream establishment operated by Emil Gordon operated in the Sing Lee block.

Shingle Mill

In 1923 Sam Sing sold the Sing Lee Block to the Powell River Company, later opening a general store at the Shingle Mill. To provide fresh produce to his many customers, Mr. Sing also operated truck gardens at Wildwood, on which he devised and installed his own irrigation system. He lived to see the successful business he founded expand, to another branch when the Fairway Market was erected and opened in Westview in 1936.

Westview

Sam Sing expanded his retail business with the opening of the Fairway Market in the village of Westview. After Sam Sing's death in 1937, his sons Paul, George, and Henry carried on the family business. During the Depression years the Sing Lee store (at the Shingle Mill) and the Fairway Market (in Westview), accepted garden produce in exchange for flour, sugar, and other basic supplies. World War II brought further expansion with the opening of the original Penny Profit grocery store in the Egan block on Marine Avenue, Westview. The postwar boom in the village of Westview resulted in Penny Profit being relocated in 1948 to a new building at the corner of Marine and Alberni.

In the 1950s May Sing recalls Sylvia McNeil, Alice Wallace, and Gloria Rumley worked at Penny Profit in the shop; outside Paul Sing, Frank Oliver, Scott Henderson, and Jack Leibenschel delivered orders.

The Fairway Market closed in 1961 and Penny Profit closed in 1987. Today the Paperworks Gift Gallery is located on the Penny Profit site.

Looking Back to Rod LeMay

Early Townsite Photographer

Rod LeMay is Powell River's most famous and earliest photographer. He came to Powell River in 1907. He later sold his studio to Maud Lane in the early 1920s and moved to Wildwood. Rod LeMay worked in the mill, drove taxi, and was an expert in blasting stumps. He died in Vancouver in the Marpole Infirmary in 1949.

"Rod LeMay always wore the same coloured suit – dark chocolate brown. He was always well dressed – he never looked untidy. He was a jovial fellow.

He was a sculptor. We were interested in what he was doing. We have a family photo taken when he had a studio by the golf course – he must have come to the house to take it.

On a Sunday, in Wildwood, we used to stop by and speak to him. He was a chatty person."

Josephine Mitchell 1987 (born in a tent in the Townsite 1912)

"As a child I used to visit him in his studio in Lutzville. I had quite a shock, on one occasion, when I saw a bust of Dr. Marlatt sitting in his studio window – it was so life-like!"

Horace Beattie 2002

"I remember Rod LeMay. He was really tolerant with the kids in Wildwood (1920s). He was involved in road building. He used to light fuses by biting the end off with his teeth! He was a wonderful photographer and sculptor. The story goes that he left his tools in his will to someone who would benefit from having the tools and had an artistic nature. The tools were kept by the Fine Arts Club which originally met in the basement of St. John's Church. The tools were eventually given by the club to Mrs. Clance, as she was deemed a worthy recipient."

Ingrid Cowie (Andersen) 2007

"Famous man, by the name Rod LeMay, lived in Wildwood. He used to do the blasting of stumps and rocks around here on the roads. He ran the first taxi.

He was a very clever man. He made a bust of Dr. Marlatt. It was shattered during the 1946 earthquake.

Rod LeMay was the guy that took the picture of salmon coming up the river, so thick they were sliding over the top of each other.

He lived in a little shack on Sutherland (Avenue) and Lois (Street). He used to sharpen my dad's saw. He had to put all the teeth back on again as my dad would hit nails with his saw. Later on, the Knights of Pythion built him a house on King Avenue.

Mr. Bidden had a small store on the corner where Rod LeMay lived. A small shed is there now. In later life, he suffered from poor health."

Duncan Bird 2007

"Rod LeMay worked for the Department of Highways, blasting stumps. He lived on King Avenue. He was a good photographer. He did his own developing, same as Gertie Lambert (friend of my mother's – Mrs. Thora Rud). Rod LeMay had good black-and-white pictures."

Ed Rud 2007

"Rod LeMay was a great friend of my mother's (early Townsite years). He had a photo studio near the golf course. One time I was in the hospital and Rod LeMay was there too. He was old, old, old. He was bedridden. Mum brought him a bottle of beer!"

Jack Banham 2007

Looking Back!
The Dice Family – Townsite from 1918

Jack Dice and Mildred Ross (Dice)

Sam Dice came to work as an electrician for the Powell River Company in 1918. In 1919 Eva Dice (Small) left Courtenay to work in the Townsite as a waitress at the Rodmay Hotel.

Sam and Eva married and had four children: Mildred (1922), Jack (1923), Gordon, and Bill. They lived in a rented house in the Townsite.

Jack:
"Our first house was on Marine Avenue next to the staff quarters (opposite the present Granada Restaurant). Later, the Powell River Company sold the house and it was moved to Westview.

*The house was heated with coal and wood — **we had some very cold winters in the 1920s & 30s**. The sidewalks were all board sidewalks. The kids used to roller-skate on the boardwalks and the people on shift were not very happy with kids going down the front street, "clickety click, clickety click".*

The mill never had a gate around it. Anybody could go in the mill anytime you wanted. We (children) spent a lot of time playing down there. Horses were still used on the dock.

I remember the Sing Lee store in the Townsite. I helped tear down the building. I remember the old theatre; I was there when it was torn down. The first show I saw at the Patricia Theatre was a silent movie.

Yes, I remember going to Dwight Hall at Christmastime. The company bought gifts for all the kids.

Ball games were next door to the Rodmay Hotel. My father used to play in the senior games. As a small boy I remember Rod Le May lived nearby

I went to the old Henderson school and then to Brooks. I left in Grade 10 and went to work in the lumber yard for a short time...I later took up an electrical apprenticeship; I worked for the Powell River Company from 1940-80. I retired as an electrical superintendent.

I met my wife, Alice Johnson in 1943 when she was working in the Powell River Company office. Alice came to Powell River in 1939. Her father, Herman Johnson started Burg & Johnson in Westview. We were married in 1949 and went to live on Butedale in Westview.

I volunteered my time as an electrician when the arena at Willingdon Beach was built by volunteer labour in the 1950s."

Mildred:

"During the 1930s when the mill was working part-time, the company only charged us for rent for the number of days the mill was in operation. We paid $2 a month for electricity.

*The early 1930s were a difficult time in the community, as we had friends who were fired from the mill because they were CCF (Co-operative Commonwealth Federation, forerunner of the New Democratic Party). My mother visited **Bob and Gladys Taylor** and generously helped out with groceries and clothes. The Powell River Company warned my father that my mother should cease her visits."*

Jack:

"Bob Taylor was a paint foreman at the mill and was fired because he supported the CCF. My father also worked at the mill and was given a message by mill management:

STAY AWAY FROM THE FIRED CCF!

*Bob was married with four children and had built his house below the Roxy Theatre (2007 – Snickers Restaurant). He was blacklisted by the Company. Eventually, the family left Powell River to make a new life in New Zealand. **Altogether, 350 men were fired before the Union was certified in 1937.**"*

Mildred:

"In the late 1930s I worked for Powell River stores. The store, on a temporary basis, was held in Dwight Hall as the old store was being torn down and a new one

built on the same location. In 1940 I started working for Kip and Taylors at the Rodmay Hotel. I worked at the soda fountain and sold ice cream and milkshakes.

World War II

During WWII my father was in the Home Guard. My mother and I trained in first aid through the Red Cross. My mother's big contribution for the war effort was making jam for Britain. Everyone knitted socks, to be sent overseas to Canadian Forces. It was important not to leave knots in the heel or toes!

I started working for the Powell River Company as a pulp tester and later, in the beater room shovelling paper in the heaters. I worked at the mill until April 1946, by this time the war was over and I helped train the men who were returning. The women, who had lost their husbands in the war, were given jobs in the Company office.

I remember in 1946 going over to Comox for a ball game in the same barge that was used in Powell River's "invasion" in 1943!

In 1946 I married Alec Ross; he worked for the Powell River Company. First, we lived in Westview; the rent was $18 a month. Then we rented a company house at Riverside from 1949-51 at $12 a month. In 1951 we rented a house on Willow Street and we bought it in 1955 for $3,600 when the Powell River Company sold off the Townsite houses. The Townsite houses were well maintained by the Powell River Company; every 7 years they were painted, and every 15 years a new roof was put on. After we purchased our company house on Willow Avenue, we raised it and put a basement underneath.

The **Riverside** company houses were built near the river; they were accessed by a bridge across the river. Mostly Italians lived in Riverside, but there were also a few Quebéckers. The houses had no insulation, and the winter of 1950 was very cold. On the dam side of the houses icicles formed, hanging off the roofs. We had an oil stove going in the kitchen and one going in the living room all winter. Some residents at Riverside closed off the bedrooms and lived by the stoves in the main rooms, in order to keep warm. The houses at Riverside were sold off in 1955 and moved to the villages of Westview, Wildwood, and Cranberry.

The Townsite garbage was dumped by the dam at Riverside. Back then, the garbage consisted of brown paper bags and wax paper and was not the same environmental hazard it is today. The majority of householders composted kitchen waste to be used in back gardens to grow vegetables. We had a great garden as Russell Lambert brought out animal manure from Paradise Valley."

Jack:

"I spent a lot of time up **Powell Lake**. We had the use of a cabin at Hole in the Wall and at the Head of the Lake.

Yes, I knew **Nick Hudemka**. He lived up the lake. He was a hand faller – didn't use any electrical tools. He was an honest and decent man. He always bought raisin bread as the raisins retarded the growth of mould on the bread. He had a radio and knew everything that was going on in the world.

*I used to go to Olsen Valley to get vegetables from **Frank and Joe Borer**. They had a great farm.*

I recall seeing the Japanese loading shingle bolts – this was before 1942 (WWII – Japanese internment).

Billy-Goat Smith

I never went by his place when he was alive because of all the stories that were told about him. The buildings were still there after he died. He had a nice barn. All the goats had gone.

I worked hard to retain the boathouses (near the Wildwood bridge). In 1982 I helped rebuild all the floats. City Hall was against it and that was the end of it."

Mildred:

"I was born in the Townsite, grew up in a company town during the Depression years, and worked for the Powell River Company during WWII.

Looking back, apart from the difficult years in the early thirties (before the mill became unionized in 1937) I think the Powell River Company was good to its employees.

The company houses were well built. In 1955 the Company gave their employees the opportunity to buy the houses they lived in. The prices ranged from $5,000 - $8,000 depending on the size and location of the house."

Jack:

"Yes, looking back, the Powell River Company was good to its employees. They built Dwight Hall and Brooks School. They provided a ball park, bowling green, tennis court, and a golf course. All the employees could use these facilities. They provided land for the churches and the fire hall in Cranberry on Lot 450.

We didn't realize how good we had it back then."

Looking Back with Hubert Rushant

The Powell River Townsite (from 1910)

Hubert's father, **Charles Rushant came to the Townsite, March 17, 1910**. He batched in the bunkhouses. In the early years, he was working on construction – he was part of the crew who built the infrastructure for the new paper mill town of **Powell River**. He spent his entire working life in the employment of the **Powell River Company**.

WWI came along and Charles and many of his friends from the construction crew joined the Army to fight in France. He was one of the lucky ones that came back to his hometown in 1918. After the war, Charles worked on the Maintenance Crew in the Townsite. Before he retired, sometime in the 1930s, he became foreman of the crew. The Maintenance Crew worked hard to maintain the Townsite area – the Powell River Townsite was a showpiece to other company towns. The rental houses were well maintained and were sought after by company employees.

Charles and Hattie Rushant lived in 361 Maple Avenue in the 300 block. They had two sons, Hubert and Jack. Hubert was born in a Vancouver hospital, December 1921. He spent his entire childhood growing up in the Townsite – attending the old Henderson School and the Brooks High School. After graduating, he went to work for the Powell River Company.

As young boys, Hubert and Ernie Hamerton delivered the *Vancouver Sun* newspaper; Bob Hatch delivered the *Vancouver Province*. After the papers were picked up at the wharf, some were left off outside the Patricia Theatre for pick-up and delivery.

'March 15, 1932 Safe Breakers Raid Powell River Townsite'

One time, Hubert went to pick up his papers when he noticed broken glass outside the theatre. He thought some mischief had been going on. Later in the day, he saw bullet holes in the handrail near the Avenue Lodge. Seemingly, the robbers, William Bagley and Gordon Fawcett made a dash for it, after the alarm was called, in John McIntyre's Model A Ford. Shots were fired at the departing vehicle; however, they had little effect in slowing down the car as the gas tank for this model was at the front, not the rear of the car. The robbers escaped by boat from Frolander Bay.

Hubert's younger brother Jack had a great interest in photography and after graduating, went to work at **Lane's studio**. The studio was located on the top floor of the **Sing Lee store**. Jack presently lives in Prince George.

The Rushant family enjoyed outdoor activities. They went skating at Cranberry Lake when the ice was thick enough to skate on. They owned a boat and at weekends, they went boating on Powell Lake. **Jack Wilson** officially took Powell River Company guests to **Rainbow Lodge**. However, if a guest was late in arriving, the Company asked Charles Rushant to take an extra passenger to the lodge.

Mail and goods were, on occasion, delivered to **Billy-Goat Smith** at the Head of the Lake. Hubert recalls his father tying up to the dock and Billy-Goat coming down to meet them. He recalls seeing the goats on the property.

Hubert knew the two **Errico brothers**. They owned property on the lake.

From July 1941 to October 1947 Hubert worked for the Powell River Company as an apprentice in sheet metal. From 1954, and until he retired in July 1981, Hubert had a second period of employment at the paper mill. Initially, he worked as a millwright helper, then a journeyman sheet worker, working up to Supervisor. He was later transferred to the G3 ground wood department as Maintenance Supervisor.

From 1947-54 (in-between the two work periods at the paper mill in the Townsite) Hubert worked for three years at Lund in the machine shop for Jens Sorensen, a couple of years logging, one summer as a telephone & telegraph linesman for the Department of Communications (Bliss Landing to Scotch Fir Point), followed by installing furnaces for Parry sheet metal and later (self-employed) installing furnaces.

In July 1954 Hubert married Jean Cattermole. The family lived at Lund until September 2005 when they returned to Powell River to reside in the Edgehill area.

It was in 1950 that Hubert built a house on a 10-acre lot half-a-mile south of the Lund School.

Hubert knew the Thulins. He remembers the dances held at Lund Community Hall, where the men wore their best suits and the ladies, their long dresses. The crib and bridge clubs played in the Hall and the scores were posted at the hotel! Lund was a very active place in the 1950s and 60s. During the Vietnam War, American draft dodgers came to Lund, many stayed there.

Today Lund has changed from the early days. Recently, three homes worth over a million dollars have been built in the area.

Looking back – Hubert recalls McMahon dairy in Wildwood when the milk was delivered by horse and wagon.

Looking Back with Jack Banham

The Banhams & Millers: Pioneer Families in the Townsite (from 1911) Four generations worked in the mill.

Jack Banham:

Townsite

Dad's family, the Banhams, came in either 1911 or 1912 to the Townsite. My grandfather, Robert M. Banham came to install clocks for the Powell River Company. He stayed on as timekeeper until he became postmaster – for something like 37 years.

He built a small post office on the site in 1915, which was later used as the Powell River Company laboratory. Grandfather was postmaster and justice of the peace. After WWI, and until he died in 1941, he lived in the heritage house across from the Patricia Theatre. The Company-rented house came with the job as postmaster.

Mum's family, the Millers, came to the Townsite in either 1910 or 1911. My mother Bessie was born in Portland, Oregon in 1899; she was 11 years old when she came to Powell River with her parents. Fred Miller was electrical superintendent for the Powell River Company. He had a band in the early Townsite years; it was called "The World's Greatest Band". Fred was the drummer. There was no dance hall in the Townsite at that time, and they used to hold the dances in the machine room. The couples danced around the packing crates!

My parents **Jack and Bessie Banham** were married in 1922. They probably got the Wildwood property around that time. They built the house in 1925. My paternal grandparents never lived in Wildwood. My father Jack worked as an electrician in the Powell River mill from 1927-62.

I continued the family tradition and worked in the mill, in the welding shop, from 1955-90. Three generations were employed by the **Powell River Company**.

The fourth generation, my daughter Susan, worked three summers in the mill as a tour guide in the 1970s. Thus, four generations of our family worked in the Powell River mill.

Looking Back with Laura Johnson (Patrick)

Walter Patrick Family – Townsite (1911) - Westview – Douglas Bay

The Patrick family are early Townsite residents (originally from Barrow-in-Furness, England). Walter Patrick, his wife Hannah Patrick (Parks) and their two children, Madge Patrick (MacGillivray) and Nora Patrick (McQuarrie) came to the Powell River **Townsite** in March **1911**. Two sons were born in Powell River, Walter (Junior) and Syd. Walter was born on December 25, 1912 in Dr. Henderson's tent hospital in the Townsite. The family lived on Cedar Street.

Walter Patrick (Senior) taught gymnastics. Hannah Patrick, an accomplished pianist, accompanied the drill exercises. Hannah was an excellent swimmer and taught many young people to swim at Michigan (Willingdon) Beach. During WWI she taught youngsters how to knit socks for the boys in France. Walter was employed by the Powell River Company as a painter. He worked for the company until he was fired in the big political purge in the early 1930s. He was one of 350 men who lost their jobs and, consequently, their Townsite rental homes. The Patricks moved into Westview village.

Walter's two sons went to work for the Powell River Company in the late 1930s (after the mill was unionized); Walter (Junior) was an apprentice papermaker and Syd an apprentice electrician.

During **WWII** Walter (Junior) joined the Air Force and went overseas. He was stationed as a mechanic at Croydon Airport. It was in England that he met his future wife, Joan Wilson, sitting outside a pub. He discovered she was in the Women's Land Army and doing, what had been a man's job, cutting down trees! They fell in love and married in England – Joan was 18.

After Walter returned to Powell River to work in the mill garage, Joan came out to Canada as a **war bride** in 1946. She travelled with other war brides across the Atlantic by boat, then by special train to Vancouver (exclusively for war brides). Nappies (diapers) were hanging in every coach. At every stop Red Cross workers were there to help. It was a shock for some war brides to be dropped off at some isolated stop on the endless Prairies – to be picked up by a horse drawn buggy! Walter (Junior) and Joan first rented one of the new duplexes on Willow Avenue (called Stork's Alley) in the Townsite; later they moved to Westview.

From the 1920s Walter and Hannah Patrick owned recreational property at **Douglas Bay**; in the early 1940s they moved there permanently. Today their many descendants continue to own property in the bay.

1930s Bosses' Row, Powell River Townsite. Far left - #6 Marine Avenue, home of Joe and Alice Falconer in the 1920s and early 30s. Photo: Lorna Miles (Falconer)

Powell River Townsite, Maple Avenue (Sycamore Street) 1920s. The Townsite was a planned community designed on the English Garden City principle with houses in the Craftsman style. Note the tree-lined street. Looking up the street (left) St. Joseph's Catholic Church (right) St. John's United. Photo: Frank Haslam collection

Hamerton's Townsite house garden (1940s): (L to R) Emma House (Hamerton)/Otavius Hamerton/Annie Pafford (Hamerton)/Euphemia Hamerton. Insert: 1929 Lucy and Ernie Hamerton with their young son Al. Ernie worked as projectionist at the Patricia Theatre. Photos: Al Hamerton

Ina and Rex Needham – 60th wedding anniversary 1990.
Rex was hired by the Powell River Company in 1934 and worked in the grinder room for 45 cents an hour. During WWII Ina worked for Boeing from Nov. 1 1943 – Nov. 1 1944 as a fitter on the PBY aircraft, then in the beater room for the Powell River Company for the duration of the war. Insert: Ken and Eddie Needham, Townsite.
Photos: Eddie Needham

Looking Back: Tourist Report 1927

The Powell River Townsite

We came in on one of the day boats from Vancouver, calling at every little point en route. We had previously heard reports of Powell River, but except for the scenery, there was not a great deal of interest along the way, and the population of the points of call did not appear to be very numerous.

It was getting dark when the boat neared Powell River and the first thing to catch the eye was the large number of lights along the shore, which at night gives the town the appearance of a nice-sized city. The usual berth of the boat at the Powell River Company's wharf was occupied, so the boat made a stop at the government wharf and discharged the passengers.

The wretched road from the government wharf to the town was not a very good impression to give the visitor. This is in great contrast to the wide cement road leading from the Company's wharf into the town, which we saw later. Arriving at our hotel we found modern improvements; a large rotunda with a great fireplace, somewhat hidden from first view by chairs. Most of the rooms have baths, hot and cold water, and telephone for the comfort and convenience of the guests.

In one respect this town differs from every other town in Canada. The large paper mill, business houses, residences, etc., with the exception of the hotel, are owned by the Powell River Paper Company who are manufacturers of newsprint. This newspaper is printed on the product of the Powell River Paper Mills. A few concessions have been granted by the Company, such as two garages, drugstore, pool hall. There is also a post office, Provincial Police building, Customs building, which have no connection with the Company and in the hotel on the ground floor is located a jeweller, barber, music store, shoe shop, and the most recent addition is the job department of the *Powell River News*. One of the greatest difficulties we encountered in coming here was to get a suitable location.

Being in possession of the Townsite and planning to build the homes of the workmen, as well as the necessary stores, etc., gave the Company a splendid opportunity of making this a model town, and in this they have succeeded. We have seen a number of towns elsewhere, where a large industry has furnished homes for their workmen. These were mostly mining camps and most of the buildings furnished by the coal mining companies were devoid of all conveniences, and were anything but models, either of comfort or convenience. In this respect, the workmen and employees of the Powell River Company are very fortunate. The houses are lovely in appearance, large rooms with all modern conveniences, modern plumbing, electric light, etc. They also have a large basement with cement floor, laundry fixtures, etc. In fact, we don't think anyone could wish for a better home to live in. The rent charged by the Company, we understand is very moderate, and at the same rate as is being charged for shacks outside the town with no improvements or conveniences whatever, and only half the size. Electric light is furnished by the Company at less than cost to their employees.

All the houses have lovely lawns, and those who love flowers have beautiful gardens. The whole town has been planned with a view to beauty as well as convenience. Schools have been built which are also models in every respect. A large hospital has been built to take care of the sick and injured. Churches have also been built by the Company, two of them being splendid edifices.

The Company has also not forgotten to provide recreation for the people. A splendid gymnasium, under the direction of a capable physical instructor, is in the heart of the town. The motion picture theatre, being one of the first buildings erected here, we understand is not in keeping with the rest of the buildings, and will shortly be replaced by a more modern and commodious building. One of the most recent additions to the buildings is Dwight Hall. We have not yet had the privilege of going through this building and have so far only seen the portion devoted to dances and theatrical productions. The exterior of the building is very beautiful and the finishing touches are now being put on the surrounding ground. The building is used for lodge meetings, dancing, and as a community hall.

The town also has a splendid bowling green and we are told that the local bowlers hold the championship of the province. We were fortunate enough to witness a bowling tournament during our previous stay. The grounds were well illuminated by electric lights and decorated by Chinese lanterns. There was a large crowd of spectators at the tournament and visiting bowlers were royally entertained during their visit here.

We noticed some excellent tennis courts in the town and have no doubt they are well patronized during the summer months.

Another great contribution to the recreation facilities of the town is an excellent golf course. Coming from the Prairies, where we have plenty of room to make the holes as long as the golfers' desire, we expected to find the links here rather cramped. We were surprised to find the golf course a very excellent one and kept in splendid condition. It was unusual for us to find the tees on platforms, some of them quite high. The course is what is known as a "sporty" course. There is a large membership and quite a number of players are to be found on the course when the weather is fine. We understand that it is possible to play golf here all the year round.

The Company conducts a large departmental store in the town. The grocery, meat, fruit, and vegetables and pastry are in a large building near the mill, known as the "main building". The hardware department occupies the basement, and the local offices of the Company are on the top floor. The furniture and stationery departments are in the corner of the hotel, while the dry goods, furnishing, boots and shoes, clothing, etc., are in what is known as the "Brooklon block". The Company does a tremendous volume of business. The clerks seem to be always busy and we found them very obliging and attentive.

One thing we have noticed here is that most of the business houses in Powell River, as well as the outside points of Cranberry, Westview, and Wildwood, seem to be cramped for room, the buildings not being large enough for the amount of business they are doing. There are, of course, one or two exceptions to this.

The town is first of all, a manufacturing town. The Company employs about 1,250 men alone and there are several small industries in the town and surrounding district. As well as being an industrial town, Powell River can boast of many beauty spots. There is a large lake nearby and there are a great number of power launches owned by the inhabitants. There are also several good beaches, food fishing, and hunting, all of which tend to make it a very desirable residential district.

Back to You, Powell River
Song By Glen Roscovich

1st Verse
Like an inland sea, Straits of Georgia, Vancouver Island, the western shore.
Her rugged mountains, cold and lonely, protect us from Pacific storms.

Chorus
Back to you, Powell River, salt chuck keeps us on our own.
Lakes and forests, sunset beaches, Texada shelters our western home.

2nd Verse
Out by Rebecca, Harwood and Savary,
whales and dolphins wander there.
Sliammon elders, the hulks at Townsite,
strong connections with days before.

3rd Verse
Powell River people, warm and friendly,
Welcoming strangers from distant shores.
They see an Eden, still close to nature.
The ocean rhythm becomes our own.

Looking Back with Amalia Gustafson (Piccoli)

The Piccoli Family – Early Townsite Residents (1911-19)

Giuseppe Piccoli left his wife **Anna Piccoli (Zorzi)** and two children, Gagliano and Mafalda in Italy in 1909 to find work in Canada. After working for the CPR he came to Powell River in 1911. Living in a tent, he worked on the construction crew, and then later got a job working in the grinder room.

Seeing the potential of a better life in Canada, he sent for his family to join him. Anna travelled steerage, with her two children, on the *La Lorraine*; they arrived on Ellis Island on May 24, 1913. The journey took two weeks.

On arriving in the Townsite "home" was three tents, and work for Anna was looking after 16 Italian boarders plus her own family. Four daughters were born in the Townsite: Angelina, Isadora (Dora), Amalia, and Mary.

They lived in a house in the Townsite until 1919, when they moved to Wildwood. Their 5-acre lot in **Wildwood** was ideal for market gardening. Anna had a greenhouse which her son had built. With the help of her girls she raised vegetables, selling them from a horse-drawn cart. Father and son worked for the Powell River Company.

Looking Back with Norma Smith (Flett)

Townsite Memories

Frank Flett came to Powell River in 1923. His job was to manage the Bank of Commerce. He had an apartment above the bank. For protection, in case of robbery, he had a gun! There were stairs to the bank below but, in case of emergency, there was a pole to slide down. After a stint of banking in Powell River, Frank went to work in other banks in B.C. He returned to Powell River in 1928 after accepting the position as paymaster for the Powell River Company.

Frank met **Jessie Kilburn** in the mill offices – she was a stenographer. They were married in 1928. They had three children: Norma, Fran, and Doreen. First they lived on Walnut Street, later they moved to "Superintendent's Row" when Frank was appointed personnel manager.

Norma remembers home deliveries of bread and milk (1930s and 40s). Milk came from McMahon's in Wildwood. Chores were done at home to earn the 15 cents admission price at the Patricia Theatre. Her parents were keen golf players and played on the company golf course.

During WWII hog fuel was stored on the Rodmay ball park. Norma knitted squares for afghans and picked blackberries for "Jam for Britain".

After the **Powell River Company sold out** and subsequent owners did not support community events, the word got out, *"**Father Christmas has left town!**"*

Looking Back with Josephine (Josie) Mitchell (1912-1991)

The Mitchell Family: Early Townsite Pioneers (from 1910)

Pietro Michelus (Peter Mitchell) was an early pioneer. He came to the area in 1910; to begin with, he lived in a tent near the old hospital site while he worked on the construction of the mill and Townsite. He later worked in the Wood Mill.

His wife Teresa came out a year later with her brother-in-law. On arriving in the Townsite, she took nothing out of her trunk for a year because she had no intention of staying! Of course, she eventually unpacked and stayed to raise a family. Two of their children were born in Italy; three were born in Powell River. In 1912 Josephine (Josie) Michelus was the second child to be born in the Powell River Company Townsite.

Josie Mitchell (1987):

"I was born in a tent. We moved from the tent to a bunkhouse and then when the house was built, we moved to Cedar Street. We were the first occupants.

*Then they built the school which was named after **Dr. Andrew Henderson**. My first teacher was Mrs. Ritchie; she was Miss Brett's sister. They only had to Grade 10 then, and we were the first class to move into Brooks. When I was in Grade 8 in 1927, I became Paper Queen.*

I remember the different blocks being built. After school came out in June we picked the blackberries – they were growing wild.

We used to play a lot of ball games in those days. We used to use Henderson School to play Anti-Anti-I-Over. I remember them having cricket teams and the men would all be dressed in their white flannels over in Riverside Oval. We had a lot of lacrosse.

*I can remember the old (first) theatre… I can always remember those hard kitchen chairs. The kids didn't have pillows. We had to sit down at the front and adults sat at the back. Then there was this pianist, **Glen Hayden**. When you think how wonderful it was, we had silent movies and he would fill in with the piano. I think you went in for a dime. Kids would go down and look for them under the slatted porch.*

We had a gramophone and the records were really popular. We had the Victrola – with the white dog – and had to crank it. After that, we had a radio. I can remember us all sitting around in the evenings, listening to serials such as "One Man's Family". The "Happy Gang" came on in the morning, about 9:30. The radio was really something.

Emil Gordon had a bake shop way down where the steam plant is. I remember going down there for bread. Then he had a shop up in the China Block. He had transactions everywhere; he was a wheeler-dealer. He was a tall, lanky man and he had a voice on him that you could hear everywhere. And he'd laugh, had such a personality. He was a real nice man, nothing bothered him. I think he made a good living.

I worked a couple of summers, while I was going to school, in the Avenue Lodge. There was construction in those days. I was in the back, doing up the milk and getting it ready for the tables.

I worked in Charlie Long's drugstore until the Company took over. **Charlie Long** was an American with great ideas and he put in a soda fountain. He brought in ice cream. One year, after he went to a World Series game, he brought back an electric waffle iron and we served waffles in the drugstore.

I had the sweet shop, during the war, at the Patricia Theatre. The rent was very cheap. I don't think the theatre opened every night. It was the wrong time of course (to run a sweet shop) – we couldn't get any chocolates. They were carrying Pauline Johnson chocolates when I took over. We couldn't buy – we were rationed. Anyway, it was quite a good experience – we would just save our rations.

We were also rationed with ice cream, so when ice cream came in, we were busy. Mrs. Alice Padgett's sister used to help out. Young girls will say, "I worked for you," but I can't really remember.

When my brothers (Albert and Marino) came home (from the war) I thought this is it. Mr. Dunning took the sweet shop over and made it into a fast meal place.

When you grow up in a town you don't realize all the changes. There was no Westview. The Townsite (today) is so sad. It was so beautiful; all the streets were lined with trees. It was so busy. Everything was centralized. Of course, there was shift work. You'd see the men coming off shift with their buckets and the men going on. **The Powell River Company was very good – marvellous.**"

Looking Back with Al (Alan) Hamerton

Townsite Pioneers:
William and Annie Donkersley (from 1911)
Octavius and Euphemia Hamerton (from 1912)

Al Hamerton's maternal grandfather, **William Donkersley**, came to the Powell River Townsite with his two boys, Harry (born 1891) and Len (born 1892) in 1911. William, by trade, was a blacksmith and shoed horses. He worked on the docks with Powell River Company horses, hauling newsprint rolls from the docks to the warehouse.

William's wife Annie and younger children came a few months later after William had saved up enough money for their fares.

William and Annie were married in Yorkshire, England in 1890; they had 10 children. Al's mother, Lucy Donkersley was born in Leeds, England in 1905; she was the second to the last of the 10 children.

William and Annie rented a house in the Townsite on Poplar Street, near Bird's funeral home, for many years. They celebrated their golden wedding anniversary in 1940. After William retired from the mill, they moved to Westview. William died in 1945 and Annie in 1954.

Lucy married Ernie Hamerton in 1925. Al (Alan) Hamerton was born in 1926.

Al's cousin, **Harry Donkersley won the DFC (Distinguished Flying Cross) and Bar in WWII.** He was the first war hero to receive the medal from King George VI in Buckingham Palace. Flgt. Lieutenant Harry Donkersley tragically died in January 1944. His plane was lost on a flight around the Stave Lake District in the Fraser Valley.

****

Al Hamerton's paternal grandfather, **Octavius Hamerton, came to the Powell River Townsite in 1912 to work for the Powell River Company**. He was the eighth child in the family, hence his parents naming him Octavius.

Octavius and Euphemia Hamerton first lived in Riverside, and then moved to the corner lot opposite the present Patricia Theatre – this lot is now the site of Ljubo's Bakery. The railroad went by their back door. After the railroad engines and rolling stock ceased going by their property, Octavius was able to add the vacated track area to the property. He raised a beautiful flower garden there.

Al's father, **Ernie Hamerton**, born in 1904, was first employed working for the **Powell River Company** in Powell Stores. He married Lucy Donkersley, who was employed as a bookkeeper for the Powell River Company.

He started, as a part-time job, working as projectionist in the first Patricia Theatre (located where the cenotaph is today). The movies were black-and-white and were silent with Stan Meade, and later Glen Hayden, playing the piano. Children sat at the front of the first theatre and adults at the back. Frank Haslam, as a young kid, worked in the theatre, cleaning the floor after the patrons had left. His pay was a free pass to the movies!

As a baby, Al Hamerton was wheeled into the Patricia Theatre in a perambulator by his mother, Lucy Hamerton (Donkersley).

Ernie became a full-time projectionist and made the move to the new Patricia Theatre in November 1928. The new Patricia Theatre continued to show silent movies until 1930, when the first talking movie shown was *Chasing Rainbows*. On March 14, 1932 the safe of the Patricia Theatre was blown and a cashbox stolen by two notorious criminals, Bagley and Fawcett.

Ernie Hamerton retired in 1960 and moved to Invermere where he worked as projectionist.

Al Hamerton married Norene Vincent in 1950. Al worked in the mill from 1947-87; initially, as an engineer on the railroad, then as a millwright, and finally as a planner in the trade planning department.

Al was on duty at the mill the night the *Teeshoe* went down on December 4, 1954. He took the following call from the pilot:

"Lost sight of the Teeshoe in the storm and night. Worried about their safety. Did they get ashore?"

Al told the pilot to phone the watchman's office as they had all the procedures to follow, in case of loss at sea. He gave the pilot the number. The next day he heard the *Teeshoe* had sunk. Three men had perished; however, one boy had survived.

Al and Norene lived in the Townsite from 1953-54; afterwards they made a permanent move to Fernwood Avenue, in Westview, not too far from the house where Norene grew up in the 1930s and 40s.

Looking Back!
Carol Jean Cotton Pritchard

The Townsite from 1911: The Pritchards and Trovengers

Albert Frank Pritchard married Irene Frances Trovenger in Vancouver in **1916**. They had first met in the Powell River Townsite. Albert Frank Pritchard worked for the Powell River Company in the electrical department. Irene worked in the payroll department and they met when she was making up the wages. After receiving two paycheques from the attractive pay clerk, "Bert" plucked up the courage to ask her out!

The **Trovenger family** came to Powell River in 1911. George, his wife Sarah Jane (nee Sweney) and their two daughters lived in a company house next door to **Frank Haslam's family** on Maple Avenue.

George Frank Trovenger initially came on his own in the early years of the Powell River Company and then went back to Oregon to get his family. George had been a papermaker in the U.S. and he came to Powell River to instruct others in his trade. He helped produce the first roll of paper which came off the machines in 1912. George and Sarah returned to Oregon in 1916.

Prior to working in Powell River, the young Bert Pritchard had worked in Ocean Falls, B.C. He came to Powell River in 1914. Bert helped start up the Stillwater plant.

Bert worked for the Powell River Company until he retired. Bert and Irene became long-time residents in the Townsite. They lived in the same house on Maple Avenue from 1916 to 1960. Next door was the Gopher Club where young single men from Oregon stayed. Parents of Mable Murray (Rowe) cooked for the bachelors.

Bert and Irene enjoyed the social amenities in the area. They owned a cabin at the Hole in the Wall on Powell Lake. In 1935 they bought a recreational property at Douglas Bay near the D'Angio property. This was a cottage they camped in during the summer. Later on, they sold the property and bought another property not too far away, in the same bay, from **Pat Buhler's parents**. This is the same location where the Pritchard house is today. Bert and Irene had many parties in their summer house. In the winter there were skating parties on the frozen pond on the **Lang farm property**. Bert and Irene retired to Douglas Bay in 1960.

Bert and Irene had one son, **Ken A. Pritchard**, born in 1925. Ken attended the old Henderson School and Brooks. Ken wrote the Thunderbird song for Brooks School. He graduated in 1943. Ken attended university in Tulsa, Oklahoma and graduated with a degree in aeronautical engineering. After university, he returned to Powell River and worked for nine months in the engineering department in the mill in order to get his working visa for the U.S. He spent most of his working life in Alberta, working in the oil industry.

Ken returned to live in the family home in Douglas Bay in 1991. In 1992 the present house was built. The old house was relocated on Padgett Road.

Ken married Carol Jean Cotton in 1950. They have three children: Patti, Judi and Ken I. Pritchard (Kip). Patti Coburn lives in Powell River; Judi Baker/Spencer in Seattle, Washington and Kip in Douglas Bay, Powell River. Ken I. Pritchard owns **Ken's Personal Touch Floor & Window Fashions Ltd.** on Marine Avenue in Westview, Powell River.

Ken A. Pritchard died in 2002, after a courageous battle with Parkinson's.

On July 18, 2007 Carol Pritchard's children hosted a very special 80th birthday party celebration for **Carol Jean Cotton Pritchard** at Douglas Bay for family and friends.

Frank Haslam – Looking Back!

Childhood Memories of the Townsite (from 1911)

The Powell River Company was formed in 1910, and in 1911 the pulp mill was under construction. In conjunction with the building of the mill, came the building of the first Townsite houses, a hotel, and a Chinese laundry.

The Company advertised for qualified tradesmen in the major newspapers. Samuel Haslam saw one of these ads when he brought his family to Edmonton in 1911. Samuel and his wife Mary had left Bolton in Lancashire, England in 1911 with their children: Bill, Tom, Phoebe, Walter, Minnie, and Frank to seek a better life in Canada. Frank was only 7 years old at that time.

Frank Haslam:

"We boarded the S.S. Victorian, the Cunard Line in Liverpool and we landed in Montreal. From Montreal we travelled by train to Edmonton. Dad saw an ad in a newspaper for skilled tradesmen by the Powell River pulp and paper company. He headed for Powell River to get a job there. The rest of the family, with the exception of Bill, followed him a month later. Bill stayed in Edmonton because he found a job in his trade (barbering).

We came up the coast on the old Union Steamship line. The Haslam family were the third family to take up residence in the Townsite. Our first home was on Maple Avenue (renamed Sycamore) and then we moved to 160 Maple Avenue.

My father's first job was in the company storage room. He later was placed in his trade, in the tin shop. Curly Woodward's dad was head of the carpenters' shop and Billy Loukes was a plumber. Billy had two boys, Joe and Jack; Joe was head of the meat counter and Jack was a carpenter.

My brother Tom went back to the old country to marry his sweetheart; he stayed there. Walter worked at the Powell River mill. Phoebe worked in the Superior Laundry and married Frank Highington. Minnie worked at the company store; she worked her way up from shop assistant to working in the office. Minnie married Courtney Powell."

The first Powell River school in 1911 was a one-room school and was held in a poolroom for five months. Miss E. Anderson was the teacher and she enrolled a class of 13 children.

The present site of the Townsite Anglican Church was designated for a school by the Powell River Company. The second Powell River school was built on this site in the summer of 1911 and was ready for opening in September 1911. Miss Murdoch and Mr. Buckton enrolled 53 students in the 1911-12 school year. The students sat two to a desk, with the overflow on benches. Frank and his sister Minnie were two of these students.

Frank recalls attending the Powell River Company school:

"I remember a room upstairs for the bigger children and a basement for the smaller children. Mr. Buckton was the Principal.

I could read and write with a pen before coming to Canada. I had attended a primary school in Bolton, England.

I transferred with my sister Minnie and all the other children to the first Henderson school which opened in 1913. Children from Wildwood attended the first Henderson school until 1926, when they had their own school in Wildwood.

Tommy Alsworth was the first principal at Henderson School until he joined up to fight in WWI. Miss Stivens became the principal while he was away in France. It was quite a surprise to me, when Tommy came back from the war, he married Miss Stivens!"

As a young boy in the growing Townsite, Frank earned some extra cash by doing a number of part-time jobs during his teenage years. He sold newspapers that came to town on the Union Steamship boats, and delivered bread and laundry in a wagon. In the early Townsite years, horses and wagons were the main means of transport.

Frank, a boy from Lancashire, helped J. Errico (known as Jerrico) deliver vegetables grown on leased land from the Company (where the tennis courts are today). Joe spoke broken English and to the amusement of the customers, Frank spoke the same way!

As young children in the Townsite, Frank and Minnie received gifts from the Powell River Company at the yearly Christmas Tree gift-giving event.

Frank recalls playing in the Company baseball teams:

"Baseball was a big game in the Townsite. The Powell River Company had built a baseball diamond behind the Rodmay Hotel where the company parking lot is today. All the men and boys played baseball. I was in both the Junior and Adult baseball teams. In 1949 I was selected for the "All Star" squad. It was a great thing for everyone in the Townsite to watch a baseball game."

When Frank was 14 he was given a job in the Powell River Company finishing room. He worked there for a year and then he joined his father to train as a sheet metal worker.

In 1927 Frank left the Powell River Company to work on his own. In 1936 he inherited his father's tin shop (where the Chopping Block is today) in Westview. In 1960 he sold his business and retired to Palm Beach. At age 102, Frank moved to the new Kiwanis Garden Manor Assisted Living community.

1940s Dwight Hall (built 1927 – largest community hall on the West Coast). Used for old-time dancing, plays, exhibitions, community events etc. On the lower floor, meeting rooms and library.   Private collection.

Townsite children 1911: (left) Minnie and Frank Haslam.   (Frank Haslam collection)
(right) Catherine McKinney (Gertie Lambert collection)

The first Henderson School built by the Powell River Company in 1913 for the fast-growing school population of the area. Insert: Dr. Andrew Henderson. Photos: Courtesy of the Powell River Museum

Old Henderson School rhythm band (1938), school playground, Oak Street houses (rear), Powell River Townsite. Today this is a playground. Leader: Barry Taylor (centre). Bev Falconer (Carrick) front row, left of leader. Doug Carrick front row – far right, near swings. Photo: Bev Falconer (Carrick)

Joe and Alice Falconer in the garden of the Mill Manager's house (known as the Cooper House) in the early 1930s. Photo: Lorna Miles (Falconer)

WWII Townsite children knitting for Britain with Mrs. Watson and Mrs. Irvine 1943. Back row (L to R) Jean Carrick/Norma Flett/Mrs. Watson/Mrs. Irvine/Margaret Allan/Barbara Woodward. Middle row: Yolande Bledsoe/Moira Carrick/Gloria Levae/Joan Thorpe. Front row: Yvonne Tunstall/Bunty Ford/Catherine Carnelly/Fran Flett/Marnie Woodward. Photo: Norma Smith (Flett)

Looking Back!
The Falconers – an early Townsite Family 1914-37

Joseph (Joe) Falconer first came to Powell River in 1914, working for a short time for the Powell River Company before volunteering to fight in WWI. Joe joined the 29th Battalion, Vancouver Regiment at the beginning of the war and did not return to Powell River until January 1919. Joe received the DCM for his bravery in action.

John Robert Banham and **Captain Bell-Irving** served in the same regiment.

Joe was originally from Portknockie, Banffshire, Scotland. In his late teens, after finishing his education in Aberdeen, he left for Canada. His first job as an accountant was on staff at the Traders' Bank, Toronto; afterwards, he transferred to St. Catherine's and Webbwood branches. Before joining the Powell River Pulp and Paper Company, Joe had valuable experience working for the Spanish River Pulp and Paper Company.

Joe worked for the Powell River Company in Powell River for two decades. His banking and accounting experience gave him top positions in the mill. In 1923 he was Mill Secretary (Bell-Irving was Resident Engineer and John McIntyre, Townsite Manager).

In 1926 Joe was promoted to Assistant Manager; by the early 1930s, manager, and in 1937 moved to Vancouver to take up the position as Powell River Comptroller at the Powell River Company head office.

Joe married Alice McKissock in 1922. Alice had worked for the CP in Vancouver on the silk train express (bringing silk from the Orient to North America). They had three children: Sheila, Lorna, and Roderick.

Joe and Alice enjoyed the social functions in the Townsite – the Papermakers' Ball on New Year's Eve was the highlight of the year. Alice bought dresses from Madame Loukes' 5th Avenue Dress Shop in Westview. Lorna Falconer remembers the Christmas Tree event at Dwight Hall when all the children in the area received a gift from the Powell River Company. Joe and Alice were involved in the outdoor recreational activities provided by the Company: lawn bowling, golfing, and fishing at Rainbow Lodge.

The Falconer family enjoyed their Savary Island summer home. Dr. Marlatt had a house nearby. The family continued to use their summer home until the 1950s when it was sold. The chimney on their house was a solid one, built by Bloomfield. In the 1946 earthquake, many chimneys moved and turned – not the Bloomfield chimney! Lorna remembers the Mace family and Jim Spilsbury on Savary Island. Jim Spilsbury sold and fixed radios – later went into the airline industry.

Looking Back with Elio Cossarin

Townsite Pioneers: the Cossarin Brothers (1920s)

In the early 1920s the three Cossarin brothers, Jack, Pete, and Joe worked for the Powell River Company. They lived in Riverside.

In 1914 Jack came to Canada from Italy. He worked for the Powell River Company from 1919-26. Jack played baseball. Jack returned to Italy in 1926 and never returned to Canada.

Jack Cossarin had an interest in photography and took a number of early Powell River (Townsite) photos during the seven-year period he resided here (1919-26). These photos would have been lost to history, however, a few of Jack's photos were sent from relatives in Italy, many decades later, to his nephew Elio Cossarin in Powell River.

Joe Cossarin, during the Depression years, left Powell River and looked for work on Vancouver Island. Joe stayed on Vancouver Island the rest of his life.

Pete (Pietro) Cossarin came to Powell River to work for the Powell River Company in 1923. He worked on the yard crew and later on the wharf. After becoming a naturalized Canadian he returned in 1930 to Italy for a visit. This "holiday" lasted 17 years before he returned to Powell River in 1948! Pete was unable to return to Canada during the Great Depression and WWII, as leaving Italy was actively discouraged by the Italian government.

After WWII the Canadian government, with friendly relations re-established between the two countries, issued Canadian passports to all naturalized Canadians of Italian origin stranded in Italy due to the war. Pete seized the opportunity to return to Canada.

On his return to Powell River, Pete tried to get his old job back with the Powell River Company but found he was too old to be rehired. Eventually, he was able to get a job as a labourer with **City Transfer**. After working for them for a few years, he returned permanently to Italy. Elio Cossarin, with a brand new Canadian passport, joined his father in Powell River in 1950.

Elio's hometown was Prodolone, a subdivision of San Vito al Tagliamento in the province of Pordenone in north-eastern Italy. In 1993 Elio retired from the Powell River mill; from 1986-93 he was Supervisor of the Shipping Department.

In the above group, left to right, are: 1st row: L.A.C. Gordie MacKenzie, Pts. "Pat" Miller, Sergt. Rod Matheson, Corp. Bob Lye, Pte. Tommy Oldala, Pte. Dick Jacob; 2nd row: Flying Officer J. A. Kyles, C.S.M. Harry Davies, Pte. Bruce Butler, Pte. O. McKinnon; 3rd row: L.A.C. George Rennie, Gunner Howard Rowe, Corp. Harold Belyea, Pte. "Gerry" Tweed, Corp. Chas. Robson, Corp. Bill Moore, Corp. Charlie MacIntosh, Pte. Joe Warman, Pte. George Drayton, Pte. Norm. Hill, Pte. Len Taylor, Pte. Fred Peterson, Corp. "Tish" Schon, Tpr. Bill Dalzell, Corp. Harris; 4th row: Pte. Ralph Kenny, Corp. Frank Manniou, Corp. Gino Bortolussi, Pte. George Haddock, L.A.C. Jackie Grundle, Lance-Corp. Art Button, Pte. Fred Harding.

1943 Powell River reunion, London, England. "Our boys" in uniform.   *Photo: Powell River Museum*

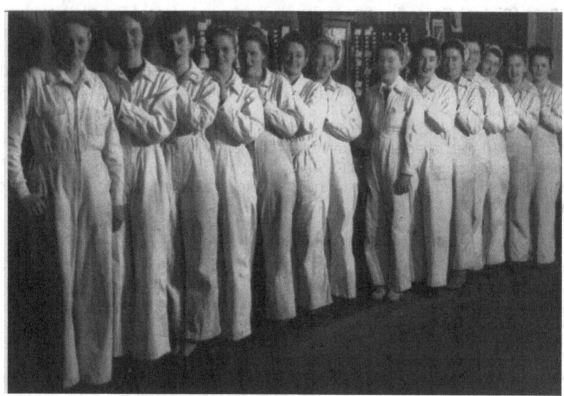

1942 "Our girls" working for the Powell River Company during WWII.
(L to R) _____/May Pauling/Pam Johnson (Cloke)/Barbara Manwood/May Wards/Hanna Johnson/_____/ Alida Fie (Simard)/_____/Elizabeth Cameron (Evans)/_____/Verna Harper/Arlene Huxter
Photo: Powell River Museum

WWII: Powell River Sub-assembly Plant Boeing Workers 1943
(L to R) Freeda Mohr (Parsons)/Jean Northey (Thompson)/Mildred Ross (Dice)/Dodie McGillivary (Anderson)/
Lynette Hayes (Toll)/Barbara Manwood/Isobel Aubre. Photo: Powell River Museum

1943 "Invasion!" A training exercise by Canadian soldiers from Comox, Vancouver Island.
Landing barges hit the beach (Townsite area). Photo: Powell River Museum

Powell River Townsite 1924 Brandolini family
(L to R) Ottavio & Erminea Brandolini/Ligia/Echara/Fides/Asswero Brandolini
Photo: Fides Prissinotti (Brandolini)

Piccoli family, Wildwood, B.C. 192_?
Front row: Mary/middle row: Amalia/Angelina/Isadora. Back row: seated (centre) Giuseppe & Anna Piccoli
Standing: Mafalda (L)/Gagliano (R). Photo: Amalia Gustafson (Piccoli)

Italian community – musical group, Riverside, Powell River Townsite 1924.
Back row: Tony Marin. Photographer Jack Cossarin. Jack worked for the Powell River Company from 1919-1926
then returned permanently to Italy.
Elio Cossarin collection

Labour Day, Riverside, Powell River Townsite, B.C. 1928
Young men (centre): Elio Shiffo/Joe Vizzutti/Angelo Turchet/Primo Gobbo
Left rear: unknown/Ottavio Brandolini/Fides Brandolini   right rear: unknown
Photo: Fides Prissinotti (Brandolini)

Employees of the Powell River Company waiting by Angelo Diana's property, Cranberry for the bus to the Powell River Townsite 1954. Verginio Pantarotto/Tony Fabris/Pete Cossarin/Angelo Diana/Giovanni Francescutti/Fedele Zuppichin/Elio Cossarin. Photo: Elio Cossarin collection

*Powell River Company mill finishing room 1926. Photographer: Jack Cossarin
Back: _____/Pete Toigo/Mike Bidin/Vico Peticco/Joe Cossarin/Giordano Canzian/Ernesto Mussio
Front: Toni Francescutti/Gildo Patrucco/Angelo Diana. Insert photo right: Left – Jack Cossarin (carrying camera)
Right – Pete Cossarin 1926. Photos: Elio Cossarin collection*

Amalia Piccoli (Gustafson) born in the Townsite 1916.
Amalia has lived her entire life (2009 – 93 years) in
Powell River (Townsite, Wildwood & Westview). Photo
1916 baby Amalia Piccoli - Powell River Townsite.
Photographer: unknown – (?) Rod LeMay.
Photo: Amalia Gustafson

Wedding of Ned Brandolini and Fides Prissinotti 1934.
Insert photo: (L to R) – unknown/Ned Brandolini:
Musicians in Riverside, Powell River Townsite, 1920s.
Photos: Fides Prissinotti (Brandolini)

Looking Back with Fides Prissinotti (Brandolini) (born 1916)

Townsite 1920's – From Bunkhouse to Riverside

Fides (at age 91) recalls first coming directly to the Powell River Townsite, from Italy in 1920, at 4 years of age, with her parents **Ottavio and Erminea Brandolini**. They travelled from Italy to Germany and from there, by boat to Halifax. They crossed Canada by train; Fides remembers the hard wooden benches on the train.

The Brandolinis came to Powell River because they had family here – Mina and Fortunato Bressenutti were Fides' aunt and uncle. **The Bressenuttis were pioneers in the community in 1910, the year the pulp and paper town of Powell River had its beginnings.** They lived on Maple Avenue.

The only available housing was in a bunkhouse and it was here the family of two adults, four children (Asswero and three sisters: Fides, Echara, and Ligia) and six boarders stayed for four years until a house became available at Riverside in 1924. Riverside expanded at this time with the addition of seven new houses. The Brandolinis were able to get one of them.

Fides Prissinotti (Brandolini):

"As children we were allowed in the grinder room – we were allowed to do that. They showed us how these grinders, these big round things, where they were throwing the fibre in there – showed us how they were making paper. They had two elevators in the mill and we would go up and down in the elevators.

We always used to bring the lunches down there. There was this old man – he was batching in one of those bunkhouses in Riverside – because there was quite a few men who didn't have their wives here. He said,

'Ermina, how about you send Fides down and bring my supper?'

And she'd make him a good supper – just like eating at home. I'd go down there and go outside, behind these big doors which opened out. I remember sitting there, talking to this old man. We were always down there, as children.

All the Italians never brought a sandwich – they had a real meal. We had a wicker basket with a lid. We'd put everything in there. They would take out this stuff – just like they were eating at home. To drink, they had milk or wine – Italians like to drink a glass of wine. We had the dish, fork and knife, and glass – just like they were eating at home. We had to get it down there fast – so it was hot. We waited until they finished and then brought the stuff back. Sometimes, my brother would go down with three lunches. The men (the bachelors) would pay (the women and children) so much money to take down the lunches.

Lots of bachelors – they were all out here without their wives. Lots went back in the early 1930s. Lots brought wives and girlfriends over here on the boat and got married over here. Some left permanently.

Some families lived in Riverside, some lived in Wildwood, not very many in Cranberry, and, of course, Westview wasn't here yet!

There was one **bunkhouse** per family; my parents lived in this long bunkhouse (#2). She (Ermina) had about five or six boarders. We all stayed in that big, long bunkhouse. When we moved to **Riverside** the house was for our family. The big room upstairs – five or six boarders would be sleeping up there. My mother worked hard, everything was done by hand – there were no washing machines or vacuum cleaners.

We had an icebox at Riverside but not in the bunkhouse. At Riverside, we moved into one of the new houses – no insulation – just heated with the woodstove in the kitchen. We had electricity and an indoor toilet. We had an indoor toilet in the bunkhouse.

Powell River Company, at the time, did a lot of nice things for their workers. They made all those nice homes there. We were allowed to use these heaters to keep the houses warm in winter – and not pay the electricity.

My dad would go out and get the wood. Everybody was going out in the bush. We would go up behind Cranberry Lake.

In 1910 they were cutting down the trees and they couldn't get them out of the bush. Big huge trees with bark six inches thick – they were still lying there behind Cranberry Lake – by this time (1920s) the bark was loose. We'd peel it off and pile it up. We'd go up there about 7 o'clock and come back at noon; that was what we did before we could go down on the beach. Dad would rent a truck and get the bark.

After school we'd go down to the sawmill and bring home two or three loads of scrap wood to burn – it (the living) was not luxurious.

In the summer we ran around in bare feet. My mother said it was healthy for the feet – it was healthy for the pocketbook!

Mother cooked from scratch – all these Italian dishes. I'm sure she cooked a lot of spaghetti. She'd cook stews and roasts. The men always got a glass of wine with their meal. My dad made wine, beer, and root beer.

We got milk from the farmers in Wildwood – a Mr. Zorzi delivered milk. Mr. (Tom) Lambert was delivering goat's milk. The Culos' from Cranberry, across from the school there – that house is about 85 years old – they delivered milk.

We either walked up to Wildwood or walked up to Cranberry on a Sunday when it was nice. Of course, we knew these people (the Italian families in the villages). We walked everywhere. No money for the bus. I have walked up to 15 miles in a day.

We all went to the old Henderson School. We walked up to Henderson School from Riverside; the Bon Ton was right there when we crossed the bridge from Riverside, behind that building and behind the apartment block that is still there on the corner, and up to Henderson. We went home for lunch for a dish of soup – it filled us up.

We bought bread. **The Farndens had a bakery in one of the long bunkhouses** – it was French bread, tasted good, there was no slice bread yet. We bought butter and flour in the Powell Stores.

The Sing Lee store was at the Shingle Mill. The bridge to go across to the Shingle Mill was at the foot of Cedar Street. Then the road would go to the Shingle Mill and up to Wildwood. There used to be this flight of stairs to the top of the hill – the kids used to slide down on the sand.

In the **old Patricia Theatre (first one by the cenotaph)** were rows of chairs stuck together at the back – when the kids got excited, they would shake these seats all over the place. We had a man playing the piano – the films were silent of course. **Glen Hadyn** played the piano. He was sitting in an enclosure behind a canvas. He was a good piano player. We would be sitting close to that enclosure – kicking it in excitement – soon the canvas was gone. We were not well behaved!

When the talkies came in at the new Patricia Theatre, I got into trouble. I think the film was 7th Heaven and we stayed to watch it twice – when we got home we got it – instead of getting home at 9, it was 10:30 p.m. My sister ran into the bathroom and shut herself in. I got a good licking for staying out for so long.

We started this Italian Club (1924). We had lots of dances in Dwight Hall (from 1928). **We depended on each other for entertainment. Quite a few had instruments – what we did didn't cost us any money.** There were very few weddings – I can't remember any – not many girls.

We had parties in the houses at Riverside at Easter and Christmas – we danced, stood around, visited, and had a good time.

Bosa was a general store – buy a little of everything. They had salami, ham, groceries, but not fresh meat. When my parents left, I went to live with my aunt and uncle, Italia and Beppe Massotti – she was my dad's sister. When my uncle got laid off, they went to Trail, B.C. They sold it (the house) to the Dini family. I had left already and went to live in New Westminster, B.C."

In 1932 Fides' father, Ottavio, was laid off in the big purge by the Powell River Company. The Brondolini family, with the exception of Fides, moved to New Westminster and never came back to Powell River. Other Italian families, laid off at the same time, moved out of town – some to Trail and others to Victoria and Vancouver; they never came back to Powell River. Some families stayed in Wildwood and a few in Cranberry.

Fides married Ned Prissinotti in 1934. Ned's father Eugenio Prissinotti came to work for the Powell River Company in 1910. Fides and Ned lived in Trail and New Westminster for three years before returning to Powell River in 1937.

In 1937, the Paper Makers Local was organized by the workers in the Powell River mill. Negotiations, in the same year, gave birth to the B.C. Standard Labour Agreement.

The only time Fides was away from Powell River were the years, 1934 to 1937. In 1937 Ned obtained a job with the Powell River Company; he had previously worked for the Powell River Company in the early 1930s. After his father had left for Italy (never to return) Ned had boarded with the Cecconni family in a house on Maple Avenue. Ned had left Powell River in 1934 and found work in Trail.

Fides and Ned lived in the Townsite for four years; first they lodged with another family for eight months in Riverside and then they moved into their own place at #8 Riverside. Then came a move to **Westview**; Ned (a wonderful cabinetmaker and carpenter) built their own house at the corner of Alberni and Joyce. They lived there for 27 years, before moving the house to its present location, near Grief Point School. Fides and Ned had two children: Nello and Anita Louise.

Note: Ned's brother Torchy Prissinotti came to Powell River in 1948 to work for the Powell River Company. His future wife, Norina Daneluz left Italy in 1950 to join him.

Looking Back with Stella Saunders (Hall/Hewson) (1914-2008)

The Townsite (1920s & 30s)

Stella Hall (born 1914) at the age of 8 came with her parents, **Alfred and Jenny Hall** from New Westminster to Powell River in 1922. Alfred worked as janitor for the Powell River Company from 1922 to sometime in the 1930s.

After living in Cranberry for a couple of years, the family, in 1924, moved to 1070 Ocean View across from Brooks School.

During the 1930s, Jenny Hall took in boarders: Curly Woodward, Hugh McKay, Harry Whitaker, and Ted Maxwell.

Stella attended Henderson School. Boys sat on one side of the class and girls on the other – no mixing! Her first teacher was Miss Brett. A Mr. Thorsteinson also taught her; he was very strict – the boys were punished by having to sit with the girls! The strap was also used. Stella played softball. Dr. Henderson visited the school and one time he spoke to Stella – he advised her to eat porridge for breakfast! Dr. Henderson lived in a house near the hospital.

The family attended Papermakers' Balls on New Year's Eve. Every Saturday night they went to the Patricia Theatre.

Stella and her two sisters, Harriet and Beatrice, married men who worked for the Powell River Company. Harriet worked at Linzey's Jewellery store and married Walter Hopkins, a papermaker who worked in the machine room. Beatrice married Ray Preston, who first worked in the finishing room, and later was janitor at Cranberry School. Stella married Laurie Hewson in 1934; he also worked in the finishing room at the mill. Stella and Laurie rented a house from the Harper's in Westview, near Marine Avenue.

Townsite Memories

"*When we first arrived in 1922, **Sing Lee had a store in the Townsite**. He later moved to the Shingle Mill.*

Mr. Florence was manager at the Powell River Company store. Mr. Semple was in charge of fruit and vegetables (Stella worked for a short time in this department after WWII). The apples and oranges came wrapped and the bananas were on a long stalk. There were baked goods, meat, and vegetables at the store. Grass seed and fertilizer were kept in a room by themselves. Money was sent up to the office in a tube and change sent back the same way.

Later on, dry goods and shoe store were downstairs – upstairs was the grocery store, Mr. Farnden had a bakery. There was a cafeteria and a shop that sold cosmetics and cards etc. Next down was a drugstore. The post office was across the lane – the mail was put in boxes (everyone had a box number). Jean Coccola had an office at the back of the store. Now, going up on the street, was the Bank of Montreal. Across the mill and across the street was Linzey's Jewellery store – the hotel – Gordon's store – around the corner a shoe store and a taxi stand – nearby, a large ball park.

Up from Linzey's Jewellery store was Kip Taylor's drugstore, and a cafeteria. Across the lane was Dwight Hall, a library below and a dance floor above. The cenotaph was next to Dwight Hall, across the street was the liquor store, post office, and at the top of the street was the Patricia Theatre – a candy store and jewellery store next to the theatre.

Bagley & Fawcett robbery (1932) – the robbers tied the man at the theatre – he managed to phone the police and the police chased the robbers. They had a boat at Stillwater and got away.

Powell River Company had a big Christmas Tree event. Santa gave all the employee's children a present that they had asked for (1920s & early 30s).

Jack Wilson used to take the head people of the company up the lake to **Rainbow Lodge**.

The bosses at the mill had two rows of houses across from the tennis court.

Dr. Lyons' dog was always with Watson McKnight until it was hurt – then it went back to Dr. Lyons to fix him up and then back the dog went to Watson!

I taught Sunday school in the old United Church in the Townsite. They ran a Young People's Society.

WWII – I worked in **Boeing Sub-Assembly plant** on the Powell River Company mill site – Mrs. Bull (supervisor) was with me when I started. **I was a fitter and I learned to handle a drill.** After the plant closed, some of the girls went into the mill to work. I applied to work in the Company store. Before I got a job in the store, I took catering at the mill – I went around the mill with milk and sandwiches to the various departments, until the cafeteria opened.

Looking Back with Faith McGuffie (Rowe)

Francis Rowe – Nurse & Midwife in the Townsite (from 1919)
Faith Rowe – owner of Rowe's Junior Style Dress Shop (1955-73)
– Westview

Faith McGuffie (Rowe) 2000:

*"My parents **Claude and Francis Rowe** worked in a Winnipeg hospital at the beginning of the 20th century. My father, Claude, was an orderly and my mother, Francis, a nurse. They came to Powell River in 1919 with their children: Eileen, Howard, Faith, and Anne. Mable and Mary were born in Powell River.*

My father had a job at the Powell River Company mill at 38 cents an hour.

*My mother took in boarders, as well as working as a midwife. **Francis Rowe brought many Townsite babies into the world.** She was a well-known and respected person in Powell River.*

For some reason, my father quit his job at the mill as he thought he would make a living by fishing. He was able to get a pre-emption six miles out of Lund. Dad built a log house for the family there. He soon found out there was no money in fishing, so he went back to work in the mill and left the family at Lund. As our property was a pre-emption, we had to live on it for five years, "to prove it" and gain title.

Dad batched out in Powell River for six years, then my mother gave my father an ultimatum, either he moved the family back to Powell River or she would move herself to an unknown destination. This did the trick, and Dad arranged for a gas boat to pick up the entire family and goods at Rassmussen Bay.

I shall never forget arriving at the government dock, in Powell River (Townsite), in the dark. I looked up and there were porch lights on, outside every house. It looked like paradise.

We lived on Cedar Street for many years. We never went back to the homestead at Lund. Dad had steady work in the mill and mother was busy as a midwife.

I attended the "old" Henderson School. After I left school at the age of 16, I went to work in the Avenue Lodge as a chambermaid. Sometimes, I was asked to waitress when out-of-town officials stayed at the Lodge.

*Later on, **I owned and ran Rowe's Junior Style Dress Shop on Marine Avenue in Westview (1955-73).** I would go to Vancouver twice a year in order to order directly from the factory."*

Looking Back with William (Bill) Jones (1900-1984)

Fired in 1932 by the Powell River Company

I was born in Birkenhead, England in 1900. When I was 10 years old, my mother took me several times to the meetings of the Independent Labour Party.

I came out to Canada in 1923 to the Prairies and worked on a harvesting expedition.

I came to Powell River (Townsite) in 1926. I lived in the Avenue Lodge. I was an electrician and I got a job on one of the phases of construction. At that time #5 and #6 machines were going in. I eventually got a job that was permanent on the maintenance crew, working as an electrician.

In 1926 there was no such place as Westview. There were a few shacks down where the park is now (Michigan Landing - Willingdon Beach). There was just a few people living there and just a sprinkling of people a little further back. There were people living in Cranberry and Wildwood. Wildwood was the first place to open up; people went up there because they could get some good tracks of land. Most of them worked at the mill and did some farming on the side. There was comparatively little farming in Cranberry.

Powell River was a real Company Town. Everything was run by the Company. There were some restrictions we had then, for instance, you couldn't have a (battery) radio without the permission of the chief electrician. The atmosphere was restrictive but nobody complained because the jobs were very good. There was definitely a class division in the town between the worker's families – you could feel it. The accommodations in the Townsite were certainly good and the rents were cheap.

In the early 1930s, the Company decided to cut down on employees. I was one of those who was cut off in 1932 before the election. But there is no doubt I would have been fired in 1933 because I was doing just as much talking as everyone else.

After the 1933 election of Bakewell (CCF) the mill management panicked and literally fired dozens of people. It was the management; it was not the Powell River Company itself, but the local management and one or two people outside. But the town, it was really a desperate place then; it wasn't a good place to be in.

I became an independent businessman (electrician) in Cranberry and later, Westview. My wife, Edith worked in the Company offices for a few years. We were both members of the Old Time Dance Club.

Looking Back with Eddie Needham

Rex, Ina & Eddie Needham
worked in the Powell River Mill (1934-1992)

Father, mother, and son worked in the Powell River pulp and paper mill: Rex from 1934-69, Ina Needham 1943-45, and Eddie Needham from 1951-92.

Edward Rex Needham (originally from Nottingham, England) came to Vancouver, after trying farming in southern Alberta, in 1926. He drove truck for Roy Selman. In 1930 he married **Williamina (Ina) Jamieson Petrie** – her family were originally from Scotland.

In 1929 Roy Selman had a contract with the Powell River Company to dig a basement for #7 & #8 machines. Rex Needham came to Powell River to drive truck for Selman. Rex returned to Vancouver and continued working for Selman. In 1932 things became really bad in Vancouver; in 1934 Rex decided to try and get work in Powell River. He got work straight away in the grinder room at 45 cents an hour.

Rex brought his family up the area but found it difficult to find rental accommodation. In 1942 he was able to rent 310 Willow Avenue from the Powell River Company; prior to that the family had lived in rental accommodation in Westview and Cranberry. When the houses were sold off in the Townsite in 1955, Rex Needham bought his Willow Avenue house for $3,400! Larger houses, with basements, were sold in the Townsite for $5,000.

During WWII, Ina Needham worked for Boeing from November 1, 1943 to November 1, 1944 as a fitter on the PBY aircraft. Afterwards, she moved into the mill and worked in the beater room (feeding paper into the beater). She worked with Margaret Lewis; their foreman was Wally Norman. When the war was over it was back to being a housewife.

Eddie Needham grew up in Cranberry and the Townsite. From April 1948, as a student at Brooks High School, he worked part-time for the Powell River Company in different departments. In 1951 he went to work full time in the finishing room for a few months. By September 1951 he became apprenticed as a millwright. Eddie worked in the Powell River pulp and paper mill for 41 years as a millwright, before retiring in 1992.

Looking Back with Ena McKenzie (Graham)

The Granada – The Graham Residence (from 1934)

The present **Granada Restaurant** was originally a house owned by the Powell River Company. William and Elizabeth Graham and their daughter Ena came to live in the Company house in 1934. Prior to their residence in the house, a Mr. and Mrs. Carr had rented it for many years.

Mr. Carr was a tailor and had worked for the Company's stores, in men's clothing, doing alterations. After the Grahams had moved into the house in 1934, Mr. Carr rented their garage to use as a shop in which to do alterations.

In 1955, the Powell River Company sold off the Company houses, however, the five houses on the Granada block and three houses across the street (the staff quarters) were kept on reserve, in case the Company required the land for expansion. The Grahams continued to rent their house from the Company.

Peter Toigo approached the Powell River Company, regarding building a motel in the Townsite. He purchased the property on the Granada block (with the exception of the Graham house). This resulted in four of the five houses on this block being sold and moved off. He later asked to buy the remaining property as he'd decided to start a restaurant adjacent to the site. The Company approached Mrs. Graham and offered to rent her a four-room apartment in the Ocean View apartments if she vacated her Company house. She was pleased to make the move; it was convenient for her to downsize at this time.

- 1972 Granada established by John Maldovanos and Demos Kaloupis.
- 1973 Granada sold to Nick and Caso Apostolopoulous – for a few years had partners Chris and Ann Philis.
- 1985 Granada sold to Gus & Joyce Lenis, and Ken & Debbie Statham (for a few months). Then Gus and Joyce Lenis had full ownership.

William and Elizabeth Graham left Glasgow, Scotland in 1919 to make their journey by boat to Canada. They crossed the country by train to Vancouver, where relatives were living. William worked in a foundry in Vancouver until the Depression years, when the foundry he worked in closed down.

In 1934, William was able to find temporary work in the Powell River mill foundry due to a skilled worker being hospitalized. The patient died and William was offered a permanent job. The Powell River Company was operating three days a week at this time.

Initially, William stayed in the Avenue Lodge; however, he was able to bring his family up when a Company house, 120 Ocean View, became available for rent. William was foreman at the foundry, worked there full time during WWII and then retired.

Like many other Townsite families, the Graham family – William and Elizabeth and daughter Ena, enjoyed the benefits of Townsite life. Ena attended Grades 2-6 at the old Henderson School and graduated from Brooks High School in 1945. The family attended concerts and dances at Dwight Hall.

The family shopped at Powell Stores. Once a year they had a scheduled holiday in Vancouver and travelled down on the *Princess Mary*. This was a time for buying new school clothes.

In her high school years Ena worked Saturday mornings at Powell Stores. She filled in as spare help in the different departments (bakery etc.) After high school Ena worked in the Company office – helping with filing etc. before taking a business course in Vancouver. After working in Vancouver for a few years, Ena returned to Powell River. She married Don Clarke.

Don had worked for the Company before joining the Air Force in WWII. He returned to his Company job after the war. Don and Ena rented, first a duplex on Willow Avenue and then a larger house in the 1100 block on Laburnum Avenue. They bought their house in 1955 when the Powell River Company decided to get out of the business of running a town. Later, they sold their house and moved to Westview.

Don was a papermaker – Don and Ena attended the Papermaker balls. They also went dancing in Wildwood Hall where **Bob Gela** taught square dancing. Many of her mother's friends belonged to the Old Time Dance Club. Ena knew **Mrs. Alexander** – she taught old time dancing – she was strict and one had to abide by her rules! She was an excellent teacher.

Ena's beautiful yellow graduation dress was purchased from **Madame Loukes** in Westview. Madame Loukes was known to dress in casual fashion when serving customers – often appearing wearing slippers and no stockings. Ena recalls one occasion seeing her dressed like a million dollars when leaving Powell River airport for a buying trip in Vancouver. Madame Loukes was dressed like a fashion plate, in a black suit with a white hat. A string of pearls and beautiful white French kid gloves set off the outfit. She wore makeup and her outfit was perfect.

Looking Back with Bev Falconer (nee Carrick)

The Townsite – World War II Years

Dad was pleased, when an opportunity came to work for the Powell River Company on the Stillwater dam. The work was only three days a week, but was steady. The Powell River Company offered an incredible opportunity to so many families who had been struggling through the Depression. Almost everybody who worked in the mill wanted to live in one of the well-maintained Townsite houses – and the price was right; the monthly rent was $4 or $5 per room plus $2 if you had a view. However, newcomers like us had to put their names on a waiting list.

We moved from Vancouver to a shack in Westview in 1935, and then in 1937 were able to get a house in the Company town, the Townsite. My parents bought the electric stove from the previous tenants of our new house. This was feasible because the P.R. Company charged only a minimal flat rate ($2 per month) for electricity; you could use all you wanted.

The Company encouraged residents to leave porch lights on all night, as there were no streetlights in early days. But after a Japanese sub was sighted off the west coast of Vancouver Island, there were some changes made. It was realized that the war zone could be closer than had been expected. The Air Raid Patrol (ARP) was set up and windows had to be blacked out. My dad made wooden frames covered with pulp board to fit snugly on the windows, and of course no more porch lights were left on. Powell River was no longer "White City" – the name given to the town because of the blaze of lights greeting people coming in by boat.

One way the government appealed to our patriotism was to encourage people to grow Victory Gardens. There were motivating articles in the newspapers. People, who had not before grown vegetables, became involved and as gardens flourished, there were a lot of over-the-back-fence comparisons of crops. Mr. Fleet produced more than vegetables in his Townsite Victory Garden; he had chickens as well. At school, teachers encouraged students to have their own gardens. My brother and I had a little plot where we planted our lettuce and radishes in V-shaped rows.

One big community effort was the "Ton of Jam for Britain" project. It was also a ton of fun. Dozens of boys and girls were taken out in big open trucks to pick blackberries. We stood up in the back, hung onto the wooden sides and sang at the top of our lungs, "Alouette", "Off We go into the Wild Blue Yonder", "Mairzedoats", and whatever else came into our heads. A cloud of dust followed our noisy convoy and when we picked berries at Myrtle Point, they were covered with dust. The pails of berries were taken to the home economics room at Brooks, where another team was making them into jam. One year I was part of that team. I think some of the jam was slightly overcooked as one of the teachers commented that we might be able to dispense with the tins and just cut the jam into blocks!

I don't recall any real hardships regarding food rationing. We were encouraged to use margarine, which was something new on the market. But my mom said they had used it in Scotland during the First World War. We softened the white margarine and mixed in the little package of colouring to make it look like butter.

A food I really did miss in the war years was Jell-O. It was still produced, but not much of it; and we never managed to get any. Mom used to make a substitute with gelatin, sweetening it with the juice from her fruit preserves, but we didn't like it. It just didn't taste like our favourite Jell-O.

In the dead of night one Sunday in June 1943, Powell River was "invaded". The "enemy troops" arrived on landing barges and debarked with Bren gun carriers on our beaches. These were soldiers being trained on Vancouver Island. Our reserves and cadets did a great job of defending our town. Cadet training was compulsory in the high schools from 1940. It was from the cadets in our class that we got information of this memorable night; and the girls had to admire the boys' extreme bravery. After all, they were stationed through the long dark night … by the cemetery… spo-ooky!

Later that morning, we found "hand grenades" (small brown bags of flour) exploded on the road. And all the kids wanted a ride on a Bren gun carrier. In the following days, every boy became a "commando". They scavenged scraps of wood and carved rifles. My brother made a machine gun and painted it with aluminum paint. One of the fathers acquired some ARP helmets for the boys, but they were quite cumbersome, so weren't often worn. The "commando" stalked each other through the bush and around the yards. There were shouts of "Bang, you're dead!" usually followed by an argument and denial, "No, I'm not; you missed!"

Finally VJ Day happened. Such celebrating! People meeting on the street shouted excited greetings to each other. And we young people had our own celebrations. The houses across the street had long front porches, so the kids on our block congregated on the Robertson's porch. I took my most precious possession – my wind-up portable record player which played 78 RPM records. We played my eight records over and over again! And we banged pot lids like we did on New Year's Eve. This is how "our gang" on the 900 block of Maple Avenue celebrated the end of the war!

Looking Back with Martin Rossander

Memories of the Townsite after WWII

After WWII, major newspapers had "Help Wanted" ads for jobs with the Powell River Company. I came to Powell River in 1948 on the Gulf Wing; my fare was paid by the Powell River Company. We stopped at every port along the way, getting further and further away from civilization.

First I lived in the bunkhouses in the east side of Riverside. They were cold and drafty and uninspiring.

Eventually, I was able to get a room in a Company-run building – it was heated by steam – instead of being cold, like Riverside, it was overly heated.

After two days of indoctrination by a Powell River Company supervisor, I was assigned to the labour gang. During the indoctrination, I was told once you are employed with the Powell River Company you are secure for life. Any bank in the world will give you a loan if you work for the Company.

We were told about the safety rules – all rules had to be obeyed without deviation.

In the two years I worked for the Powell River Company – it was the most mind stifling thing I ever encountered.

I was at the bottom of the pole as far as status was concerned. I was assigned to the roofer – as long as there was no paper or sulphur to unload on the dock – my job was to be on the roof and "look busy".

My boss was quite a night hawk and he needed his sleep. I had bought an acre of land on Fernwood and I needed my sleep too. The roofers had a small bin that was steam heated and there was only one key. After the boss had been in the bin in the morning, he would lock me in for the afternoon. There really was nothing to do on the job, just a question of "being busy". The supervisors knew about the nap times, but they had summer cottages which needed new tar roofs.

The mill was making so much money, they hadn't a clue what was going on. **There was tremendous loyalty to the Company – while, at the same time, disloyalty was going on** (using mill workers and supplies for summer cottages).

There was a social structure in the Townsite. There were various levels, mill supervisors, doctors, school principals, and teachers were at the top.

I was hungry for social events – events at Dwight Hall. Entry was strictly at a social level. The social stratum was guarded from the top. It would be seen as imposing to attend these events. The Papermakers' Ball was attended by the Papermakers and those at the top of the social structure. Two hundred dollar ($200) dresses had to be bought from Madame Loukes – only to be worn once – not to be given to charity – no one else had to wear the same dress.

I was at the bottom of the social structure, living in Riverside, and working in the labour gang. Within the mill itself was a social structure.

It was a question of loyalty – one was expected to fit in. If you didn't, you were punished. It was just there (the social structure) – no one discussed it.

During "the purge" a number of employees had been fired. They were now doing business in Westview – Bill Jones was one of them. Westview got its beginnings from there – that was the basis for those little villages.

Wildwood was different – Italians settled there for social reasons, and the opportunity to grow large gardens and have dairies. It was a different culture compared to Cranberry and Westview.

There was a bunch of shacks in Cranberry, called Parryville. Small houses were built in Cranberry for retired mill workers (Moose Village 2008). We (Powell River Company roofers) did the roofing up there.

The Powell River Company provided houses but there were never enough to go around. They had an upper limit of 500 in the Townsite. One of my first jobs was to put hot tar on the duplexes on Willow Avenue.

Married women worked in the mill during the war because there was a crisis. They were assembling aircraft. After the war, women were sent back to the kitchen. I knew **Olive Devaud** – an independent personality with her own set of values. She was attracted to Unitarian principles; she gathered clothing for orphans overseas. She was global in her thinking – to others Powell River was the world. Her late husband, **Alphonse Devaud** had run a dairy and set up a water system in the area (near the present Olive Devaud nursing home).

I took a bus, one day, and went right to the end of the line (Edgehill). I had a childhood experience of desolate places in Saskatchewan – I couldn't hack it – Edgehill was like "the end of the world". I saw some shacks with mill canvas on them – a lot of work with very little reward. I didn't get off the bus.

WWII V-E Day May 7, 1945 What a wonderful day!
Jim Tait and Roy Leibenschel drove the Cranberry kids around Cranberry with the siren wailing. Wilshire's store is in the background. Evening dancing in street. Sid Wilshire (standing by cab door). Running board: Les McDonald, Mike Mathews. Tail Running Board: Allan Price (twin) Gloria Riley (Daly). Next row (back to front): Bruna Aprilius/Delina Raimondo/Betty Harding/Arnold Price (twin)/Flo Gaganoff (Heavener)/Hazel Wilshire/Pat Tufnail/Dimitri Tetarenko/Archie Blacklock (holding flag). Behind Archie – Bill Donkersley
Photo: Archie Blacklock collection

Gerri & Charlie Parsons
Open Air Market, Powell River
Photo: B.A. Lambert 2000

Cranberry Village

Cranberry Village, commercial centre 1930s   *Courtesy: Powell River Museum*

Leibenschel garage, Cranberry 1940s.   Photo: Roy Leibenschel
Insert: Cranberry Days, Lindsay Park 2007 Pam Brown/Roy Leibenschel. Photo: B.A. Lambert

Looking Back!
Roy Leibenschel – the Pioneer Years in Cranberry from 1910

Cranberry was called Cranberry because of all the cranberries by the lake.

There were lots of cranberries where the present trailer park is today. Even today cranberries can be found by the lake.

Cranberry was a pioneer suburb and could boast a shopping district of 21 businesses.

To begin with, Cranberry was one big forest near the lake. George McFall, George Smarge, and Olson made a claim for minerals (1910) but nothing came of it. There was no road from the Townsite to Cranberry. Some Russians put one through from Errico's vegetable patch (present Lawn Bowling Club in the Townsite) by Lot 450 to Cranberry. According to Roy in 1929 (when the Leibenschels moved to Cranberry from the Townsite) there were still a few planks around on the old road.

The Company put in an orchard on Lot 450. George Radford lived in a house near the present fire hall. He leased the old orchard from the Powell River Company and he ran a chicken ranch. Roy was just a young boy (early 1930s) when he went with his father to deliver chicken feed there. As a kid Roy used to steal apples from the old orchard!

The old orchard house, after the death of Ma Buttery in 1939, was rented out to Company employees – this included Jack Scott and his wife who rented the place in 1942. The Isolation Hospital was there too. Altogether, there were three houses on the property (1920s & 30s). After WWII the veterans' houses were built on Lot 450. The Powell River Company gave the land to the vets.

Smarge (1912) built a house by the lake; a couple of years later it burned down and they moved to Wildwood.

McFall also built a house by the lake. It burned down in the 1920s, so he built another house on the other side of the lake. He kept pigs and cows. He sold milk to the early settlers – had an old horse called Monty. Monty knew every trail around the lake.

There was a couple of shingle mills – one at Mowat Bay (Mowat & Wasser – 1915) and one near Cranberry Lake (Profitt & Somerton – 1920s). In the late 1920s, there was a saw mill at Mowat Bay. Somerton did the logging for the Marlatt brothers (Dr. Marlatt and his two brothers, Roy and Paul.) Somertons logged in the Edgehill area and boomed the logs across the lake. The sawmill was behind Bill MacKenzie's on Marlatt. By 1931 the sawmill had folded up. A huge pile of sawdust was still there in the early

1930s. Roy helped put out a house fire near the site – the concern was the sawdust might catch fire. The bowling alley was made of wood from the Mowat Bay mill.

In the 1920s, Bloedel, Stewart & Welch logged near Haslam Lake. There was a rail track from there, through Paradise Valley to Myrtle Point. Also a line by Duck Lake. Palmer and Whipple logged in the 1930s.

1921 - the government subdivided the Cranberry Lake District into lots for returning soldiers. They were sold in a lottery at the Patricia Theatre for just $1.

1929 - Leibenschels moved to Cranberry from the Townsite. Cranberry was a well-developed place. Went down after 1955 (amalgamation with Westview).

There were lots of stores in the 1930s and 40s in Cranberry. It was a booming place. Lots of cafés in Cranberry; you could never go hungry.

Cranberry Motors had gas pumps and a body shop. Sold Shell gas.

Jimmy Goddard ran the post office. His father, Eddie ran the grocery store. Roger Goddard delivered groceries for his father, Ed.

1926 - The Goddard Community Hall was built.

Alsgard had a furniture store, burned down. Rebuilt on same location. Café and pool hall located in new building run by John Nicotoff (known as Fat). He had a pool hall and ran a one-car Taxi. Later Foursquare Gospel (Church) took over the building.

Alsgard built a new furniture store further down the street, which later became Cranberry Hardware after being bought out by Aholas. Aholas came from Ocean Falls.

H.J. (Bert) Parry brought his family to Cranberry in 1922. He bought land adjacent to Lot 450 (the old orchard) and opposite, what is today Cranberry Pottery. The family lived in a tent while their house was being built. Parry built and rented out small cottages. These cottages were in high demand, due to the shortage of rental accommodation (Joe & Hanna deWynter lived in Parryville after WWII).

Across the street from Parryville, Bert Parry built the first business block. The following businesses were located there: Haddad (dry goods), a meat market, a delicatessen store, and the very first Alsgard Furniture store. In 1929 the block burned down.

Roy remembers when he was fire marshal, being called out to chimney fires at Parryville. The chimneys were bracket chimneys and the bricks were held together with lime and water instead of cement. Roy attended the fires, was easily able to pull out a couple of the bricks from the chimney. He then condemned the building by putting a sticker on the door. Roy had been appointed from Victoria to inspect for Underwriters Insurance – he was not popular!

Bill Beattie owned the Caledonian Bakery on Crown Avenue. The shop has gone but the house is still there.

Mr. McCleod and his father, Max, built the Cranberry store (Goddard block). Besides apartments, there was an office for Cranberry light and water, also, upstairs, a dentist, a Dr. Rideout.

Mid 1930s – Kip Taylor's drugstore in Cranberry.

Reeds Men's Wear was in the Wilshire building, and then they moved across the street, the house is still there.

The first location of Quality Printers was opposite Wilshire's, in a building owned by Molly Tupper McClaren; it had been a clothing store and a laundry. Eventually, the building was condemned. Quality Printers then moved into a building behind Leibenschel's garage at the corner of Manson and Cranberry; the building was leased from Ernie Leibenschel. Quality Printers printed by the job. It produced the Buyer's Guide, put out twice a month on mill paydays. The shopping flyers were mailed and delivered by the post office to each household. Sometime in the 1980s, the business was sold by the owners, Jack Hanna and Eva Mosley to Colin Palmer. Mr. Palmer moved the business to Westview.

Sid Wilshire came to Cranberry in 1921 and built a house (still there) and a confectionery store later (opened 1931). In 1946 he sold the business to his nephew, also called Sid Wilshire. Later, it was sold to Archie Blacklock – the shop was still called Wilshire's. Wilshire's was alongside the Goddard block. Small building, at the end, was Smith the butcher (in-between Wilshire's and the Goddard block).

Present – Dog grooming shop (2007 Snack Shack) was Max's shoe repair in the 1940s. Made out of bricks from MacGregor's brick factory. Roller rink on site before the brick factory.

One time there were five sets of gas pumps in Cranberry!

Brick plant operated by Don MacGregor. Brick plant behind the dog grooming shop. Now operating as an apartment building.

Across from Smith's butcher was Steve Koehut – had a dry cleaning outfit and café upstairs. On the site of Cranberry hardware was a three-star garage operated by Emil Gordon and Mrs. Ward. They bought nine Graham Pages in 1931 and sold everyone.

Bernier's shoe store was operated by Ed Bernier. Ed sold shoes and the old man, his father, repaired them. In the 1930s the old man (Thomas Bernier) moved into Westview. Young moved into Bernier's store. The present Seniors Centre is on the site of the old shoe store.

W. Pitt Cross came to Cranberry in 1921. He saw a way of making a few bucks, so he built a grocery and meat store in 1926 (later became Woewoda's Cranberry Sheet Metal). He also built a garage at the corner of Manson and Cranberry. After it burned down in 1938, Roy's father, Ernie Leibenschel purchased this site and put up his own garage in 1940 and started Manson Service Limited. It operated two computer pumps which computerized the gas sold. They sold a lot of gas.

After Pitt Cross, the store was carried on by Bill Young as a dry goods store. Later on, Kip Taylor moved into the store. Eventually, Kip Taylor's old place became a café which served steak and kidney pies.

Goddard sold the Goddard building out to a French family.

Next to the shoe repair shop was the Cozy Corner Café.

Joe Derton had a barber's shop, and a pool room. In 1960 it became the Jehovah Witness meeting hall.

Bosa originally lived at the back of Joe Derton's place – originally he went door-to-door selling groceries. He then opened up shop near the old United Church. Eventually, the store moved to present location of Mitchells. It was originally Bosa and Mitchell. The site was originally Joe and John Errico's vegetable farm. The corner of the farm went as far as Lindsay Park. Mitchells bought out Bosa.

Etalo Dini, an Italian, ran the bowling alley upstairs in the present Crown Inn building. Downstairs, the Brown Brothers ran a grocery store and Jack Tunstall ran a furniture store. Overwaitea moved into Browns' store. Overwaitea then moved into the Townsite and eventually into Westview.

Across from the bowling alley was the old Cranberry Lake Village office, at the corner of Drake and Cranberry. Light and water bills were paid there.

Near Drake Street was Mrs. Ethel McKenzie's women's dress shop.

1946 – Mitten had a body shop – taken over by Mike D'Cleary.

The old building near the corner of Drake Street was Cranberry's first fire hall. The first truck was bought in 1942.

On Church Street was Eagon's grocery store. Reece took it over. He made ice.

There was another little store on Park Avenue run by Bob James in the 1930s.

In 1924, the Culos family built a big house opposite what is today the old Cranberry School. The house was built on two lots – each lot cost $50. The concrete bricks were all poured by hand. Anthony Culos also bought property on the lower side of Park Avenue – known as the Culos dairy farm. One time, when Roy was a teenager, he stole some apples from the orchard there. Culos came to visit his father and apples were found in Roy's car. As punishment, his father took Roy's driving licence away for a month! The cows came up twice a day from the pasture on Park Avenue to be milked. There was a barn behind the Culos' farmhouse. The road from the farm to the house was coated with cow manure. The Edgehill kids had to walk up this trail to go to Cranberry Lake School. Sometime in the 1950s Tal Haan bought the Culos' farmhouse.

Where the Scott farm is now, McFall had the original property in the 1920s followed by Norman McIntosh.

1949 – St. Hugh's Church Hall – Anglican Church was a Powell River Company bunkhouse, cut down. It is now a house on Nelson and Cranberry Street.

There was quite a bit of bootlegging in the 1920s and 30s in Cranberry. Roy knew a young fellow who drove a grocery truck back then with "special orders" at the back of the truck (behind the groceries!)

There was a cat house in Wildwood (1930s & 40s) Roy recalls one time stopping at the Wildwood establishment with a delivery. Later in the day, Roy's father got the message that his son had left his hat there! Roy had some explaining to do.

In the 1930s there was a cat house in Cranberry, on Drake Street, known as the Russian Heights. It was a little house behind Joe's pool room.

In the 1940s Alsgard, who published the *Town Crier*, bought out the *Powell River News* from Tommy Green. Alsgard's building became the present-day tile shop.

Ice on Cranberry Lake from 1931-33. Leibenchels delivered ice from the lake. Roy used to skate on the lake – still has his skates somewhere. Also had a 10-foot boat with outboard motor on the lake. Roy used to fish for small trout in the lake – before it became a tangled mess with lily pads.

Post office was first in the Goddard Block, run by J. Goddard. Moved to Mitchell's, then Wilshire's, and then passed out.

Belgian Mike packed beer bottles, sold chickens – he sold everything. He was quite a character and had trouble with drinking. For a while he wasn't allowed to drive so he had a dog and cart. One time he had a horse and wagon – but he would forget to feed the horse!

In the 1930s and early 40s Tommy Lambert from Paradise Valley used to go door-to-door delivery with goat's milk and eggs. Tom Fong (Valley Road farm and later Westview) delivered vegetables. Bread was delivered then. Everything in those days was door-to-door delivery.

Cranberry was a booming place during WWII. For a couple of years there were no street lights. Folks in Cranberry had shutters on the windows. Roy learned to drive trucks with little narrow strips on the headlights.

When the war was over, the fire truck drove all the way round Cranberry to celebrate the victory. Some guys got drunk for a couple of days. There were two celebrations – one for VE Day and the other for VJ day.

Roy worked at Manson full service garage from 1945-52. In 1952 he was employed by the General Motors dealership under Powell River Motors. In 1969 Gary Motors took over the dealership. Roy retired from Gary Motors in 1975.

After 1955 (amalgamation) Cranberry went downhill. In 1955 Cranberry was the only village with money in the bank.

Westview stole Cranberry's Christmas lights after the amalgamation of the Townsite and the villages.

In the 1950s some Cranberry merchants moved to Westview.

Cranberry Lake was clean until it became a bird sanctuary – then all the birds in the country came there. Water lilies became a problem.

Roy moved to Edgehill in 1951. To this day, most folks affectionately call him Mr. Cranberry. Roy always goes to Cranberry Days which are held in Lindsay Park. In 2007 he was given the honour of cutting a very large cake. With a smile, he told Mrs. Brown of the Cranberry Ratepayers Association, to hand him a chain saw so he could do the job right!

Looking Back with Charlie Parsons

Fred and Lucy Parsons – Cranberry Lake Farm (from 1924)

Fred Parsons started his farm near Cranberry Lake in 1924. He came to work for the Powell River Company in 1923; however, he was determined to own his own place rather than rent a Company house for his family.

Fred and Lucy Parsons had nine children: Fred, Walter, Lucy, Margaret, Eileen, Charlie, Kathleen, Robert, and Ernie. Charlie was born in 1932.

The family managed through the Depression years with Fred Parsons working part-time in the mill (50 cents an hour) and produce from the family farm.

Charlie:

"We had a big garden and Mum did a lot of canning. There was always a big root cellar full of groceries (canned goods). We kept cows, pigs, chickens, and rabbits. There were plenty of pheasants around in the 1930s. We traded veggies for fresh salmon from Sliammon First Nations. Dad always had plenty of potatoes in the garden. He traded spuds for salmon. Mum put in an order, once a month, through Woodward's for basic supplies – flour, sugar, etc. It was delivered from the dock for 10 cents a box.

Mother found clothes for us at the Sally Ann (Salvation Army). She had a hand-cranked sewing machine; she made dresses for the girls out of flour sacks. We all wore "cut-me-downs". Mother taught me to darn socks, this was later useful in the army as I charged the other men a $1 for every sock darned.

I was one of the first students to attend the brand new four-room school **Cranberry Malaspina School in 1930.** *I can remember when I was in Grade 6, taking my bicycle to school and delivering a few quarts of milk on the way.* **Mr. Holmwood was the principal.** *We always had chores to do, before and after school.*

Cranberry Lake *was the centre of all our fun. We (the kids – James and Don MacGregor) made our own transportation on the lake using cedar slabs from a skid road nearby. We sat astride the slabs and paddled around the lake with two-handed paddles. I paddled around the lake on my float long before I learned to swim.*

Two places I have fond memories of are, the Rock Bar and the Mud Hole. At the Mud Hole was a cedar log and we dived from the log into the mud hole. We emerged, covered in mud, and then swam in the lake to clean ourselves off. Another fun thing to do, just before going home, was to pelt out friends with soft mud balls – of course, they had to go back into the lake to clean themselves off again! I remember making a zonga attached to a tree; we'd swing out on the rope and the make a big splash into Cranberry Lake.

*If we had a penny to spend, we bought candy at **Wilshire's**. We performed extra chores to earn the 50 cents for the show in Powell River at the **Patricia Theatre**. Thursday nights were buddy nights – two could get in for the price of one!*

In 1942 Charlie went to work for the **Powell River Company**. He was an apprentice machinist, earning 16 cents an hour- eventually earning 26 cents an hour before receiving his call-up papers for the army. Charlie received cigarettes from the Powell River Company when he was overseas in Holland. He sold them for $1 a pack. After the war, Charlie went back to work for the Powell River Company for a couple of years before starting his own business with a farm tractor, plough, and cultivator. Later on, he bought a front-end loader and a back hoe.

"In 1948 I was working on my second machine, and I got married the same year to Gerri Cooke.

In the winter of '48 the ice froze 18 inches and it was as solid as a rock. Gerri was expecting and I built a chair on skids, so she could safely have a trip on the lake. We put benches near the lake for the skaters to sit on. As many as two dozen cars were parked on our property. We sold doughnuts and hot coffee. The water from the coffee came from a stream and the washing up water came from the lake. We only operated our "Ma & Pa" coffee stand for that one winter, as the Municipality informed us we required a business licence!

In the 1950s there were opportunities for independent trades people. The outhouses disappeared around town and new houses went up in Cranberry, Edgehill, and Westview."

■ Serving a growing list of customers for Ready-t-oWear

Drygoods, Wools, Novelties, Etc.

THE CORNER SHOP

MRS. E. McKENZIE   CRANBERRY

1942 The Corner Shop (Ladies Wear), Cranberry, operated by Ethel McKenzie. The store was rented from Ed Bernier.   Photo: Al McKenzie

— 1944 —
Cranberry Bowling Alleys
9 Alleys to serve you - Coffee Shop
Mr. and Mrs. E. Dini

Cranberry Recreation Centre, Manson Avenue. Velma Dini serving mouth-watering hamburgers at the bowling alley (1950s). Photos: Dini collection

SCOTTY'S TRANSFER LTD.
Est. 1940   Phone HU 2-3701
Freight, Express and General Hauling
Sand - Gravel - Wood and Top Soil

Scotty's Transfer, Cranberry 1950s. (L to R) Bill Kayle/Joe deWynter.   Photo: Hanna deWynter

The Rees family, Church St., Cranberry 1950. (L to R) Bill & Lil Rees with their children David and Bill Rees. Bill was the "ice man" – delivering ice to the villages.   Photo: Dave Rees

Looking Back with Stanley (Rusty) Peters

Cranberry Pioneers – the Peters Family (from 1924)

My father, Charlie Peters, came to Cranberry in 1924 to work as a steam engineer at **Marlatt's Sawmill**, just off Hatfield Place, near Cranberry Lake. My mother, Ethel Peters, came up to Cranberry in 1925. My parents first rented in Cranberry, and then in 1930 they built a house on Marlatt and Cranberry Street.

After the area was logged off around Cranberry Lake, logs were winched up from Mowat Bay to the mill by a steam engine on a float on the lake. After the Marlatt's sawmill closed, my father went to work at the Yellow Cedar sawmill at the Shingle Mill. After it burned down he then worked for Doc Jameson at the Shingle Mill as a night engineer. During the time he worked at the Shingle Mill, Dad owned a Model T Ford. Sometimes on a weekend, in the 1930s, we drove down through Paradise Valley to **Douglas Bay** for a picnic on the beach; Dad always took a couple of spare tires in case of a blow out!

I remember Goddard's store, Dick's Dry Goods, Smith's butchers, Alsgard's hardware, Mr. Beattie's Caledonian Bakery, and Wilshire's. **There were more businesses in Cranberry than in Westview in the 1930s.**

I'd go up with my pals to search for beer bottles at the old shingle bolt camps at Haslam and Duck Lakes. Joe Derton paid one cent a bottle! If we saved up enough pennies, we went to the show at the Patricia Theatre (15 cents - afternoon show, 25 cents – evening show). Otherwise, we spent our money at Wilshire's: 5 cents for an ice cream, 10 cents for a float, and 15 cents for a milkshake. Near the door was a rack of penny candies; some were three for a penny, one could fill a bag for a whole nickel!

In the 1930s Joe Wing (Grief Point), Sing Lee (Wildwood), and Tom Fong (Paradise Valley) grew vegetables with Chinese labour. They sold veggies from a truck parked in the street and did house-to-house deliveries, carrying the vegetables in a wicker basket, held over the shoulder with a rope.

After amalgamation in 1955, the Municipality cleared out the creek that went through Scott's farm to Willingdon Beach. **The water level in Cranberry Lake fell two feet and the lake never recovered from this loss.**

In the 1940s I was a driver for the Powell River Transfer. **During the 1946 earthquake I was parked outside Bayers store in Westview with the Sunday mail delivery. Suddenly, the road was moving in waves – the telegraph poles swayed back and forth – then all the guys from the Marine and Westview hotels rushed out in their pj's and shorts!"**

Looking Back with Peter Mitchell

Cranberry Village: Mitchell Brothers (from 1946)

In 1929 A. (Gus) Bosa was selling groceries from a cart in the village of Cranberry. During the 1930s he built a store on Manson Avenue, in Cranberry, a short distance from the location of the present Mitchell Brothers store. Bosa was a successful businessman; he posted Woodward's grocery advertisements in his store and matched their prices. During the 1940s Bosa took as partner, Lindi Cecconi. Lindi left the partnership after a few years. In 1946, in the postwar boom of the area, Bosa took in two new partners, Marino (Babe) and Albert Mitchell. The new company was known as:

A. Bosa & Mitchell Brothers, General Merchants

The same year, Babe Mitchell spent time in Vancouver at a butcher shop in order to learn the trade. This allowed the store in Cranberry to sell fresh meat.

In 1949 A. Bosa and Mitchell Brothers built a new store on its present location on Manson Avenue, Cranberry. It was the first independent self-serve grocery store in the District of Powell River.

In 1951 Gus Bosa left for Vancouver and formed A. Bosa & Company.

In the late 1940s and 50s the company van was driving as far as Stillwater to deliver grocery orders.

A. Bosa and Mitchell Brothers placed orders for groceries and dry goods with Malkins, Slade & Stewart, Canada Packers. The company reps travelled to Powell River by Union Steamship, to write up the orders. Some orders were placed locally with Jack Harper Limited, Westview (tobacco and candy) and Lambert Brothers, Paradise Valley for eggs. 1950s merchandise included: meat, groceries, televisions, and furniture. It was the second oldest Inglis appliance dealership in Canada. Wine grapes were imported for the local Italian community. Orders were filled for logging camps. "Tug & grub" orders were filled in the late 1960s for Kingcome Navigation.

In 1961 Babe and Albert Mitchell bought out A. Bosa & Company. In 1981 Peter Mitchell purchased the store and gave it the name:

Mitchell Brothers Merchants

Looking Back with Mayor Stewart Alsgard

The Alsgard Family – Pioneers in Cranberry (1920s-50s)

Stewart Alsgard:

Growing up in Cranberry Lake was a marvellous experience. I count myself fortunate to have grown up in that community at that time. It was a wonderful village and I look at it today and I try to think of what it was when I was just a kid riding a bicycle around there. There are still a few things that look something like they were. I can go along to Wilshire's and pick out every store. I remember taking our ration coupons and getting butter. I worked in one of the grocery stores when I was a little older and I used to set pins in the bowling alley.

My grandparents, Martin and Lucy Alsgard came to Cranberry Lake in the 1920s. They had two sons, Al (my father) and Frank (my uncle). My grandfather established Alsgard's Hardware at the corner of East Road (Crown Avenue) and Cranberry Street. King's Collision is part of that structure. The hardware part was at one end. It was destroyed in a fire. Martin built a new building and it still stands today right beside Wilshire's. It was built by my mother's father, **Brady Wick**. It opened and flourished in the 1920s and struggled during the Depression years. The business was sold to Tom Ahola.

Business was growing, and by this time my father had married a young teacher, **Anne Wick**. She was a graduate from Normal School in Vancouver and had come to teach in Westview. My parents had met at a dance in Dwight Hall on St. Patrick's Day, and shortly thereafter were married.

When they were first married they lived in one of the little houses across from Derton's. Later, they moved to Nelson Street then to Church Street. As a little boy I remember growing up with all these wonderful Italian families. We then moved to Manson and Cranberry Street. My parents had enough of a down payment to buy a house from **Fred Pitt Cross**. The **Leibenschel** family lived on one side and the **Cattermoles** on the other side.

Back to Church Street. Dad worked for the **Powell River Company** at this time. He then decided to help his father in the hardware store. Then he got the idea that he would like to get into the newspaper business. There was an old mimeograph machine in the attic and Dad would type up stencils and draw it out. My mother and two sisters helped fold the papers. The first copy of the *Town Crier* is in the museum. Then the paper was moved to the building now known as Powell River Custom Tile & Marble on Cranberry Street. I remember this marvellous place where things used to clang and bang and they had the old hot metal process complete with linotype and handset chases. One winter day while I was skating on Cranberry Lake a kid yelled out that my

Dad's paper was on fire so I ran all the way home from the lake wearing my skates only to get there and see the fire just about out. The building was badly damaged but they worked hard and the next day the paper came out on time.

My sister Gail was born in 1945. By that time Dad had moved his newspaper business down to Westview.

Earthquake!

I came to Westview with my dad one day in 1946. I was 11 at the time and was sitting downstairs in the newspaper building, waiting for him, when all of a sudden the building started to shake. All I heard Dad yell was:

"GET OUT NOW!"

I ran out of the door. Dad was there and grabbed me. We stood there and I watched the building separate from the foundation, and then everything settled back down again. Back in Cranberry, my mother dashed up the stairs to get Gail. The whole neighbourhood was outside in their yards.

We had a great garden back then. Money was in short supply. One of my jobs was to pick vegetables and weed the garden.

Cranberry Lake School

I attended kindergarten at St. Joseph's in the Townsite. Going to Cranberry Lake School was a marvellous experience. I started Grade 1 in 1941. One of the best teachers I ever had, one that I admire to this day, who had a marvellous effect on what I did and how I approached it, was **Jim Devlin**. He was a wonderful role model for kids. Every boy played soccer whether you wanted to or not.

In winter, snow came and the whole school headed down to the lower playing field. We'd have these snowball fights, battles royal, and build great snow forts. We skated on the lake when it froze over. We went as a class – the older ones only, Grades 4 to 6. We'd formed long lines, link hands and skate across the lake, and get the ice to roll – not realising the danger – we were immortal!

Golden Stanley was another person I admired. Golden started the **Cranberry Lake Scout Troop** and was the Scout Master. **Frank Clark** was his assistant. We sold Christmas trees as a winter activity to raise money for the scouts. We all belonged to the Hawk patrol. Golden Stanley was great; he was a naturalist and had this wonderful knowledge of plants. He grew up in Horseshoe Valley. We became Junior Forest Wardens and had to go down to the Townsite for our meetings. The older boys became Army Cadets at Brooks School.

Cranberry Lake

Because of the lake's warming cycles, swimming began at Rock Bar and later moved down to Drake Street where two rafts were located. Then the lake would get too warm and we'd all get a rash, so we went swimming at Mowat Bay where the Turnbulls lived. It was nothing like it is today. There were boom sticks there; we paddled up to First Bay and then hiked up to Lost Lake on the railroad grade.

I remember having a hot dog stand with a school friend. My grandmother boiled the wieners and ran them out to us in a bucket. We sold them for 10 cents to the truck drivers hauling logs up from Mowat Bay. They gave the order coming up with a heavy load. When they returned empty, we ran alongside the truck and delivered the hot dogs.

I saw the construction of the Veteran's Village at the Powell River Company orchard site at Cranberry Lake. I remember them building the houses because I had a paper route and I delivered the *Town Crier* there. My challenge was to get everyone there as a customer. I got them all!

When the *Gulf Stream* ran aground in 1947, my father did a special edition of the *Town Crier*, reporting the tragedy. *Movie Tone News* sent a camera crew to film the wreck site. Dad took them up to the scene and a few days later at the Patricia Theatre, during the news portion of the program, there it was.

The Dini's operated Cranberry Lake Bowling Alley. There was a poolroom below. **Velma Dini** made the best hamburgers in town. Many boys set pins at the bowling alley. There were nine lanes; four boys set two lanes, and one favourite boy had only one lane to set. Setting two lanes meant hopping from one lane to another; we'd all get splinters and go home for mum and dad to pick them out!

I remember **Mr. Goddard**, the Postmaster. The Post Office was a fascinating place. He had this big safe and a pistol visible in the open safe, always there for us to see – as if it was ready to be fired! We'd all go in, just to check if the gun was still there! The rest of the building was a grocery store.

Al Smith, the butcher, had a shop next to **Brown Brother's Grocery**. I remember the sawdust on the floor. That building is still there today.

I remember the ration books. Purple coupons for butter. They were like gold. They were dated. We got about one pound of butter a week.

We had very good friends, the **Hamertons**, who had a son, Bob, about my age. The Hamertons had goats and we used to milk them. Mrs. Hamerton mixed the milk up with Eagle brand condensed milk and chocolate crystals, ice cold in a pitcher. It was a lovely drink, never lost the taste for it.

Wilshire's

Wilshire's was "the holy of holies". It was a fascinating place. Even during the war years, Wilshire's was able to get ice cream for the store. We saved up our allowance, about a nickel a week. Four of us would get together and pool our money. Behind the counter, in the special fridge, were all the exciting flavours. We were not allowed to sit at the counter but could stand at the end. We looked down into the bottomless pits of ice cream and then we'd buy a couple of cones and pass them around the group. Sometimes we'd buy a cherry soda drink and mix it with a cordial. We were allowed to sit at a table with our drinks. When it was done, it was "Goodbye boys," and out you went.

Joe Derton's Barbershop

Joe Derton cut my hair. He put a board across the arms of the chair. He'd lift you up and put you on the board. Next a towel went around your neck and he'd cut your hair. Chocolate bars were rationed but he always had a few bars. The word quickly got out if he'd just received a shipment in. All the kids, even if they did not need a haircut, would be lined up at the door and he'd have to referee this. It resulted in one chocolate bar being shared three ways. We learned to share a lot in those days.

Joe had a poolroom that was curtained off behind the barbershop. There was no way that any kid could get in there. It was forbidden territory for small children but, whenever he was not looking, we were always peeking in to see what it really was.

Brown Brothers Grocery moved in under the bowling alley. I had an after school job in there; I worked in the produce department and got paid 25 cents for a couple of hours work. Mrs. Lambert, who ran the Edgehill store, bought bananas from Brown Brothers while she was waiting for her regular shipment. She'd come in and place an order and I would have to put it on the next Powell River Stages (bus) that was going to Edgehill. Mrs. Lambert ran that store for a long time. Edgehill seemed a long way from Cranberry Lake in those days.

The **Bosa's Store** was very close to Cranberry Lake School. It was here we would buy one Pep Chew and share it between at least six of us. Later, the store located to its' present site as Bosa and Mitchell Brothers, and then eventually became Mitchell Brothers. Their sister, **Josie Mitchell** ran the Sweet Shop in the Townsite's Patricia Theatre building. My greatest desire was to serve ice cream. I watched the process for years at Wilshire's. Then Josie hired me for no wages to scoop ice cream. I got a free ice cream at the end of the day. When my friends came in, she watched me like a hawk!

Looking Back with Piroska Bartley (Kovacs)

Cranberry Pioneers (from 1930): Leon and Suzanna Kovacs

In 1926, at age 24, **Lazlo (Leon) Kovacs** (1902-1978) and his brother Louis (both Hungarians) immigrated to Canada from Berzéte near Slovensko, Czechoslovakia. They travelled to Edmonton to work on a farm where Leon had to drive a 12-horse team. After one season of farm work, they left and walked via the railroad track to Chilliwack, B.C.; there they found work picking hops. In 1928 they landed in Powell River, sleeping in the old Townsite cemetery while waiting to get work at the mill.

In the late 1920s, 80 Hungarians (mainly bachelors) were hired as casual labour, installing #7 paper machine. A few stayed in Powell River, while the majority (including Louis) returned to Vancouver; many went to work in the saw mills. **Joseph Kolezar** was one of the Hungarians who stayed. In 1928 he sent for his wife Margit, and their two boys, Joe and Jim, to join him.

In 1929, **Zsuzsanna (Suzanna) Marcus** (1909-1995) travelled by herself from Mád, near Tokaj, Hungary to Powell River on the promise of a job at $15 a month. This did not work out; without any money to rejoin her fellow Hungarian travellers in Vancouver, she met and married Leon Kovacs within three days of her arrival. Often saying, had there not been *no* ocean, she would have walked home! Walk they did, attending dances at Lund and Stillwater.

During the early 1930s, Leon waited on standby for casual work at the mill. He was able to get one or two days a week; just enough to buy flour and coal oil. In the late 1930s Leon was finally able to get permanent work with the Company.

The Kovacs first lived at **Riverside**, sharing a house with other immigrants. In 1930 they bought their first house in **Cranberry**, 448 Manson Avenue (known as the yellow house). This house had been built by **Mr. Spetari** for his bride, but on completion she refused to leave Italy, so he sold it to the Kovacs.

The Kovacs were hardworking and self-sufficient people; raising chickens, rabbits, and a large vegetable garden. To supplement her husband's sporadic employment, Suzanna had supper boarders and she ironed dress shirts for 10 cents a shirt. During the Depression Suzanna applied for relief. The government agent told her to, "Eat your house!" She replied, "My house not chocolate!"

In 1949 Leon sponsored his youngest brother Joseph and his wife Margaret to come from Hungary to Canada. The newcomers also settled in Cranberry. In 1956 the Kovacs moved to **Westview**. Today, their daughter **Piroska Bartley (Kovacs)** lives in the family home in Cranberry.

Looking Back with Bill Rees (Junior)

William (Bill) Rees – the Ice Man in Cranberry

Bill Rees came to Powell River with his mother in **1926**. William worked for the **Powell River Company** from 1926-48. His uncle, Hank Stinson, also worked for the Powell River Company. In 1937 Bill married **Lil Dunn** in Seattle, Washington. They had two sons, David and Bill (Junior); both sons worked in the Powell River mill, David for 35 years and Bill from 1957-77.

The **Dunn** family came to Powell River in **1926**; Lil was 10 years old at that time. **Robert Dunn** worked as an electrician for the **Powell River Company** from 1926-43. **They first lived in a cedar shack, on the beach, at the foot of Alexander Street (near the Legion), due to the shortage of rental houses.** The Dunn children rode on the flat car to the old Henderson School in the Townsite. The boys pushed the flatcar there and back, while the girls sat on the deck. In 1927 the Dunn family built a house on Harvie Avenue in **Westview**.

In 1937(?) **Bill Rees** bought property from the Egans, on Church Street, in **Cranberry**. A grocery store and a house were on the property. In 1948 William quit his job in the mill and became the "Ice Man". In order to develop the property, William sold the old grocery store to Ted Wilson. Bill believed by being an independent businessman in Cranberry Village he could make a better living.
The ice plant was on **Gus Courte's** property on Marine Avenue in Westview. Bill delivered ice to the villages and the outlying areas north and south of town. Hank Stinson looked after the compressor in the ice plant. Three storage lockers were built in the ice plant in order to store ice cream and frozen foods.

In 1952 Bill built a storage unit on his Cranberry property with cement blocks from the **MacGregor brick factory**. He sold ice cream and frozen foods to Brown Brothers, Wilshire's, and Mitchells in Cranberry and to stores in Wildwood and Westview. As a teenager, Bill Rees worked for his father for four years before finding a job in the quarry at Blubber Bay for six years.

Bill Rees met Mowat Bay resident **Andy Anderson** on one very memorable occasion. Andy and Clara had just moved into the bay after their lease for the Lakeview Lumber Company, at Haywire Bay, expired with the Powell River Company in 1960. The house was on blocks and the mill equipment on floats.

Bill was going fishing up the lake and went to dig for worms on the Anderson property; he was suddenly aware that Andy was nearby, helping him find worms! Andy was into herbal medicine because he pointed out to Bill that the "weeds" in his garden were actually herbs!

Looking Back with Marion Henderson (Beattie)

The Caledonian Bakery in Cranberry (1930s & 40s)

My father, **Bill Beattie, owned the Caledonian Bakery in Cranberry**. I would help in the bakery when I was not attending Malaspina Cranberry School. In those days, a loaf of bread cost nine cents a loaf! The penny change meant a great deal in those days, and had a lot more value than today's one-cent coin.

Dad delivered bread in the mornings to Emil Gordon's store, below the Rodmay Hotel, and the Sing Lee store at the Shingle Mill.

Cranberry, in the 1930s, was a self-sufficient village. Anything you could possible need you could find at one of the independent businesses in the village. It had a church, a school, a community hall, and a post office. There was Weir's drugstore, Harry Dick's dry goods store, Butch Smith (the butcher), Wilshire's store, Buckerfield's store, and Martin Alsgard's furniture and dry goods store (later sold to Tom Ahola in 1937). Cranberry Lake had 21 businesses in the 1930s and 40s.

The big house across from Malaspina School was built in 1924 by the Culos family. They owned farm property by the lake. The Culos' cows were well known in the locality and would provide fresh milk for Cranberry residents. I remember, as a school child, visiting the farm and being afraid of the bull!

Going to Wilshire's on a Saturday was a real treat. I would rush down with a nickel in my pocket and buy five penny candies! Added treats at Wilshire's were ice creams and milkshakes.

Of course, there were the matinee shows, held at the theatre in the Powell River Townsite, for a nickel a ticket. *Hop-a-long Cassidy* was my favourite show.

For a special Christmas present, I would take the bus with a friend, to shop at the Five-and-Dime store on Marine, in Westview. It was a popular place to shop and we had to line up in a queue to be served. For those fortunate enough to have a big trip to Vancouver (by steamship), Woolworth's the big Five-and-Dime store was *the* place to shop.

I started in Grade 1 at Malaspina School in 1935. I remember the following teachers: Miss Livingstone, Miss Hosea, Zella Stadi, Miss Roberts, and Mr. Holmwood.

When WWII was officially over, the fire truck drove around Cranberry Village and all the children had a ride on it.

Looking Back with Kay Hodson (Parsons)

Malaspina Cranberry Lake School (1930s)

My father, Fred Parsons, was one of many parents with children who pressed for a school to be built to serve the families of Cranberry and Edgehill.

I remember I was 5 years old in 1930 when the ribbon was cut by Mr. Scarlett, the government agent for Powell River. The school was named "Malaspina" after the body of water between Powell River and Texada Island.

My first day of school was September 1931. My first grade teacher was a Scottish woman who used the pointer to emphasize phonics; for words that started with "wh", like *which, where* and *why*, she whipped the pointer down, making a "wh---oosh" sound! It was quite scary but very effective in keeping discipline in the classroom!

I had the following teachers: Miss Malli (Grade 2), Miss Haliday (Grade 3 & 4), and Mr. Alan Holmwood (Grade 5 & 6).

There was a large oil heater in an alcove of each of the four classrooms. Coat hooks were also in the alcove for drying coats over the heater in wet weather.

Only the teachers were allowed to use the front entrance to the school. The back door, at the basement level, was for the use of the students. There was a stairway of about 12 steps which led to the classroom level.

We had outside toilets until 1933 – and no place to wash our hands!

I remember the whole school assembly, outside by the flagpole, with the old Union Jack at half-mast when King George V passed away.

Each morning before class we said the Lord's Prayer and sang "O Canada".

Culos' Dairy was located across the street from the school, and the cows were herded to pasture from the barns, down the hill at 8:30 in the morning to the pasture at McFall's field (now the bird sanctuary) and back at 3:30 each afternoon. So, we met the messy critters everyday, both coming and going!

It was a long walk for a little 6-year-old from my home in Edgehill, opposite McGuffie Avenue through the maze of cows and droppings, to school every day.

Looking Back with Lorraine Jamieson

The Jamieson Family – Pioneers in Cranberry (from 1931)

"My father worked for the Powell River Company in the 1930s and 40s. He had a really hard life in his job – he worked on the wharf, five days a week. My parents first started out living in **Parryville** before purchasing a house at 525 Cranberry Street). They bought the original house in about 1932. My brother, Allan, was born in 1934; I was born seven years later, in 1944.

My mother worked as a housekeeper for Cook's motel, the famous Madame Loukes, and at the original Beach Gardens.

Madame Loukes' 5th Avenue Dress Shop – Marine Avenue, Westview

I met her lots of times; I have been in her store and house. When my girlfriend was getting married, we bought our suits and gloves from Madame Loukes.

Mother worked for Madame Loukes for quite a while and was very happy working for her. Madame Loukes (in the shop) dressed in a dishevelled way with buttons missing. When she went away on business trips, she flew out from the airport, dressed in a beautiful suit, hat, and shoes – and looked like a lady.

Cranberry School

I went to Cranberry School in 1952. The old school is now in a very sorry state. I have many happy memories of May and Sports' Days.

Teachers at school (1950s) were: Miss Docker, Mrs. Larsen, Mr. John Phillip, Cis Larsen, Mike Mooney, and Fred Doupe – teacher and principal. Dorothy Merrifield was my Grade 5 and 6 teacher. When my brother was attending in the early 1940s, Mr. Devlin was teaching there.

It was a big thing to finish Grade 6 in June – without any formalities. Then, one morning in September (after Labour Day) we walked to Brooks School for Grade 7. We quickly adapted to being in a new school.

We went to Cranberry Community Hall on Marlatt Avenue; the whole family went everywhere in my childhood years – kids had a good time. The adults went Old Time Dancing in Cranberry and at Dwight Hall in the Townsite.

The fire siren for Cranberry Lake fire department was near my bedroom window, at the back, near Drake Street. It went off with a loud and unusual sound. A phone call alerted the voluntary firemen to assemble at the fire station.

We shopped at Powell Stores in the Townsite. We shopped once a week, every Saturday. The groceries were put in the rumble seat. Later, we shopped in Cranberry Food Market.

We skated on **Cranberry Lake**. I remember one sad accident – one of the Padgett boy twins went through the ice and died. The fire department came, but was not successful in getting him out of the lake alive.

Before Lindsay Park there was **Whyte's Beach**. We swam in the lake at Whyte's Beach. We celebrated with our first swim at Easter time. There was a big diving platform there (at Whyte's Beach). Safety was not an issue; it (the swimming) was safe and wonderful.

On Cranberry Street was a little **post office**. I do remember Mrs. Daly; she had a daughter named Gloria (Riley). Mrs. Daly knew all the children. There were two wickets, one for letters and one for boxes and parcels.

Wilshire's had high stools at the counters. They made delicious milkshakes and sodas. All the kids (in Cranberry) went there. There was an area with trinkets and gadgets; we looked and were mesmerized. Even as teenagers we went there. I went there with my nephew and niece.

We'd go and order a beer – a root beer!

"I want a beer, please."

I shall always remember going to Wilshire's and ordering a beer!

There was the **roller rink off Crown Avenue**. It is now a curling club. It was a great place for teenagers to meet. Friday night was couple's night – a great place to go with your boyfriend and not be surrounded by little kids.

There was a **bowling alley** above the **pool hall**. Boys and girls went to the bowling alley; however, girls were not allowed in the pool hall!

My parents were married in the Cranberry United Church. I remember the Foursquare Church – I went there for a while. I also remember the Anglican Church in Cranberry.

Looking Back with Ron Dini

The Cranberry Recreation Centre on Manson Avenue

Townsite 1919-1941

Etalo Dini (known to everyone as Dini) was born in 1896 in Lucca, Florence, Italy. He immigrated to Canada in 1914 and worked for the Yellow Head Coal Company in the Peace River country, Alberta. Dini came to the Powell River area in 1919 and initially operated a men's club (pool room) at the Shingle Mill and later a pool room at the Rodmay Hotel.

Velma Dini was born in 1911, immigrated to Canada from Rivignano (near Venice) Italy in 1923. Velma came directly to Powell River, B.C. because she had cousins (the Biosutti family) living here. Velma worked in the post office in the Townsite.

Dini and Velma married in 1935. They moved to Cranberry in 1941 and lived at 5621 Manson Avenue.

Cranberry from 1941

Mom and Dad purchased a home on Manson Avenue and also an old building that Dad, a journeyman carpenter, renovated and expanded. This facility became known as the **Cranberry Recreation Centre**. The **bowling Alley** located on the second story, opened with two bowling lanes and was operated by Mom. As business grew over the years, Dad built seven more lanes, constantly sanding and refinishing to keep it in tiptop condition.

The **pool hall** on the street level was run by Dad. One-half of the street-level portion was the location for the **Overwaitea Grocery Store** and **Joe Derton's Barbershop**.

As young boys, we all sought pin setting jobs at the bowling alley. We were paid 25 cents per game. The bowling alley was a popular social gathering place and always enjoyed full capacity, as various bowling leagues from the paper mill and local businesses enjoyed the vibrant surroundings and happy atmosphere. Mom, an avid gardener, always had fresh vegetables and fruit for the customers. Mom was renowned for her culinary skills and received praises in various B.C. travel magazines for her choice hamburgers (with fresh-from-the-garden tomatoes and lettuce), lemon meringue and oven-baked apple pies topped with ice cream. My sister Elaine spent many hours helping Mom and Dad at the bowling alley. It was always a thrill to hear that someone from other Canadian provinces or the U.S., would come to our isolated town and make it a point to stop by and experience what the locals had already been enjoying for years.

Our home on Manson Avenue was lived in by Mom until she passed away in 1996; Dad died in 1971. There were three children: Elaine, the youngest Marlene, and myself, Ron.

In Cranberry Lake, we enjoyed: roller skating at the Hall, swimming in Mowat Bay on Powell Lake and Rock Bar at Cranberry Lake. In the winter, Cranberry Lake would freeze over and we enjoyed ice-skating. Many of us recall the day a plane landed on the ice ... and didn't even sink. Soccer was a passion sport for many of us and the trips to Sechelt and Vancouver were particularly exciting. We became men when we were ready to play soccer against the Sliammon Indians.

A Saturday treat was seeing a movie at the **Patricia Theatre** for 25 cents; Cokes, ice cream or a chocolate bar cost 5 cents. When I wasn't at a movie on Saturdays, I loved to ride my bicycle to Westview and listen to my cousin Dick Biasutti sing country songs and play guitar. His influence directed me to a career of country music-related work that I still enjoy with a passion.

Our mode of transportation in those days was typically walking. My buddy, **Domenico Piccinin**, and I walked to school most everyday, rain or shine. It was several miles through the woods past Timberlane Park and the occasional bear, always too busy enjoying blackberries to bother us.

My sister Marlene remembers swimming at Cranberry Lake, playing the piano and trombone in the Brooks School band. She was also an avid hockey fan at the games in the old arena. She often walked to Wilshire's store for a magazine or a treat. Along the way was Bernier's shoe store, Ahola's Hardware Store and the Sweet Shop run by Jack Dunning. Bosa and Mitchell was just down the street from our home and Marlene helped Mom with the shopping.

As a 15 year-old, I worked on a deep-sea ship as a deckhand during the summer months. We transported paper rolls from the Powell River mill to Long Beach, California, each trip took four days. The following summer I took a job logging up on Haslam Lake. When I was 18, like most all other boys in the area, I went to work in the MacMillan Bloedel paper mill. I spent some three years on the jackhammer.

During the Paper Mill strike in 1956, I was part of the benefit concerts we offered, featuring the great music and dance talent of many locals.

While performing at the regular Italian dances with the **Jack Ellis** band, piano player, **Joe Tait**, accordion and myself on stand-up bass and guitar I met and married **Gina Vitellone** from **Wildwood**.

Looking Back with Anita Zuccato

The Culos Family – Lakeview Dairy Farm
Cranberry (30s & 40s)

Anita's maternal grandparents **Antonio and Anna Culos** were originally from Italy. Antonio came out ahead of his wife and family in 1903 to find work in Vancouver. It was difficult finding a job and Antonio told his family about "tough times" in Vancouver. Anna came later with the children in 1913; they went through immigration in the Ellis Island terminal in the U.S.A.

In 1919 the Culos family were living in a company house on Cedar Street in the Townsite and Antonio was working for the Powell River Company.

In 1924 Antonio bought two lots in Cranberry for a total of $100. He continued to work in the mill to sometime in the 1920s. It was hard, tough, back-breaking work preparing the site. First, a road had to be hacked through the bush to get to it. It was not easy getting water and a well 60 feet in depth had to be dug by hand. Antonio made all the cement bricks for building the house by hand. Young Italian men in the community helped Antonio build the house. Finally, Anna and their family of four sons and a daughter moved into the big house (opposite the old Malaspina Cranberry Lake School). A large barn was built near the farmhouse.

Antonio also bought property near the lake from **McFall** (the old bird sanctuary). He planted an orchard there and pastured his cattle by the lake – hence the name, **Lakeview Dairy**. The cows went back and forth to the pasture each day; they were milked in the barn, at the top of the hill, twice a day.

"The Culos cows were well known in the locality and provided fresh milk for Cranberry residents. I remember as a school child visiting the farm and being afraid of the bull!" - Marion Henderson (Beattie) 2000

"Culos' farm was located across the street from the school, and the cows were herded to pasture from the barns, down the hill at 8:30 in the morning to the pasture at McFall's field and back at 3:30 each afternoon. So, we met the messy critters everyday, both coming and going!" – Kay Hodson (Parsons) 2000

Henry Culos lived in the big house until 1951. It was then sold to Mr. and Mrs. Tal Haan. Henry built himself a house near the lake, on the pasture area. Enrico Culos subdivided lots on Park Avenue; Tom and Jean Hobson bought a view lot on Cranberry Lake.

Looking Back with Al McKenzie
The Corner Store Ladies Wear in Cranberry
Owner - Ethel McKenzie (1940s – 60s)

Ethel and Archibald Thomas McKenzie came to the Townsite, Powell River in the mid 1930s. They rented a house near City Motors from the Powell River Company. Archie was a sawer in the Saw Mill and worked there until he retired in 1958.

At the beginning of WWII they moved to Cranberry and rented a house on Cranberry Street. In 1942, Archie built their family home at 5820 Mowat Avenue, the second house down on the street. The McKenzie's had three children: Gordon, Mary, and Al.

In 1942, Archie joined the Canadian Army and was posted overseas to Scotland, where he worked for the Forestry Corps.

It was during the war years that Ethel decided to start a Ladies' Wear Shop in Cranberry. She rented the store next to Bernier's shoe store and called it 'The Corner Store' (at the corner of Manson and Cranberry Street). The store was a success and in 1955 she bought a house and lot at the corner of Drake and Manson and built a new store. This store was called 'The Corner Store Ladies Wear'.

Sometime during the 1960s, Ethel sold the store. Later, she went to work at Sweet Sixteen on Alberni in Westview as manager. She continued as manager when Sweet Sixteen moved to the new Safeway Mall (now Crossroads Village). Ethel died in 1968.

After Ethel's death, Archie left the family home and moved to a cabin on Haslam Lake. Gordon took over the family home; he died in 1981, and for a short time it was lived in by his widow, then it was sold.

Al, the youngest of the McKenzie children (born 1938) remembers the happy days growing up in Cranberry. He attended Cranberry School and had fun at the lake. He remembers the Vets' village being built after WWII. His uncle, Ted Jones worked for the Marwell construction and built the houses there. Uncle Ted had a big Cat (Caterpillar) which scooped out the basements; Al was the envy of his school friends as he was allowed to ride on the big Cat.

An adventure Al will never forget was riding in the rumble seat of Les Jamieson's Model T Ford to Westview. It was an exciting trip!

Another adventure was a drive to the McQuarrie place in Paradise Valley.

Bernier Shoe store, Cranberry 1930s. Cranberry Centre built on the Bernier lot at the corner of Manson and Cranberry St.   Photo: Bernier collection

The Senior Citizens Association B.C. #49 (formed 1953) Olive Devaud, President.
The association met (i) Moose Hall 1953-76 (ii) Recreation Complex 1976-2001 (iii) 2001-2006 Barowsky Place
(donated by Hertha Barowsky) (iv) From January 1, 2006 Cranberry Senior Centre.
Executive 2008: Rear: Rick Bradley Back row: Anna Scott/Joan Makowichuk/Jim Rose
Middle row: Ann McKenzie/Margaret Cousins/Lenore Arneson/Alice Cramer. Front: Dave Myers
Photo: #49 Seniors Association

1941 Mike Van Bunderen (Mike the Belgian) outside Town Crier Office (published by Al Alsgard), Cranberry. Mike was the first to recycle in Powell River, collecting bottles etc. with his dog and cart.   Photo: Powell River Museum

Early photo of Cranberry business section – including Parryville (rental cottages) now demolished – shows Wilshire house (behind the shop). The original building of the Town Crier is shown. Photo: Private collection

Mrs. Martha Lavina Mosely with her daughters Bernice Virginia Steele and Grace Estelle Hudson, Cranberry 1940s.   Photo courtesy of Sandra Hanson (Olson)

*Martha's youngest daughter **Eva Lavina Mosely (1918-2009)** jointly owned Quality Printers in Cranberry with Jack Hanna; she was one of Powell River's first businesswomen. Eva was a local historian and humanitarian – spending countless hours volunteering in the Extended Care Unit.*

"The Lambert and Mosely families were close friends. Both families came to Powell River in the 1920's. George and Martha Mosely came from the black community on Salt Spring Island. I attended the first Westview school with Eva. Eva graduated from Brooks school with top marks but the year she graduated was the only year the Powell River Company did not give a scholarship. George tried to get employment with the Powell River Company but was never hired, no reason given.
Initially, Eva worked for the Town Crier newspaper in Cranberry; later, she went into the printing business (Quality Printers) with her lifelong partner Jack Hanna. Eva and Jack were in love but not judge or minister, at that time, would perform an inter-racial marriage.
Eva worked hard for the Wildwood Hall (CCF) - keeping the accounts up-to-date."
Stuart Lambert

Looking Back with Jean Hobson (Melville) (1915-2007)

Hugh Melville – Dairy Farm at Myrtle Point (1930s & 40s)
Chicken Farm at Cranberry Lake (1947-53)

Hugh Melville (1883-1967) was born in Sonoma County, California, U.S.A. **Elizabeth Melville (1884-1952)** was born in Edinburgh, Scotland (of Irish decent). Their children Mim (1906-1951), Kathleen (1912-1982), and Jean (born 1915) were born on Texada Island.

From 1917-28 the Melville family lived in a **Bloedel, Stewart & Welch Company** house at the Myrtle Point logging camp. Hugh Melville worked for the company. After the closure of the company in 1928, the family moved into the main company house and lived there from 1928-47. Hugh Melville was caretaker of the company property. During the 1930s and WWII, Hugh ran a successful dairy business on the company property. He delivered milk to Westview and the Powell River Townsite for 15 cents a quart.

"I used to make out bills for the dairy business. We sold milk for 15 cents a quart and gave away the skim milk. There was one lady (who was married to a big boss at the mill) who journeyed all the way down to Myrtle Point in order to get free skim milk!

No one, that I knew, had difficulty in paying their milk bills during the Depression. There was steady money coming into the Powell River area with the Powell River Company working half-time during the Great Depression."

Jean Hobson (2002)

Cranberry Lake

After the company property at Myrtle Point was sold to Miles McLeod in 1947, the Melville family moved to Cranberry Lake. Hugh Melville ran a chicken farm in Cranberry from 1947-53. He raised 1,500 hens and sold the eggs to the fast-growing community of the Townsite and Villages for 50 cents a dozen. Hugh had a door-to-door delivery system.

In 1953, after the chicken business was sold, Hugh (now a widower) moved in with Jean and Tom Hobson at Park Avenue, Cranberry.

"In 1941 I married my husband, Tom Hobson. He was Father Leo's brother. Tom had previously suffered a serious accident and the Foley's (owners of the mill) gave Tom a permanent office position. Tom became a long-term employee and eventually retired from the mill after 40 years of service.

*We bought property on Park Avenue from **Henry Culos**; it was originally part of his farm. He was not keen to sell it to just anyone, however, he knew and liked Tom Hobson. Henry agreed to sell to Tom as a personal favour.*

The old Culos farm became a bird sanctuary (later abandoned). The property is presently owned and looked after by the Municipality of Powell River."

Jean Hobson (2007)

Later on, **Lindsay Park** became a popular swimming place for young people. In 1978 the Parks and Recreation Department recommended to Council that the large rock in the centre of the wading pool at Lindsay Park be removed. **Bill Alton, Ruth Mattick, and Isobel Elliot** organized the signing of a petition against its removal and presented it to Council. On April 10, 1978 Council defeated a motion for its removal.

Jean and Tom had three children: Marie, Dave, and Sheila. Jean's nephew, Dean, was also raised by the Hobson's. The kids in the 1950s and 60s had wonderful times on Cranberry Lake. The lake was a focal point of their leisure activities. There was rowing, fishing, swimming at **Whyte's Beach**, and skating when the lake froze over. In the 1950s float planes landed on the lake.

Today, these activities have almost stopped due to the infestation of lilies. Sometime, possibly it was the 1980s, a lady who lived on the lake planted lilies on her property. In the 1970s and 80s, Cranberry became known as a "depressed area". In the Townsite little has changed, except the demolition of the old hospital. Today, there are huge mega stores in Westview. Jean continues to shop at Mitchell's grocery store in Cranberry.

Looking Back with Ellen Scott and Family
The Scott Dairy Farm (1940s & 50s) – Cranberry Village

Thomas (Tom) and Ellen Scott (nee Gustafson) bought a 5+ acre property, near the old bridge which went over the McFall Creek, in 1943 from a **Mr. McIntosh**. This beautiful meadow and homes continue to be owned by Mrs. Scott and family – it is directly across from the old bird sanctuary (the old **Culos** property). The McFall Creek is the dividing line between Cranberry and Edgehill.

Ellen Scott (Gustafson) was born in Saskatchewan in 1911.

Ellen Gustafson, at the age of 18 years, came to live in the Powell River Townsite with **Alec and Adele Gustafson in 1929**. Initially, Ellen worked in the **Townsite** doing housework. Ellen was the downstairs maid and Christine Willis, the upstairs maid.

Ellen and Tom married in 1937. **Tom worked for many years, for the Powell River Company, in the grinder room.** He later worked as wharfinger for **Johnston Terminals**.

They lived in Wildwood and Paradise Valley before a permanent move to the farm in Cranberry.

Ellen and Tom had six children: Barbara, Douglas, Elaine, Jean, Mary, and Mable (known as Snookie). In 1947 Kay Benner came to live with the Scotts and became part of the family. Kay helped with the cows and looked after the kids.

The Scott children have many happy memories of visiting **Papa Goski's cabin at Finn Bay**, Lund in the 1940s and 50s.

Besides the 5 acres they owned, the Scotts leased 11 acres, adjacent to their property on **Lot 450** from the Powell River Company for a dollar a year. In the 1950s they rented the old Culos farm property (old bird sanctuary) to pasture their cows – this was after the Culos Dairy closed down.

The Scott Dairy in the 1940s and 50s ran a herd of 16 cows. It was a mixture of breeds. Some were milked by hand, but most by an early type of milking machine called a surge milker. A strap went around the cow, the surge milker attached and four inflations attached to the four teats.

One huge Holstein had big bags (udders) and she had to be milked by hand with a dishpan underneath to collect all the milk.

In the 1940s there was a dairy on the property with a boiler room. The milk was bottled at the dairy, and the raw milk delivered to the customers by truck for 15 cents a quart.

In the **1950s**, when pasteurization was required, the milk was put into eight-gallon cans and delivered to **Tip Top Dairy on Marine Avenue**. Scott Farm then received a milk cheque for the amount of raw milk delivered. They were no longer in the door-to-door house delivery business.

The Scott children received **piano lessons from Mrs. MacGregor**. Payment was made in cream and milk.

After the dairy closed down, the pasture was used for boarding horses. Ellen Scott always kept a few chickens for home consumption.

Looking Back with Vivian Bernier (Pulsifer/Calder)

The Bernier's Shoe Business Cranberry & Westview (1920s – 70s)

The Berniers of Cranberry are an old-time family, first living and operating a shoe repair business in Parryville in 1926 and then moving in 1928 to the corner of Manson and Cranberry (now the Seniors Centre) to establish a shoe repair and retail business.

Thomas and Cassie Bernier

During WWI Thomas Bernier (1874-1958) enlisted in the 16th Canadian Scottish Highlanders in Lethbridge, Alberta, January 11, 1916. He was discharged on December 10, 1919 – age 45 years.

Thomas Bernier first came on his own to Powell River in 1926 to scout out the business possibilities in the area. Satisfied there were economic opportunities in Powell River, he sent for the rest of the family.

In 1926 Cassie came to join her husband Thomas. Their son Edward, his wife Mae, and their two children, Vivian and Ray, joined Thomas and Cassie in Parryville. The Bernier family started a successful shoe repair business. Cassie and Mae operated a treadle sewing machine with brushes for polishing the shoes. Shoes for repair were picked up in the Townsite, fixed, and promptly delivered back.

Harold Bond remembers, as a boy, riding his bike to the Townsite to deliver shoes for Bernier, in a canvas sack. He was paid 50 cents a trip.

Ed Bernier (the early years):

"It was mighty rough for a while as we had no water or electricity. We used to get our water from a well at the back of the house. And we rigged up an old sewing machine with an emery-covered spool to finish off the shoes.
I can remember the road to Powell River. The Cranberry Lake road was just a trail.
There was a construction camp down by the old government wharf. Every night I used to trudge down there, pick up the shoes in sacks, and carry them home. Then I'd work half the night repairing them, and they'd be ready for my trip back there the next night.
There were no roads to Westview, and there was no Manson Avenue through Edgehill."

In 1928 the family moved to a house on the corner of Manson and Cranberry – previously owned by Jackson. It was a large piece of property; the house was on the corner and the shop on Cranberry Street. Both father and son repaired shoes and boots – sometime in the 1930s work boots and logging boots were sold.

In the mid 1930s Thomas Bernier moved to Westview to start a shoe repair business on Westview Avenue. The population of Westview was increasing and he saw the need of a shoe repair business in that area. After Tom moved to Westview, a Mr. McKibbon had a shoe repair business in the old store.

In 1931 Edward Bernier added a second shop, adjacent to the first original shop; both shops were on Cranberry Street. Initially, the second shop was a grocery store rented by Youngs. Later, Ed Bernier moved his shoe shop into the new building. **The Cranberry shop was now a retail shoe shop.**

In 1934 the front part of the old shoe shop became a beauty salon rented by Annette Plisson (Evans). In 1937 Annette sold her business to Gladys Woodward (Clayton). Gladys also rented two rooms in the upstairs of the Bernier home for the short time she operated the beauty salon. During WWII Ethel McKenzie opened a dress shop in the old store and called it the Corner Store, later she moved her business to the corner of Manson and Drake.

In 1946 a Mr. and Mrs. McCluskey and their daughter Alice opened Cozy Corner Café on the same premises. The business was later sold to Bob and Ethel Wilson and Nedra Leach in 1950; they ran the café for about a year. Corky Coburn, at one time, had a pizza shop there. The old shoe shop became a laundromat in the 1970s.

In 1953 Ed Bernier and Elva McDonald opened a shoe store on Marine Avenue, Westview, near the Roxy Theatre (2007 – Snickers Restaurant). It was called Ber-Mac's. Elva McDonald later married Staff Sergeant Otto Bigalke and sold the business to Al and Gwen Lock in 1956.

Other Cranberry Businesses

The first business block was built by Bert Parry directly across from his house and across Cranberry Street. It contained the following businesses: Haddad's Dry Goods, Len Weir's Drugstore, Al Smith Butcher, Joe and Minnie Ferraro's Grocery Store. This block burned down in 1929.

Mr. Somerton had a jewellery store in Cranberry.

Wilshire's was sold to Archie Blacklock.

Fred Parker ran the garage on the corner of Cranberry and Crown (later moved to Marine Avenue in Westview). Charlie Bennett later owned the Cranberry garage.

The Owl's Roost Café was located in the present Cranberry Pottery.

Emil Gordon had a furniture store on Manson across from the Berniers but closer to Drake Street. Later, Barry Lang had a furniture store and second-hand store in the same premises. This was before Etalo Dini built the bowling alley that housed Brown Brothers. That business was bought out by Overwaitea.

William Pitt Cross built the building that now houses the Tile and Marble store. He had a grocery store. Later, Brown's Grocery had their business there. Al Alsgard moved into the house next door and the Pitt Cross building produced a local newspaper, the **Town Crier**.

Don Woewoda had a sheet metal shop in this building, called Woewoda's Cranberry Sheet Metal Limited.

Pitt Cross also owned the garage on the corner of Manson and Cranberry. The site was burned down in 1938 and Ernie Leibenschel bought it and rebuilt Manson Service Limited in 1940.

The area at the top of Drake Street was called Russian Heights.

Goddards had a grocery store in the Goddard Block which also housed the post office.

Harry Dick had Dick's Dry Goods, later sold to Harvey and Nellie Shafer.

Koehuts had a small dry cleaning establishment; they lived in a house behind it. Next door to Koehuts was Harry Reed. He had a men's store and the family also lived behind the store.

In the 1930s Bosa's grocery store was in a small building in front of their house on Manson, near the Cranberry United Church. There were a number of houses built close to each other and Italian families lived in all of them: Vicelli, Bosa, Aprilis, Patrucco, and Raimondo. In 1949 Bosa and Mitchell brothers built on the present site of Mitchell Brothers – the business was called Bosa & Mitchell. Later, Bosa moved to Vancouver.

Ed and Mae Bernier and family

The Bernier property was sold to Whipple, the real estate agent, in the 1970s. Ed and Mae retired, south of town, to the Black Point area.

Ed and Mae Bernier had six children: Vivian, Raymond, Leroy, Arnold, Yvonne, and Elaine. In 1983 Thomas and Mae celebrated their 60th wedding anniversary.

Ed Bernier was active in village life. In 1931 he helped start the first Fall Fair, which was held in Cranberry. In 1966 Ed was presented with a desk set, by Ray Weaver, for his dedication in working for the fair for three decades. From 1934-74 he was sheriff for the area. During WWII Ed worked for Boeing and served with the local Duke of Connaught's Own Rifles.

Ed worked hard for the amalgamation of the Villages of Cranberry, Westview, Wildwood District, and Powell River Townsite in 1955. He was selected to be on the local Court of Revision by the Corporation of the District of Powell River.

In 1958 Vivian Bernier was appointed as accountant at the main branch of the Canadian Bank of Commerce in North Vancouver. She was the first woman in B.C. to be promoted to this rank.

In 1966 Vivian Pulsifer (Bernier) was named Sheriff's Officer for the County of Vancouver with jurisdiction from Sechelt Peninsula to Acton Sound, some 150 miles north of Powell River. The Sheriff's Office is responsible for civil actions. The appointment was temporary with Mrs. Pulsifer taking over while her father, Ed Bernier was recovering from a heart attack.

Looking Back – Cranberry Village!
Scotty's Transfer - Joe deWynter

Scotty deWynter started Scotty's Transfer in the 1940s in Cranberry village. Joe, and later Mike deWynter, joined the business. Scotty later sold out to Joe and he went into the insurance business – Scotty operated the insurance business from his own home in Cranberry. Mike also left the business and he bought and operated Harnel's Dry Goods store in Cranberry.

Joe owned and operated Scotty's Transfer from 1946 until he sold out in 1969 to Mr. and Mrs. Rod Cable. Bill Kaye was his secretary. Joe started with one truck and ended with a fleet of seven vehicles.

The deWynter brothers came west to B.C. as the family farm became a dust bowl in the 1930s. Mike deWynter sold out in 1947.

Joe came to Powell River in 1940 and worked on the maintenance crew in the Townsite before he was called up. He was in the Canadian Army and saw service in Italy, Belgium, and Holland.

It was while running a canteen for the army, out of a hotel in a village in northern Holland that Joe met his future wife, Hanna. Hanna's father was the principal of the village school. Hanna came as a war bride to Powell River, Canada in 1947. Her journey was not easy; by air to Gander, Newfoundland, a stopover in the U.S. and then, finally Vancouver, B.C. – with her was her son, John.

It was a difficult time after the war to get accommodation. First, Joe and Hanna stayed for a short time in Mowat Bay, and then later that same year moved to Parryville, Cranberry (the rent was $24 a month). In the late 1950s, the company office was in the building which is part of Cranberry Pottery today. In 1950 the deWynters bought their own home at 5683 Nelson Avenue. They lived in Cranberry until 1972 and in December of the same year, moved to Westview. In 1974 they started building their own home on beach property south of town, at the end of Stark Road. On February 1st, 1975 the deWynter family moved into their new house. They had owned the beachfront property, with cabin, from 1960.

Scotty's Transfer was a successful business in post-war Powell River. New houses were built and Joe hauled gravel. Scotty's Transfer initially moved garbage for a few years, delivered feed to farms, delivered freight from Westview wharf to businesses, and moved household goods. Any big jobs that came up for Scotty's Transfer, **Frank Best** and **Charlie Parsons** worked together on the project. Scotty's Transfer helped with the building of the breakwater at Westview and the old Arena at Willingdon Beach. They worked on logging roads and construction at the mill.

Hanna was busy raising a family of five children and taking the calls for the business. She very quickly adjusted to living in Canada – in Holland she had been taught a number of languages, including English.

The family shopped in Cranberry, and apart from visits to the doctor and dentist in the Townsite, everything they needed could be found in Cranberry Village. They swam at Whyte's Beach in the summer and skated on Cranberry Lake when the lake froze in the winter. Hanna had skated on the canals in Holland and had brought her skates with her.

Hanna is a skilled potter and her wares can be seen at the Farmer's Market.

Hanna was organist at Cranberry United Church. In 1971 Hanna was one of the lucky few who was given a ticket to attend the service at Westview United for the Queen's visit. She remembers having an excellent view from the gallery of the Royal party.

Looking Back with William (Bill) Peebles (1913-2007)

Cranberry Veterans' Village from 1946

Bill Peebles (2006)

"It was after WWII that I moved into the Cranberry Vets' homes in 1946. I was demobbed in December 1945, just before Christmas. The Powell River Company offered me a job (I had worked for them before enlisting). They wanted me to start right away but I told them I'd start after Christmas.

There were 19 homes built for the vets on half-acre lots on the old Company orchard property. Nine were built at the front of the property and ten at the back. They cost $6,000 to be repaid over a 25-year period at $20 a month.

I lived with my wife, Eva at 6630 Cranberry Street. Eva died in 1998 after a marriage lasting 37 years. The property was adjacent to the old fever hospital (demolished) – the pipes were still there. I lived in the vets' village for 54 years.

After the war, Cranberry was a thriving community. One could shop for all one needed in Cranberry. There was a post office, bakery, dry cleaning outfit, bowling alley, a pool hall under the alley, fire hall, two lodges (Odd Fellows & Pythian Lodge), school, Ernie Leibenschel's freight business (later Harold Long's), Ahola's hardware (now glassworks), and Overwaitea's cash-and-carry (where the pub is today), Bosa & Mitchells (now Mitchells), Wilshire's, Cranberry United Church (now Otago Club), and two gas stations (Leibenschels on the corner of Manson and Cranberry Street and a second one on the corner of Crown and Cranberry Street).

Cranberry had beautiful Christmas lights. I don't know where they went to. There was a rumour that the Marine merchants in Westview stole them after the amalgamation in 1955.

I was foreman for the clothing (repair) crew for the Powell River Company. There were 15 men in the crew. I retired in 1976 as a 30-year company man.

In the year 2000 I married Sylvia Keets at Westview United Church.

I am a member of the Powell River Legion Branch 164 and received my 50-year pin at a ceremony on January 12, 2001."

Kovacs family: Suzanna, Laszlo, Louis, Margaret and Joseph Kovacs.
Child: Piroska Kovacs (Bartley)   Insert: Kovacs house #448 Manson Avenue, Cranberry.
Photo: Piroska Bartley

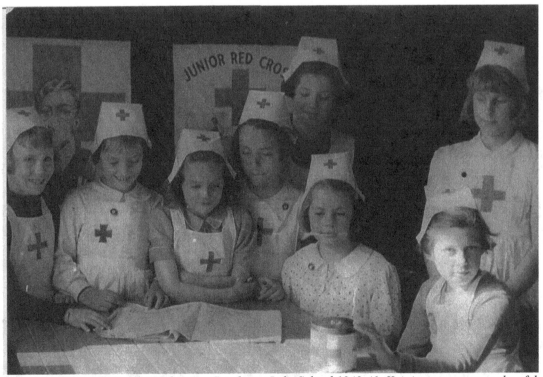

Junior Red Cross Grade 3 girls, Malaspina Cranberry Lake School 1940-41. Knitting squares to make afghans,
saving toothpaste tubes, and buying war savings stamps. Front: (L to R) – Rita Negrin/Vera Daly/Joan
Gibson/Lucy Culos/Betty Harding.. Back: Gloria Daly/Pat Garret.
Photo: Gloria Riley (Daly)

Parsons family 1930s, Cranberry Lake.
Back row: (L to R) – Margaret/Fred/Eileen/Walter/Lucy/Charlie. Front row: Kathleen/Ernie/Lucy (mother)/
Fred (father)/Robert. Photo: Parsons family

Scott farm, Cranberry. Tractor: Katy Burton (Benner) and Tom Scott 1940s.
Scott Children standing near Buckerfield's feed truck: Mary (Matthews), Jean (Marcaccini) and Elaine (Steiger)
Photos: Scott family

The Pest (Pestilence) hospital located in the Powell River Company orchard on Lot 450, Cranberry, Powell River. Note the fence to the right of the house – to keep visitors out! Ma and Pa Buttery looked after the needs of the patients.   Courtesy: Powell River Museum

Powell River Company Orchard Lot 450, Cranberry 1930s. Pa Buttery was on the company payroll to take care of the orchard. Fruit from the orchard went to the company store. After WWII the company gave the land for veterans' homes. Insert: Veterans' Village 1947.   Photos – Courtesy Powell River Museum

Looking Back with Barbara Lambert

Pest Hospital & Orchard Houses (1920s – 40s)

In the 1920s **Mrs. Lucy Buttery** was the first nurse in attendance at Powell River's isolation ward located by Cranberry Street in the **Powell River Company orchard** on **Lot 450**.

Bessie Banham:

> "The white, wood-frame building, surrounded by a high wire fence, was in clearing in the old orchard. The bare, painted walls of "V" joint and the uncurtained windows made the three-bed ward, the room for the nurse, even the pantry, bleak and unfriendly. There were no electric lights, or phone, but it did have the luxury of a bathroom. The water supply was hand-pumped from a well into a tank each day by Frank Radford."

It was known as the Pest (Pestilence) hospital, a safe and secure place for those with diseases which could be spread by contact with others and cause an epidemic.

Today the old orchard is a site in Cranberry known as the Veterans' Village.

Ma Buttery was born in Marsh Chapel, Lincolnshire, England on May 24, 1849. In 1919, Ma and Pa Buttery lived in the first orchard house owned by the Powell River Company. Ma not only nursed isolation cases in the Pest Hospital but performed housekeeping duties in the hospital and provided patients with meals. It was only a short walk from their orchard house to the hospital.

The Butterys put in a productive garden and this put fresh vegetables on the menu for the patients in isolation. In the 1925 & 26 edition of Wrigley's directory, Pa (Bill) Buttery was listed as a gardener and in the 1927 edition as a poultry man – probably feeding and watering chickens for the Radford brothers.

As of May 25, 1925 the Radford brothers leased the orchard and the chicken runs from the Powell River Company. Prior to the company lease of the orchard the Powell River Company directly employed and paid the "orchard man" an average monthly wage of $122. As Pa Buttery lived in the orchard house and worked on the property as a gardener and poultry man, it is more than likely that he was the first "orchard man" to be employed by the company.

It was a lonely existence for patients sent to the Pest Hospital. They were not allowed visitors as they were deemed contagious; however, Gus Schuler broke the rules! He was in the hospital because he had been exposed to scarlet fever; however, his friends came to visit him and together they passed away the time playing cards. This went on for some time until Dr. C.R. Marlatt caught them all "red-handed" and promptly ordered the visitors into isolation! The men continued to while away the hours playing cards as well as shooting apples off the trees in the orchard with a .22 rifle.

Ma (Lucy) Buttery lived to the grand old age of 90 and died soon after being admitted to St. Luke's Hospital on August 5, 1939. Her funeral was held at St. John's Union Church with the Pythian Sisters providing a tea after the service. Pa (Bill) Buttery died in Kamloops on May 28, 1942 at age 83. His obituary referred to him as a Powell River pioneer, a familiar figure in the Cranberry orchard. He came directly to Powell River from the "Old Country" in 1919 "when the paper town was but a healthy infant."

The Buttery's orchard house was the first and oldest of a number of orchard houses the company owned and rented out on the orchard property. In 1946, **William Peebles**, a WWII veteran, found the pipes of an old house near his home at 6630 Cranberry Street in the Vets' Village – probably the site of the old orchard house.

After the death of Ma Buttery, the old orchard house was rented to Powell River Company employees – this included a Mr. and Mrs. Frank Scott in 1942.

The Pest House was moved sometime in the 1930s to a new location, probably a site on the present Cranberry fire hall. Its use as an isolation ward was over; it was now a rental house for Powell River Company employees. It was now known as #1 Orchard House.

From 1945-48 it was rented to **Walter Patrick. Mike and Millie Crilly** rented the house from 1949-58. Their eldest son, Brian Crilly, recalls it as a house with two very small bedrooms with a bathroom added onto the back. The front porch had a distinctive picket fence. The Crillys had a telephone which was used by their next door neighbours the **Neilsons** at #2 Orchard House.

In 1955 the Powell River Company sold the Townsite houses and also put up for sale the houses they owned on the old orchard site. These houses were slow in selling. In the late 1950s, #1 Orchard House was simply torn down for the lumber; this was bought and used by a Mr. Christiansen to build a garage on Lakeview Street in Wildwood. Number 2 Orchard House was sold in the late 1950s and moved to Southview. Number 3 Orchard House was also sold in the late 1950s; it was bought by Rudi Pexton and moved in the vicinity of Haslam Street.

Number 3 Orchard House was probably built in the mid 1920s and remained on site until it was sold in the 1950s. The first occupants were Mr. and Mrs. Frank Radford. Wrigley's directory lists Frank Radford as residing at the orchard in 1926 and specifies his trade as raising poultry.

The Radford brothers leased the orchard and chicken runs from the Powell River Company for $30 a month.

Lease of orchard, including chicken runs to Frank Radford, formerly an employee of ours with his brother who will operate the premises. Our rental is nominal. Radfords to take it over as this will relieve us of the heavy operating expenses which we have suffered the last few years.
Powell River Company weekly letter – May 30 1925

Frank Radford had considerable previous experience in managing a poultry yard in Freeman, Ontario and later a fruit and poultry ranch in Burlington, Ontario. Initially, he was employed as a carpenter for the Powell River Company before taking up the lease on the old orchard site.

Mr. and Mrs. Frank Radford ran a successful business operation; this was described in detail in the *Powell River Digester* July 1925 edition and the *Powell River News* August 1928. Their poultry operation in 1928 consisted of 1,400 adult birds and 800 pullets. The chickens were kept in several runs and moved periodically. One run was sown each year with kale which later helped feed the chickens. The chickens were kept as laying hens for two years and then sold as broilers. Mr. Radford was an expert in dressing chickens – a total of six minutes to prepare one fowl!

Mrs. Radford collected the eggs twice daily. In winter, gas lights were used in the coops to lengthen the day for the fowls. Mr. Radford delivered 200 dozen eggs twice a week to the company store and other customers. Water was supplied to the chickens by a 22-foot well on the property.

In addition to the chickens, Mr. Radford looked after 300 fruit trees, consisting of apples, cherries, plums, and pears; a greenhouse for growing pot plants and beehives for producing honey.

Old timer **Roy Leibenschel** recalls his father **Ernie Leibenschel** delivered chicken feed to Frank Radford in the early 1930s. Ernie, a young boy at the time, went along for the ride. He remembers the gardens and chicken houses being in the vicinity of, what later became known in the 1950s, as # 3 Orchard House.

Number 3 Orchard House was later rented to the **Farleys** and in the 1950s to the **Cattermoles**:

Monty Cattermole:

"The Cattermoles have always lived in Cranberry. The Orchard house, their present home (1959) --- was originally the home of the orchard man who looked after the big

acreage of fruit trees, maintained by the Powell River Company which supplied all fruit to the local stores. Next door to it (Orchard House) was the Pest Hospital for isolation cases."

Powell River News February 19, 1959 (Glacier Ventures)

Number 1 Orchard House was located on the site of the present Cranberry Fire station at the corner of Cranberry Street and Dieppe Avenue. The location of **Number 2 Orchard House** was near the fire hall – in the adjacent parking lot. A boggy area of about 200 yards separated #2 and #3 Orchard House.

Number 3 Orchard House was located further along Cranberry Street, going towards the Townsite. The Cattermoles' driveway is still visible today, half-a-century after the house was moved.

Part of the old orchard can still be seen in what is known as the **Veterans' Village** which was built in 1946 after WWII.

According to the 1946 *Digester* Fall edition, the houses were built under the Veteran's Land Act with the Powell River Company donating the land to the Canadian government. In order to secure a home, the veteran had to occupy the property for 10 years and no re-selling was permitted during this time period. These homes were designed by several leading Canadian architects. The average price was $6,300 and a deposit of $600 was required. At the end of 10 years, provided the veteran had complied with the terms of the Veteran's Land Act, the price of his home was reduced by $2,000 – thus the vet paid a total of $4,300 for his property if he elected to pay for it at this time.

"There were 19 homes built for vets on half acre lots in the old company orchard property. Nine were built at the front of the property and ten at the back. They cost $6,000, to be repaid over a 25 year period at $20 a month."

William Peebles, WWII Vet (2006)

Eventually, with home ownership, the veterans subdivided their large lots. Thus, the area, known originally as the Veterans' Village, has today many different styles of houses.

Today the **Pest Hospital** and the **Old Orchard Houses** owned by the **Powell River Company** are just fading memories of Powell River's fascinating past.

Looking Back with Archie Blacklock

Wilshire's (1962-1991) – Cranberry Village

Archie Blacklock

*"My parents, **William and Agnes Blacklock, came to Powell River in 1924**. My father worked for the **Powell River Company** as a longshoreman. He retired from the mill in 1961.*

When I was a baby, we lived at One Mile Bay, Powell Lake, in a float house. We then moved to Mowat Bay in 1932, when I was 2 years of age. After that we moved to Cranberry Street, at the top of the hill.

*I attended Cranberry School, **Mr. Holmwood** was principal. I remember swimming at Whytes Beach and Mowat Bay. I skated on Cranberry Lake – it was a lot colder then – Cis Hayes landed a plane on the ice one time. Kids I remember from school were: Les Kolezar, Jack and Dech Tateranko, Bill Donkersley, Pete and Tom Phillips. I delivered the Province paper to all of Cranberry in the late 1930s and 40s.*

I remember the Butterys – they lived on Lot 450. Farleys also lived on Lot 450 – near where the present fire hall is. Later on, the Cattermoles lived in Farley's place.

The Pest Hospital was located halfway between Buttery's place and the Farley's.

Cranberry businesses I recall:
Smith's Meat Market, Dicks Dry Goods, Wier's Drugstore, Cranberry Hardware, Three Star Garage, Brown Bros, Ray's Superior, Bosa & Mitchell, Shell Station (Fred Parker), Caledonian Bakery (Bill Beattie), Parryville (H.J. Parry).

*As a teenage, I painted houses for **H.J. Parry** at Parryville. I was paid 25 cents an hour. There were about 15 buildings there; 14 houses and one long building which housed six mini apartments.*

In the late 1940s, I worked for B & B Logging, south of town; Goffin Logging at Gold Lake, and later deliveries at Tip Top Dairy.

*Hart Innes was the pasteurizing plant manager at **Tip Top Dairy**. The milk was delivered in bottles to the customers. I was on the Cranberry run and part of the Townsite. Sometimes we switched around delivery routes.*

In the late 1940s and 50s I worked for **Scotty's Transfer**. Deliveries included: general freight, animal feed (grain) to local farmers (Lambert's in Paradise Valley, Springbrook Dairy at Myrtle Point, Lewis and McMahon's in Wildwood), and hay (Blue Mountain, Lambert's and Pitt-Cross). Freight was hauled from the company dock to Powell Stores.

From 1953-63, I worked initially for Cranberry Village, and later the Municipality of Powell River.

I bought Wilshire's store in Cranberry in 1962 from Rhoda Wilshire. Syd Wilshire had just passed away and Rhoda was not in good health.

Grace Melvin made sandwiches and milkshakes. We served soups, sandwiches, subs, coffee, hot chocolate, milkshakes, and floats. In the early years, we had toys and a few groceries. Later on, we moved into meat, veggies, fishing tackle, hardware, giftware – more like a modern convenience store.

Russ Lambert brought in eggs to sell in the store.

We had the **post office** in the store for seven years during the 1980s. Betty was in charge of the post office. We sold lottery tickets: 649 and B.C. 49 scratch tickets.

Many helped serve at Wilshire's from 1962-1991: Grace Melvin, Penny Robertson, Jenny Sheldon, Joanne Burge, Lil Norman, Mrs. Allen, Karen Cosgrove, Valerie Riley, Cathy Westy, Jan Crocket, Gerry Wilson, and others. Our own kids, Gail, Brenda, and Kim worked in the store.

Wilshire's was sold to Gary and Brenda Kremsutter in 1991. They ran it as Wilshire's.

Looking Back!

Cranberry did fairly well until the shopping centres came to Westview. In the 1960s Cranberry started to go downhill. Today, there are a few businesses in Cranberry, but it's not like it used to be."

Edwin Profitt's shingle mill at Mowat Bay, Cranberry, 1915.
Insert: Harry Riley at Mowat Bay, Cranberry, Powell River 1923. Harry lived on a float house with his family.
Photos: Gloria Riley collection

Archibald and Ethel McKenzie's house, 5820 Mowat Avenue, Cranberry 1942.
Insert: Mr. and Mrs. A. McKenzie with their children: Gordon, Mary, and Al – Cranberry 1938.
Photos: Al McKenzie

Italian wedding reception for Mr. and Mrs. Angelo Culos at the home of Antonio & Anna Culos, Cranberry (opposite Cranberry Lake School). The bride journeyed all the way from S. Giovanni, Italy to marry the groom on the day of her arrival (May 16, 1927). Front row: (L to R) Mrs. M. Francescutti/Mrs. Helena Culos/Mr. Angelo Culos/Mr. L. Castellarin. Photo: Powell River Digester 1927 Insert photo: B.A. Lambert 2008

Golden Stanley (Horseshoe Valley pioneer – historian) leading Scout troop, Cranberry 1940s. Private collection

Cranberry Days July 14, 1969, Cranberry.
Left: Fay Aitken. Right: Andy Anderson
(Andy lived at Mowat Bay).
Photo: Jack Hanna   Powell River Museum

The deWynter family having fun skating at Cranberry
Lake. Prior to the 1960s the lake froze during the winter
for periods up to six weeks. It was a popular spot to
skate before the Arena at Willingdon Beach, Westview
opened in 1955. (L to R) Shirley/Jean/
Joe (father)/Cheryl deWynter.
Photo: Hanna deWynter 1957

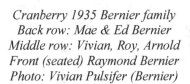

Cranberry signpost: Lake Road to Mowat Bay 1947
Lorraine Jamieson (age 3) playing in front yard.
Insert: (L to R) Allan Jamieson/Betsy Jamieson
(McGuffie)/Lorraine Jamieson
Photos: Lorraine Jamieson

Cranberry 1935 Bernier family
Back row: Mae & Ed Bernier
Middle row: Vivian, Roy, Arnold
Front (seated) Raymond Bernier
Photo: Vivian Pulsifer (Bernier)

Scott Dairy Farm 1947
Ellen Scott with Doug, Jean, and Mary Scott
standing on an old well cover.
Photo: Scott family

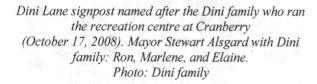

Dini Lane signpost named after the Dini family who ran
the recreation centre at Cranberry
(October 17, 2008). Mayor Stewart Alsgard with Dini
family: Ron, Marlene, and Elaine.
Photo: Dini family

Looking Back with Al McKenzie
Memories of Mowat Bay

I have many memories of Mowat Bay. I go back to the days when grass and trees grew right down to the water's edge. When I was a small child, my mother would pack us kids up and head down to the Bay. She would spread a blanket under a tree and watch over us while we frolicked in the water.

For years, Old Man Turnbull rented cabins on shore and float houses on the water. He also rented leaky rowboats for a dollar a day. As a young lad, I would go there first thing in the morning and bale them out. For my labours, I got the use of an eight-foot punt for the day. I spent many happy hours fishing and exploring the bottom end of the lake.

To the left was a row of boathouses. One day, a low moaning could be heard way in the back of Chippewa Bay. It grew louder, and what we call a 'Chippewa Howler' came screaming down the lake and hit Mowat Bay like a Kansas tornado. The next day the carnage was devastating. There were logs and half-sunk boathouses everywhere and boats at the bottom of the Bay. Some are still there.

Turnbull moved out and along came Andy Anderson. Andy promptly flattened everything and moved in with a whole sawmill in pieces, turning the place into an antique junkyard, complete with rotting piles of lumber. There was no admittance unless you had business with Mr. Anderson.

When old Andy passed on, the Municipality acquired the property and it has evolved into the beautiful park it is today. The only things I miss from the old days are the shade trees near the water.

Just up the street, John Gaganof crafted beautiful clinker-built boats. For $300 or $400 you could get one with a 5 h.p. Briggs engine in it and a set of oars, just in case.

In those days, most boats were handmade in backyards. At launching time, an 18' cruiser would be manhandled onto the back of one of Scotty's Transfer's three-ton flat decks. We would back the truck as far as we could into the bay. With great fanfare, the boat would literally be dumped into the water.

Then one fine day a very smart fellow invented the boat trailer, and the launching ramp was born. Then along came fibreglass and a boating revolution was born. A revolution we still enjoy today.

Powell River is a boating town. Our harbours are full and every second yard has one or two boats sitting on trailers.

Looking Back with Gloria Riley (Daly)

Cranberry (1930s & 40s) & Mowat Bay (1920s – 40s)

Gloria Riley 2008 - *"Cranberry was a nice little community, we had everything."*

Ed Daly came to Powell River in 1929, after hearing, by word-of-mouth, about hiring by the Powell River Company. In 1930 Ed was able to get steady work in the grinder room; this was hard, physical work, so eventually he took a job, for health reasons, in the locker room. **Ed and Kay Daly** lived on a two-acre property in **Cranberry**, near **Haslam Street**. Gloria was born in 1931, and her brother Terry in 1933.

Ed was a CCF supporter but was not fired in the political purge in the mill (1933-37). Working in the mill, during, and after the purge, "was not nice for a while". Ed talked to other workers to get support for a union – having a union would give employees job security. **The Union was certified in 1937.**

During WWII Kay operated the **Cranberry Beauty Salon** in what is now Cranberry Pottery. Later, Kay worked with **Bertha Thutin** (Norman) in the **Cranberry sub-post office** in the Goddard building.

Gloria attended **Malaspina Cranberry Lake School** from Grades 1 to 6; from Grades 6 to 10 she attended **Brooks**. From 1947-51 she worked for Powell stores. In 1951, Gloria married **Harry Riley** who worked for the **Powell River Company** for 40 years. Mrs. Hugh Daly, Gloria's cousin, during WWII worked in the mill. Gloria and Harry had five children: Patrick, Clifford, Danny, Bonna, and Martin.

Gloria and Harry first lived in the Goddard (Mountain View) apartments; in 1952 they rented three rooms at 101 Poplar Street. In 1956 they bought 5766 Maple Avenue (Evan Sadler's old home), then they made a final move to 5504 Marine Avenue in 1964, buying from Lois and Bob Murray.

In 1923 **Tom Riley** was hired by the Powell River Company as bandmaster; he worked at various jobs in the mill. In 1924 he helped move the graves from the Townsite to Cranberry. Tom and Min Riley had two children, **Eddie** (born 1917) and **Harry Riley** (born 1922). **The Riley family lived in a float house in Mowat Bay.** Harry, as a toddler, frequently fell into the water – there were no floatation devices! In 1925 the Rileys moved onto land behind the float houses.

In 1930 Min married Bill Rees. The family lived in Mowat Bay.

Looking Back at Mowat Bay

Andy and Clara Anderson

Andy moved to the Powell River area in **1908** after he had heard about the hunting, trapping, and logging operations on the Canadian West Coast. He was originally from Sweden and came over with his family to the U.S. in 1892.

In 1927 Andy married **Clara Olson**. They became a team; together they hunted mountain goats, bear, and deer in the Powell Lake watershed. They knew **Billy-Goat Smith** and helped transport his goats up Powell Lake to his cabin. They operated the **Lakeview Lumber Company** from 1932-60. This was a successful venture during the Great Depression and after WWII. They supplied lumber to the growing villages of Wildwood, Cranberry, and Westview. Clara drove a truck and managed the company books.

They were forced to move from this location in 1960 because the Powell River Company did not renew their lease. After the lease was cancelled, the entire mill was moved to the Anderson's 16-acre property at **Mowat Bay**. Unfortunately, for the Andersons, the Powell River Municipality refused to allow the operation of a mill on this site. Gradually, the machinery rusted away with disuse.

In 1976 the old mill equipment found a permanent home in Burnaby's Heritage Village. Sadly, Andy watched from his wheelchair as the flatbed trucks picked up the machinery and drove it away. Andy died at 89 years of age in 1977. Old-time Cranberry residents remember Andy, as an elderly man, walking with dignity and determination in the 1968 Cranberry Fun Days celebration.

Larry Hanson (2007):

"I knew Andy when he lived in Mowat Bay. I used to help in his yard. Andy told me a few old stories:

One time Andy was out trapping in the mountains near the upper part of Powell Lake. It started to snow, kept on snowing and he could not move out of the area. So he hunkered down in a hollow cedar tree he found for a number of days until it was safe to leave the area.

Andy was a great believer in folk remedies. He attributed his good eyesight, in his old age, to drinking dandelion juice."

Looking Back at Cranberry Cemetery

Postscript: Billy-Goat Smith

On March 21, 2006 a marker was placed on Robert Bonner Smith's grave in Cranberry. It was dedicated by Rudy Pearson, past president of the Powell River Museum. A small etching of a billy goat appears on the stone.

The mystery surrounding Robert Bonner Smith is explored in *Old Time Stories* by Barbara Ann Lambert. The following stories are a brief addition to the published account by Trafford Publishing, Victoria, in 2006:

Duncan Bird (2007):

"Before WWII, during the 1930s, when I was about eight or nine years old, I met Billy-Goat Smith. **Bill Roberts** *took Walter Elly and me up the lake. Bill Roberts was a wonderful guy; he was a good friend of my dad's.*

We started early in the morning. I remember seeing all the trees and stumps around Powell Lake. **Billy-Goat Smith** *had dried raspberries on trays made out of shakes. He had vegetables hanging up – corn and onions. Old Billy-Goat Smith wanted to give us some goat's milk – it had a very strong smell. Walter and I threw it over our shoulders when he wasn't looking! The smell of everything around there was not very pleasant. He had a stream coming down by his place. He scooped fish out of the stream with a little net and placed them in a frying pan. We went into the house to deliver groceries.*

Winters up there in Powell Lake were worse than the ones here in Wildwood. Things used to freeze up something terrible. Lots of firewood was needed, and it all had to be cut by hand.

Living alone like that (Billy-Goat Smith) – there were lots of rumours – did some murder back in the States. That's the reason he found that isolated area, up at the lake.

My cousin worked in the bank. Billy-Goat brought in some funny old paper money – old $2 bills.

Billy Roberts and **George Simpson** *brought up Billy-Goat Smith's groceries and supplies to his place, up the lake."*

Jack Banham (2007):

"Everyone went to the **Patricia Theatre***. The band used to play there.* **One time Billy-Goat Smith came into the theatre. Everyone clapped!** *Mum was there. It was one of those rare occasions when he came into town.*

My mother's sister, Ann Francis, visited him once. He gave her a glass of wine in a dirty old glass.

Charles Pember – a religious guy – was a good friend of Billy Goat's."

Looking Back with Gerri and Charlie Parsons

Wonderful Memories of Cranberry (2000)

Cranberry Business District

Around 1921, Sid Wilshire Sr. and his wife built a home near the new road (now Cranberry Street). Then they moved the house to the rear of the lot and built a confectionery shop with a novelty department and a workshop in the rear. The same store is there today, with the same soda counter, where people still buy milkshakes and workers still stop for coffee breaks.

Bert Parry saw the possibility of Cranberry Lake as a residential suburb. He invested in some property adjacent to Lot 450, brought his family from Vancouver and lived in a tent while he built their home. Mr. Parry built some small cottages that he rented. Then, across the street from his home, he built a business block which housed four stores: Haddad, a dry goods merchant; Farara's Grocery and Delicatessen; a meat market operated by A. Smith, and the first Alsgard Furniture Store. This was Parryville. The Parryville houses, which over the years had been homes for people who needed places where the rent was not too high, were demolished. The area is now just a vacant lot next to Evans Park. The meat market and furniture store are no more.

Bob Simpkins erected a building which was known as the Goddard Block and is now an apartment block. It was a store that later became the Cranberry Post Office and a barbershop, with an apartment block above. The Goddard Brothers, Eddie and George, built a community hall, which later became the Foursquare Church, and is now another apartment house.

Jack Dykes ran a bus service with a truck that had benches along the sides.

W. Pitt Cross built a home and grocery-meat store that later became Cranberry Sheet Metal Shop. He also built a garage, on the east corner of Manson and Cranberry Street, which later burned. The property was purchased by Ernie Liebenschel, who erected a garage and gas station with the first computing gas pump. Ed Siska operated the station for a time and then entrepreneurs sold motorcycles and rented cars. The building no longer holds a commercial enterprise.

Martin Alsgard started a furniture store in the Haddad block and moved to a building adjoining Mellieur's Garage on the corner of Crown and Cranberry Street. He then moved the business to Goddard Community Hall and, when the hall burned, erected a new building. The new building later became Tom Ahola's Hardware Store. Still later, it was taken over by Tom's son, Ed, and then used by Harold Tuck as a music and TV repair shop. The building then became a second-hand store, a home improvement building and is now empty.

Malnick built a store on Manson Avenue and, later, sold it to Bosa. In 1946 Bosa went into partnership with Marino (Babe) and Albert Mitchell. The company was known as Bosa & Mitchell. In 1961 the Mitchell Brothers bought out A. Bosa & Company. In 1981 Peter Mitchell purchased the store and gave it the name Mitchell Brothers.

The Garage by the cemetery was first owned by Joe and Frank Mellieur then Emil Gordon and others. It became a body shop run by Stan Slater and remains a body shop today.

Where the Cranberry Pottery shop is now, there was a little restaurant, the "Owl's Roost," run by an Englishman and his wife. It was a place where many young people hung out, even though the Englishman was very strict about their conduct; any swearing or other nonsense, and out you went. Many of the kids disciplined each other, and all had great respect for the owners. It was a pleasant place for young and old, a place where everyone had fun.

Joe Derton had a pool hall and barbershop on Cranberry Street. It later became the Kingdom Hall, the Pythian Sisters Hall, and is now the Unitarian Church. Joe later operated the barbershop near the post office. Sara Garash had a hairdresser's parlour. Bill Beattie had the Caledonian Bakery on Crown Avenue.

In 1928 Harry Dick sold dry goods and sundry items door-to-door. Bert Parry suggested he start a store in the same block as Wilshires. Mike deWynter bought him out and the building is no longer there.

Ernie Liebenschel had a business known as Liebenschel Transfer & Coal. He brought coal from Nanaimo by barge to a depot in Powell River. Scotty and Joe deWynter operated gravel trucks.

At the intersection of Manson Avenue and Cranberry Street, was the original Town Crier building. It has been occupied by a drugstore, an art gallery, a second-hand store, and a card shop. It is now home to a tile store.

Near that corner, Brown Brothers had a grocery store with a bowling alley above. Len Wallace and Jim Lamb took over from the Browns. Then Overwaitea occupied the building. It is now the Cranberry Tavern, with a hotel above.

The Tom Bernier family built their home, with a shoe store and repair shop next door, on the east corner of Manson Avenue and Cranberry Street. For many years, the store was operated by Tom's son, Ed. Eventually, the house and store were torn down to make way for the Cranberry Centre.

Cranberry had a complete shopping district with 21 business establishments.

Cranberry Village

Andy Culos Sr. built a rather unusual white cement-block house for his family on Manson Avenue, across from the Cranberry School. The house, later owned by the Haans family, is now an apartment block. The Culos family also purchased land by the lake, where they built an orchard and kept cows to supply the milk-starved community.

In 1976 the Municipality opened the wildlife sanctuary on land once owned by the Culos family. For about 20 years, local people and tourists visited the sanctuary. It was closed because of lack of funds to run it and complaints from people that geese and ducks were detrimental to the lake. Some people believe the present water lily problem in the lake was caused by excess nutrients from the sanctuary.

The Cranberry Centre was built under the Neighbourhood Improvement Plan with funds from the Federal and Provincial governments and a grant from the Municipality. The building housed the local library, offices of the Improvement & Housing groups, and a meeting area. It was officially opened on March 4, 1977. The Centre, although still used for meetings and as a polling station during elections, is mainly a daycare centre. The library was moved to Westview when all the district libraries were merged into one.

In 1928 the Cranberry United Church was built with subscriptions and much volunteer work. Initially, a student pastor came from Vancouver on weekends. For a time, the building was a youth centre. Then it was sold to the Otago Rugby Club. In 1942 the Foursquare Church was built across the street from Parryville. It then moved across the street and now the building is an apartment. St. Hugh's Anglican Church, on Nelson Avenue, was a converted bunkhouse donated by the Powell River Company.

The four-room Malaspina School, but inevitably called "Cranberry School", was built in 1930 to eliminate the long hike students had to make to attend Henderson School. In 1950 another four-room building was added, with a covered walkway between the two buildings. The school's auditorium was built in 1956. The school was closed in 1986. Presently empty, the building's future is unknown.

E.J. Ryan installed a 50,000 gallon water tank on the hill on Third Street (now Lombardy in the Townsite) and 100 residents were hooked up to the new water main. Water was pumped to the tank from the Powell River Company tanks. Cranberry today is on the Haslam Lake water system.

David Harkness was hired by the Cranberry Light & Water District to install electricity in 1931 for 150 consumers. The telephone company had difficulty installing telephones, but finally overcame the problem by changing the type of transformers and lowering the voltage on the hydro poles.

Ernie Liebenschel organized volunteers to form a fire brigade and was elected first fire chief. Local businesses bought the first hoses and equipment. A fire truck came later. The fire hall was on Drake Street, just below Manson Avenue. It later became the Cranberry Library when a new fire hall was built. The old fire hall is still there and houses the Infant Development Program run by Artaban. The fire hall on Cranberry Street, beside the Veterans' Homes, is now used only as a storage place. The Provincial Police first provided police service. Then the RCMP took over. Today, the Powell River District force numbers about 24.

The Powell River and District Agricultural Association was started in 1931. With a grant from the government and donations of prizes by local merchants, the first Fall Fair was held in the basement of the school. There was a great display of fruit, vegetables, and needlework. It was the beginning of many successful Fall Fairs, which later took place in the Willingdon Arena. They ceased for awhile and then returned at the Farmer's Market in Paradise Valley.

From the earliest days, Cranberry Lake was a popular place for ice-skating in the winter. People can remember years when there was good skating from mid-December to early February. After Willingdon Arena was built, in 1955, ice time was available year round. But when the lake froze, they enjoyed outdoor skating, especially with a full moon and a bonfire on the shore for roasting marshmallows and warming hands. One year, 1948, there was coffee and doughnuts for 25 cents at Parsons' place. One year, from December 5th to New Year's Eve, three feet of snow fell and lots of ice formed. People, including mill workers and school children, travelled from one end of the lake to the other along paths dug in the snow. In the summer, Cranberry Lake and Mowat Bay were popular swimming holes. Unfortunately, today it is not wise to do so in Cranberry Lake because of the pollutants.

After Andy Anderson died, Mowat Bay Park was developed for swimming and a boat ramp installed. Lindsay Park was named after Tommy Lindsay, who took on the job of clearing the site and installing swings to provide a safe playground for children. It is not used much today, as ducks and geese have taken over. D.A. Evans Park still sees as many ball games as it did in the past.

Pete and Ruth Parry built the first roller rink, a popular place with young people. It was a wooden structure with cement floor that burned down about 1946. It was rebuilt with cement blocks and wooden floor. When the rink closed, it was used for awhile as the Odd Fellows Lodge and today it is the curling rink.

Cranberry Lake was incorporated as a village in 1942 with three or four commissioners and Ray Weaver as chairman. Weaver remained on the council until the Municipality was formed in 1955.

From 1953-55 improvements were made to the streets from taxes collected. The committee of such people as Jack Brooks, H.J. Parry, Archie McKenzie, Bob Gela, and Ernie Liebenschel co-operated to make Cranberry a prosperous place. Bob Johnson was committee secretary for many years, until 1955, when he took a position with the municipality.

In April 1947, the Village Corporation started compulsory garbage collection. Garbage was collected once a week, more often if required for businesses. Building owners were billed once a month. Any unpaid debts were added to tax bills. Outlying districts were responsible for their own garbage. The dump was then on the present Inland Lake road.

The original cemetery was located near the old golf links, at the brow of the hill on the road to the old Townsite breakwater. All available space within the white picket fence was used and, as the Company wished to expand, the cemetery was moved to its present location at Crown Avenue and Cranberry Street. In 1932 the new site was being neglected and the Cemetery Improvement League was formed. With donations, a charge for plots and volunteer labour, the grounds were landscaped. Today, both the Regional District and the CDPR keep the cemetery.

After World War II, the Powell River Company donated an old orchard site in Cranberry for the construction of 19 homes for veterans. The site had once been known for "The Pest House," for patients with contagious diseases; it had no lights or telephone and was surrounded by a high wire fence. Patients were provided with good meals. Families of the patients were kept there too, and people who visited patients were isolated. Opposite the Veterans' Homes, on the other side of the street, the Powell River Sick Benefit Society built little homes for retired Company employees. The Moose Lodge took over maintenance of the homes, now known as Moose Village and it is still used for retirees.

In 1955 Cranberry Lake was one of the outlying districts that amalgamated with others to form the present Municipality of Powell River. At a meeting held in the Odd Fellows Hall in Cranberry, the ratepayers expressed their concerns about the incorporation of a municipality. Many were against Cranberry joining, as they felt the area was successful in the way that it was progressing. They felt they could pay for their own needs and saw no purpose in joining. Others felt it was an advantage to join, as the communities could stick together and share expenses of schools, utilities, etc. as well as police costs. Some were afraid that revenues collected would go to improvements in Westview and Townsite instead of Cranberry. Although Westview did receive more road improvement, Cranberry profited by receiving sewers, better garbage disposal and better water works from Haslam Lake.

In 1967 a group of Cranberry Ratepayers got together and organized a "Cranberry Day" that was held at Lindsay Park. Activities started with a pancake breakfast and a parade from Timberlane to Lindsay Park. Then followed the official opening ceremonies; a sail past and races; tours of the *Cranberry Queen* (Parsons' houseboat); a Community Band concert and a tug-of-war between Cranberry and Edgehill schools. After dinner, there were baseball games at both Timberlane and D.A. Evans parks, followed by dancing at Lindsay Park and a community dance at the Odd Fellows Hall. Prices for hot dogs, ice cream, etc. were at 1940 rates. All old-timers were honoured. Andy Anderson was there, with his goat pulling a cart, and he gave some of the children rides in it. Fun was had by all.

In June 1969 the Ratepayers again had a Cranberry Day. There were 50 vehicles in the parade, which was only eight minutes late; a great honour to the parade master, as being on time is rare. Each block area in the district had a float in the parade. Included were: the three Cadet Corps; the Highland Laddies; Cranberry School with 60 students; floats from various lodges, a float with good citizens and floats from various Cranberry businesses. The Miss PRE contestants were there, and the Cubs and Scouts were there to help where needed. The Rotary and other lodges had fishing derbies. Steve Mason and his band played for the big crowd that gathered for the celebrations, and the Trailriders came out to show their abilities. The two-mile route was lined with people of all ages from grandparents to little tots. Gerry Gray presented Tommy Lindsay with a cake to honour his 80th birthday and his efforts in creating the park. There was a bathtub race on the lake between "Admiral" Gerry Gray and "Commodore" Bob Gela. The small boats glided back and forth across the lake and underwent their various tests. The Powell River Recreation Department swim classes gave demonstrations. Hundreds enjoyed the *Cranberry Queen*, a raft with seats on it, as it made its trip around the lake. Charlie Parsons donated the raft as a swimming float when the day was over. All enjoyed an open-air concert by the Community Band, a group of people who had a hankering to play instruments for pleasure. Many people remarked that Lindsay Park should have a band shelter, so that there could be afternoon and evening concerts.

Over the years, Cranberry has held its own as a little community town. There are not many businesses, as most of the shopping is done at the malls in Westview, where one can do "one-stop shopping". When the lake freezes, young people still come to skate; people still go to Wilshires for a milkshake or a cup of coffee; there is still a barbershop with one or two barbers; Bosa Mitchell have upgraded their store and the store is now known as Mitchell Brothers, but still have many of the offspring of older customers shopping there.

Westview Village

Westview Village 1950s, Marine Avenue.
Businesses on Marine Avenue (left side) Bank of Montreal/Madame Loukes 5th Avenue Dress Shop/Black's Drug Store/Rowe's Junior Style Shop.   Photo: Hindle collection

Madame Loukes 5th Avenue Dress Shop, Marine Avenue, Westview Village 1940s – distinctive clothes for women.
Courtesy of Powell River Museum

179

Business section, Marine Avenue, Westview 1930.   Courtesy of Powell River Museum

1951 Labour Day parade led by the Powell River Company sponsored pipe band, followed by Local 76 on Marine Avenue, Westview. Businesses: Doran's Furniture, Cant's Shoes, Dr. Vonarx, Muir's Hardware, Mart's Music, and Jack Fletcher's clothing store.   Courtesy of Powell River Museum

Mavis and Myrna Goddard, Westview residence. Myrna, as a child, brought fresh flowers to decorate Madame Loukes' shop windows; later (as a teenager) she worked part time in her shop.
Photo: Myrna O'Hearne (Goddard)

Invasion! Marine Avenue, Westview June 6, 1943. A training exercise by Canadian soldiers from Comox, Vancouver Island. Bags of flour were used to mark the "dead". A memorable experience for Powell River residents.
Courtesy of Powell River Museum

Michigan Landing (Willingdon Beach) 1924. Cabins and tents were all year-round homes to families on the waitlist for Townsite homes. The fenced area to the left was a dairy farm – cows grazed on Willingdon Beach!
Burroughs family photo – courtesy of the Powell River Museum

Michigan Landing (Willingdon Beach) 1922. The Poole family spent a winter in a tent (right of photo) before moving into the Townsite. (L to R) Victor/Ruth/Sylvia/Dorothy Poole – all dressed in their best for Sunday School – a walk along the railroad tracks (Willingdon Beach Trail) to the Townsite.   *Photo: Victor Poole*

Westview Village, Grief Point & Edgehill Districts

- **For thousands of years Sliammon First Nations lived in summer and winter camps in the Westview and Grief Point areas.**

From 1880 Timber Leases

- **(1883) Jim Springer:** the focal point of civilization in the district revolved around two small logging camps, owned and operated by the **Moodyville Saw Company**. Behind present-day Willingdon Beach was **Dineen's Camp**. Fifteen men worked the camp using 12 oxen to drag the logs through hastily-built skid roads. Endless vistas of forest stretched for miles (present-day Westview).
- **(1890s) William (Billy) LaVoie** (1864-1942) logged in the Grief Point area. On returning from the Yukon gold rush, worked for the Powell River Company 1910-15.
- **(1897) Harry Nickel (Nichols)** (1845-1933) bought a **Crown Grant of 150 acres** – Lot 1423 Gp 1, New Westminster, at present-day **Grief Point** for **$150**. He arrived by steamship from Texada Island, lowered in a boat and rowed ashore; however, his animals were thrown overboard and left to swim there. Harry established a farm. He delivered butter and milk by rowboat.

1900 – 1920 Squatters - Pre-emptions - Stump Ranches

- **1900 – 1920** the Westview area was mainly run-out timber leases. Alberni Street was originally Elders No. 1 Logging skid road. Squatters lived on the old timber leases – including the **Fishleigh** family (from 1915).
- **1911 – 1918 George Burgess** (booming grounds foreman for Michigan & Puget Sound Railway) ran a small dairy farm at Michigan (Willingdon) Beach. In 1918, when logging operations ceased, **George Adey** acquired the farm.
- **1913 William Joyce** purchased 40 acres from the government at $10 an acre (from Joyce Avenue and down to the ocean, bordered by Duncan and Fairmont). He installed a local water distribution system with a water wheel and tank at **Squatter's Creek** – supplying his own farm and homes on Egmont Street.
- **1914 <u>Government Pre-emptions of 40+ acres</u>**, first come – first served basis: 13 lots in Wildwood and 14 lots in Westview. Applicants waited in line on the steps of the Vancouver Courthouse for 40 days and 40 nights. **Jim Springer** took the roll call every four hours. The Westview lots went to:
- Phillip George Bren, Gustav Courte, Joseph Dorval, Arthur James Fraser, John Loukes, Milton Munn, Hiram Goodwick Norton (abandoned by Albert Waldron – 1915), John F. Kilvert (1922 – abandoned by W. Bozen, 1923 - John Lambert), Sidney G. Stewart (1926 – abandoned by W.M. Henderson, 1926 – Reuben Daniel Fidler), W.M.C. Willis and Jane Willis.
  Gustav Courte: 49-acre block on Marine Avenue, between Massett and Nootka. Marine Avenue was just a bush trail in the 1920s.

Joe Dorval: 50-acre property: established Westview Dairy on Marine Avenue.
John Lambert: 1923, 50-acres end of Westview Avenue. Goat Dairy.

- **1916 – 1927 First Westview School** attended by Courtes, Fishleighs, and Lamberts.
- **1919 Jack Harper (Harper's Limited)** bought six waterfront lots from the government in Westview – had the first light plant and gravity water system.

1920s – Westview Tent Village at Michigan Landing (Willingdon Beach)

- **Victor Poole, Burroughs, Burgess and others – lived year-round in tents on the beach – leases from the Powell River Company – cancelled 1926.**
- **1921-2 <u>Government lots for sale</u>.** The lucky numbers were drawn from a hat at the Rodmay Hotel.

<u>Land Grants were made to ex-servicemen of 5, 10 and 20 acres:</u>
Robert Taylor (DCM, MM) – Five acres of waterfront land (behind Snickers).

- **1920s – Tom Rickson** bought out McGuigan's, Westview's first store on the site of the present Marine Inn. He built the **Traveller's Rest** in 1938 – first hotel.
- **Westview United Church** congregations met in the Westview School annex.
- **1927 -** *Powell River News* printed and published by T.W. Green.
- **1927 - 1950 <u>Second Westview School</u>** – land donated by William Joyce.
- **1927 <u>Willingdon Beach (previously called Michigan Beach after Michigan & Puget Sound Railway) – dedicated by Lord Willingdon.</u>**
- **1927 – 1999 Log Cabin** on Joyce Avenue – purchased by Olive Devaud.
- **1928 – Felix Van Vleet** purchased Malaspina Stages.

1930s Utilities – Commercial area on Marine Avenue

- **1930 <u>Westview Light, Power and Waterworks Improvement District was formed</u>.** The trustees installed a lighting system and a water system. **The Squatter Creek System** abandoned after water was piped in from **West Lake**.
- **1931 <u>Telephone Service</u>** provided by North-West Telephone Company.
- **Fred Cooper** bought Lot 5109 (south half) 20-acres for $200.
- **1932 Olive Wood (Devaud)** bought Lot 5109 (north half) 20-acres for $200.
- **1933 <u>Anglican Church built at the corner of Joyce and Duncan</u>**.
- **1935-1968 <u>Roxy Theatre</u> (present-day Snickers Restaurant).**
- **1936 Madame Loukes** 5th Avenue Dress Shop on Marine Avenue.
Frank Haslam – sheet metal shop on Marine and Alberni.
Sam Sing – Fairway Market on Marine Avenue.
Knight News (1930s) on Willingdon Avenue (1966 Marine Avenue).
- **1938 <u>Westview volunteer Fire Department organized</u>**.

1940s Village Status – Shops on Marine – Farms

- **1942 Earthquake!**
- **1942 _Westview incorporated as a Village_**. The first village commissioners were: George Irvine (chairman), T.H. Nuttall, Bob Lyon, and J.A. Clapp.
- **Leslie and Mabel Steeds** bought three lots for $400 on Joyce Avenue.
- **Tom Fong** leased land from Olive Devaud for market gardening.
- **1946 – new wharf opened in Westview**. In 1948 Westview small boat harbour officially opened.
- **1946- 1963 Vic and Shirley Courte** owned large acreage at **Grief Point** – below Malaspina Avenue, from Texada Street to Victoria Street. The Courtes sold vegetables wholesale to grocery stores – tomatoes grown in old school buses.
- **1946 Alexander House opened by Lord Alexander – HQ of the Canadian Legion.** The house had previously been the **Van Vleet** residence.
- **1946 Earthquake!**
- **1948 Herb Hindle opened Stationery and Gift store on Marine Avenue.**

Corner stone laid for the Westview Baptist Church.
Sing family re-located Penny Profit to corner of Marine and Alberni.
Paul and Jean Fiedler bought a four-acre stump ranch. Sold lots for $400.

- **1949 Grief Point Sunday School** (Interdenominational) opened on Marine Avenue.

1950s Amalgamation – Transportation – Farms

- **1950 J.P. Dallos School**
- **Tip Top Dairy** – modern pasteurization plant (J. Dorval and Frank Adey)

Stuart and Russell Lambert – Blue Mountain Dairy farm
Gobbee Blue Mountain Poultry farm

- **1951 Frank Roscovich** purchased a house on Cooper Road (Huntingdon Street) for $6,000.
- **1952 Westview Airport**
- **1954 Ferry via Saltery Bay and Sechelt Peninsula to Vancouver**
- **Beach Gardens Drive-In**
- **1955 Ferry Service between Texada Island and Westview**

Powell River Television Company (black-and-white TV reception)
Willingdon Arena

- **1955 _The Amalgamation of the_ Townsite and the villages of Westview & Cranberry and Wildwood District to form the Corporation of the District of Powell River**. At the time of amalgamation, Grief Point and Edgehill were districts managed by Westview Village.

Edgehill District

1920s

- **1921 – Robert and Nellie McGuffie** obtained land by present-day **McGuffie Creek**. The family lived in a tent until their house was built.
- **1924 – John MacGregor VC** bought a five-acre lot in Edgehill. He chose Edgehill as he considered the price of land in Westview as far too expensive. MacGregor Avenue is named after this WWI war hero. John MacGregor worked for the Powell River Company. After WWII he established a brick factory in Cranberry.
- **1925 – Peter Pearson** bought four acres on Manson Avenue from John Siguresen. The house was one of the first pre-fabricated homes to be shipped into the area. Peter worked for the Powell River Company.
- **1929 - Oren Olson** went to work for the Powell River Company. Later, he bought land in Edgehill and built a house on Manson Avenue.

1940s

- **1940 – John Kenmore** owned a large stump farm in the vicinity of Edgehill School. Young piglets were raised and sold.
- **1941 - Luigi Zuccato and Katie Zuccato (Culos)** moved to Edgehill. They bought a house and 3+ acres of property from the Lotus family.
- **1944 – 1959 the Bergot family owned and operated a 16-acre farm in Edgehill.** It had previously been known as **Brooker's farm**. Raymond Bergot worked for the Powell River Company. Marianne Bergot rode her horse to ratepayer's meetings in **Westview**.
- **1945 - Edgehill Store established by Mrs. Nina Lambert.** Store and house built on a seven-acre property. Nina's husband worked for the Powell River Co.
- **1946 - Alex Gustafson** built a house in Edgehill. According to his wife, Adele, "they were living in the bush". Alex worked for the Powell River Company.
- **1948 - Ben Ogden** bought a half-acre lot in Edgehill for $150. The family lived in a tent until the basement was finished – then they moved into the basement. At this time there was no electricity, sewer, water, or phone connection for this area. Abbotsford Street did not exist. There was a small skating pond nearby.

1950s

- **1951 Roy Leibenschel** moved from Cranberry to Edgehill. Recalls delivering ice to Edgehill Store. Mrs. Lambert kept goats at one time.
- **1954 Ernie Carlson** purchase a house and one acre of property at #10 North Lake Road. Ernie worked for the Powell River Company.
- **1955 Edgehill School opens.**

James & Elizabeth Hildebrand purchased their first house at 4713 Michigan Avenue in 1957 from Lloyd Roberts.
This house is featured in Powell River' First Fifty Years – the first house built in Westview by Lloyd Roberts.
Photo: Hildebrand 1960

This house on Marine Avenue was originally the Courte farmhouse built in the 1920s-30s. The Courtes had a large
productive farm in, what is today, a residential area of Westview.   Photo: Ann Bonkowski 2008

Vonarx family home on Westview Rd, Westview 1930.
Photo: (L to R) Mrs. Vonarx with baby Doreen/ Bob Vonarx/Dr. Vonarx.   Photo: Vonarx album

Jean Fiedler at Tip Top Dairy (1946), on Marine Avenue (near present-day viewpoint). Cattle were pastured in,
what is today, a residential area of Westview. Tip Top Dairy was owned by Joe Dorval.
Photo: private collection

Log Cabin (1927-99), Westview, Powell River. Olive Devaud gifted the cabin to the Unitarians. Jack and Myrtle Vineham were the first caretakers. A meeting place for Unitarians (Martin Rossander, Stuart Lambert & others), CCF, seniors, and low-income groups.   Photo: B.A. Lambert 1999
Insert photo: (L to R) Glen Roscovich/Martin Rossander 1996

Olive Devaud (in nurse's uniform) 1950s, photo group Westview.
(L to R) _____/ _____/Gertie Lambert/Mrs. Ross/Olive Devaud/_____/Joan Neeves/Hannah MacGillivray.
Photo: Sonia Olson   Powell River Museum

189

Second Westview School (burned down in 1950 – arson?)
Insert: William Joyce – Westview pioneer – donated land for the above school. Joyce Avenue is named after him.
Photos: Mary Carlson (granddaughter of William Joyce)

Ruby Roscovich 80ᵗʰ birthday 1996 Photo: Roscovich album. (L to R) Mary & Al Carlson/Ruby Roscovich
Inserts: Left – 1948-64 Carlson's house, 6892 Burnaby Street, Westview
Right – 1950 to present-day Roscovich residence, 4191 Manson Avenue, Westview.

Looking Back with Mary Carlson (Douglas)

Westview – The William Joyce Farm (from 1913)

Mary Douglas and her sister, Irene, came to live in Westview in 1931 with their grandfather **William Joyce**. They were raised on a farm, 30 miles west of Red Deer in Alberta. By staying with their grandparents in Westview, British Columbia, the children were able to get a high school education (not generally available in isolated areas) at Brooks High School in the Townsite.

Joyce Avenue is named after this early pioneer.

Mary Carlson (Douglas):

*"In 1931 my sister and I came to Powell River to stay with my grandfather and to finish our education. We came on the **Princess Mary** which was an overnight trip from Vancouver.*

We left Vancouver around 10:30 p.m. and arrived in Powell River around 6 a.m. The Princess Mary served Powell River for twenty years, making three trips a week from Vancouver. Also, it made three trips a week to Courtenay, docking at Union Bay.

Most of the staterooms on the Princess Mary were small – two bunks. The cost of the stateroom was $3 per night. If you cared to share a stateroom, the lower bunk was $2 and the upper bunk was $1.50. There were few staterooms, so you had to book early or sit in a chair all night – or even sleep on the floor. The meals on the Princess Mary were very good. You could get a real good meal for 50 cents, served on lovely dinnerware. Also, they had excellent silverware.

In 1913 my grandfather, William Joyce, purchased 40 acres of property from the government for $10 an acre. This property ran from Joyce and down to the water and was bordered by Duncan and Fairmont.

This was wild land and there were many large trees on the property, so he bought a team of horses and with the help of Walter Lasser and Bill Fishleigh, they cleared some of the land.

They built a log cabin with a lean-to at the back for wood and storage. He also built a large log barn with a lean-to for storing feed for the horses and to be a chicken house. Many Westview old timers will remember these log buildings. He had this team of horses for some time and worked with them for the Powell River Company, hauling newsprint on the wharf etc.

Through the years he cleared quite a number of acres on this property and had a large lovely garden, an orchard of 200 fruit trees, plus many beehives.

In 1931 a small house was built at the end of the log cabin. Mr. Eric McKella helped with this building. This house was later moved to Egmont Street. Some of this property was cleared and subdivided into lots which were sold to local people. These lots were along Joyce Avenue and Duncan Street and down to the waterfront.

Approximately two acres on Duncan Street was cleared and donated for a school. The Westview Elementary School was built on this property in 1926. Unfortunately, this school was burned to the ground in 1950. Eventually, the present Municipal Hall was built on this property. With the help of Mr. Eric McKella and his team of horses, Mr. Joyce built a log dam at Squatter's Creek, close to where the J.P. Dallos School (E'cole Côte du Soleil/Powell River Christian School) now stands.

A water wheel was installed and a water tank built close by. With a water pump, power was provided for a local water distribution system. This system supplied water for his own farm plus many homes on Egmont Street and also to a bake shop on the corner of the old Westview road.

Incidentally, this was Westview's first bake shop and was operated by Mr. and Mrs. McFiadzean. The charge for water at that time was 25 cents a month. This dam and water wheel and water tank was demolished in 1945 and the creek was filled in so that it was not dangerous to children playing in the area.

In 1937 the log barn was tore down. Around the year 1945, a large portion of the farm was sold to the Westview Playground Association.

The remaining parcel of land was sold to the school board for a new Westview primary school. This is the present J.P. Dallos School. Part of the J.P. Dallos School is built on the spot where Mr. Joyce built the log cabin so many years ago. Joyce Avenue was named after the late William Joyce."

Memories of Brooks School (1930s)

"We went to Brooks School by bus. We walked from where we lived, down Egmont (-it was a trail then) and caught the bus at the corner of the old Westview road and Marine. The bus fare was five cents!

My homeroom teacher was Mr. Thornstenson. He was a colourful individual and loved to play golf. He often came to school after lunch, dressed in plus four and plaid socks, ready for a game of golf as soon as school was out.

In Grade 9, Max Cameron was my homeroom teacher. He was principal of Brooks at that time. He was a quiet man and we all liked him. Max Cameron (Senior) High School was later named in his honour.

My home economics teacher was a lovely lady named Miss Robertson.

Max Cameron and Miss Robertson finally married and left Powell River.

Miss Ethel Green was my Latin teacher. She was also gym instructor in the old gym in Powell River. This old gym was close to Dwight Hall and the building was half a gym and half a liquor store! A Mr. Brown instructed the boys in the gym. We walked from Brooks School to the old gym and later caught the bus home to Westview. Miss Green married Ed Peacock and they moved to Victoria.

The library at that time was in the basement of Dwight Hall. We walked there from Brooks. I remember a Mrs. Miller as librarian, followed by Mrs. Skirley.

The French teacher was Miss Molly Tupper. She was very businesslike. She later married Alex McClaren. For some years she had a lovely little gift shop on Marine Avenue. In 1956 she became a municipal councillor at Powell River Municipal Hall.

While the girls were busy sewing, the boys were taking manual training with Mr. Gwythers.

There was no particular dress code for the pupils of Brooks School. Mostly, the boys wore long pants and a shirt or sweater. The girls wore skirts, (and) short-sleeve sweaters or blouses. Some of the girls knitted their own sweaters.

Some of the students worked while they went to school. When I was in Grade 10, I worked for a family named Reece. Mr. and Mrs. Reece had twin boys, Melvyn and Raymond. My job was to get their breakfast and prepare the boys for the day, before I left for school. On returning from school, I made the dinner, tidied up, and put the twins to bed by 7:30 p.m. Then it was time do my homework!"

Mary and Al Carlson

"   Al and I were married in 1945. Once our children were raised, we did a lot of travelling. We were bridge players and we joined the ACBL (American Contact Bridge League). It was wonderful to travel with them to large tournaments in Canada and the U.S. We became bronze masters in the bridge world.

We lawn bowled for years in the summer and spent the winters in Palm Springs (California) like many others from Powell River.

Also, we enjoyed dancing. We danced with the square dancers – took lessons from **Bob Gela**.

We danced with the Old Time Dancers for many years. Dwight Hall was full of old time dancers from 1941-43. It took two years to get in with them (there was a waiting list). For years we had a live orchestra. **The orchestra consisted of Al Carson, Johnny Cramb, Alex Townshend, and sometimes Mary (Johnson) Crosley joined them. Later on, Murray Black and orchestra played for the Old Time Dance Club. Later on we had records; Harry Neaves and Woody Runnells looked after the music.**

The Old Time Dancers moved from Dwight Hall to the Moose Hall, then to J.C. Hill School, then to St. David's Hall.

We joined the **Seniors Association Branch #49** in 1975. We belonged for over thirty years. In the beginning we were located on Marine Avenue, in the upstairs of the Eaton's Building. Later on, we moved to the Moose Hall and then to the Complex. **In 2001 Mrs. Barowsky left us her house on Courtenay Street. We then made a final move to our present location in Cranberry."**

Looking Back with Joan Wilson (Christian)

Memories of my Fishleigh Grandparents
West Coast (1910) and Westview Pioneers (1915)

Emily Louisa Fishleigh (Tuppen) died in Powell River in 1982 at age 102. She had lived a truly remarkable life as a West Coast pioneer after arriving in Canada in 1910 with her three children: William, Arthur, and John.

William (Bill) Fishleigh, a cabinetmaker, came out ahead of his wife in the spring of 1909 to Ontario. At first, he had no difficulty in finding work in his trade, but when the Canadian winter set in he found the building crew he was working with quit for seven months! He lived off his savings during that first winter and then made a decision to go west on a cheap CPR excursion. Bill took up a pre-emption at Ucluelet on the West Coast of Vancouver Island and worked seasonally, herring seining for the Kelly-Douglas Saltery.

Emily Tuppen was born on June 5, 1879 at Tottenham, London, England. She was proud of her parents: Susan Ann Cox was a surgical nurse in a large London hospital; William Tuppen, a Scotland Yard detective sergeant (1872-97), who had single-handedly apprehended a serial murderer known as the "Hampstead Heath Killer". He also worked on the notorious "Jack the Ripper" case. After her father's retirement from the police force, the Tuppen family moved to the Isle of Wight.

At the age of 18, in 1887, Emily went to work in London as a nanny. One of Emily's favourite stories was the memory of a morning walk in Hyde Park, with her two charges, and being overtaken by **Queen Victoria** in a horse drawn landau with a footman riding pillion.

Emily married William in 1904. From 1905-10 Emily ran a guesthouse on the Isle of Wight. **Mark Twain** stayed there several times. Emily found him to be "a grumpy old man".

In 1909 William decided to emigrate to Canada for a better life for his family. Emily's parents were against Emily going with two young children and a baby to the other side of the world, but Emily was determined to follow her husband.

In the spring of 1910, after the birth of John (January 1910), **Emily made the journey to Ucluelet from England, with her children entirely on her own. It was her determination and fortitude that kept her going and to eventually arrive in Ucluelet on the West Coast. She was the first white woman in the area.**

The Fishleigh family stayed for a few years in Ucluelet. There were no schools or roads; just a store with a post office managed by an old Norwegian sailor. Eventually, they left Ucluelet as young Bill was of school age.

It was in Alberni that their youngest child, Ruth, was born in 1913. It was while in Alberni that Ruth had a fall which resulted in a small cut on her chin; Emily sewed up the cut with her own hair.

The Fishleigh family travelled to Comox before arriving in Westview in 1915.

Emily Fishleigh:
"We had to get out because Bill (Junior) had to go to school. We sold our five acres of bush; he and I cleared for $90. We took it and got out, and that's how we got into Westview.
We squatted in Westview. We couldn't go into Powell River (Townsite) as we had no money. We were on a timber limit, they told us. Mr. Smith (the land agent),
'You know you're on a timber limit.
And until the timber is released, it won't be out (for homesteading).'
'We've got to stay here. We've nowhere to go,' I said.
That's how we came to stay there."

Initially, William found work building a bridge on Marine Avenue, near Eighth Street. He also worked with Alec Bell clearing "the cut" from the breakwater in the Townsite to Westview.

He then went to work for the Powell River Company. At first he was offered a job in the grinder room but turned it down; a few days later, he was offered a job in the barker room.

Bill Fishleigh rode to work on a horse from his pole-and-shake shack on Michigan (Willingdon) Beach. He worked for the Powell River Company for 30 years, retiring in 1947.

Powell River's First 50 Years golden jubilee edition describes early Westview:

"William Fishleigh's shack, behind where is now Black's drugstore, was one of Westview's earliest homes. Mr. Fishleigh originally had a pole-and-shake shack on the beach. When the land, on which he had squatted, was subdivided for sale he was given first chance to buy eight lots on which he had done improvements. He later built the first house in the area where he now lives. The Westview area was mainly run-out timber leases. Alberni Street was originally Elder's #1 logging skid road. In 1921-22 lots on logged-off timber leases were sold by the government. Land grants were made to ex-servicemen of 5, 10, and 20 acres and most of them were eventually subdivided. Other early settlers with

William Fishleigh were Jack Turner and Mrs. Mullen, who had a home on the beach."

Bill sold some of the lots he purchased for $100 each. He used this money to build a bigger house for his family (located where Shaw Cable is today).

Emily:
"When it was cleared, Westview hadn't got its name then, Wildwood had and Cranberry had. There were a few shacks in both places – mostly Italians in Wildwood.

The first one to come in (to Westview) was a jeweller – then the Fidlers came in, then the Loukes, then the Brens, then the Waldrons.

Mrs. Courte, my next-door neighbour, she had a horse and buggy, and that was the first thing on the road. The next thing, Mr. Bren had a car, and that was the only car we had in Westview.

***They had to build a school for my children**, because they had no other school there until the Courtes came, and there were the two little boys, and Irvine, he went before he was 6. Of course, Ruth had to go when she was 5 to make the number. We had all young teachers just come out of Normal – all nice girls. We had Miss Evans, Miss Baker, Miss Cook, and a Miss Kabalsky."*

The Fishleigh children attended the First Westview School. The school was built in 1916 and paid for by the parents for a total cost of $100. It was a one-room school just off the old Westview and Nootka roads. Mr. Waldron cleared the land with a team of horses. A grand opening for the school was held in Fidler's Field and all the settlers with their children attended.

Emily was hospitable in her big house, behind Black's drugstore. She hosted neighbours and visitors (some from Sliammon) with cups of tea.

"The Native People were only at Sliammon. They used to come out with fish and baskets. I had several baskets – they were good. They used to come to my house and have a cup of tea. One was Louise and one was Mary. They used to walk all the way from Sliammon."

Young men, looking for work in the district, could always find bed and board with the Fishleighs before they found something more permanent.

The Fishleigh grandchildren, Joan Wilson (Christian) and David Christian, stayed with their grandparents for four years during the early 1940s. Joan attended the second Westview School (where City Hall is today). She either walked or rode her bike there with her friends, Annie Marie Harris (Gibson) and Larry Borroughs.

Joan Wilson enjoyed the tea parties and meeting all her grandmother's acquaintances. She recalls the businesses near her grandparents' home on Marine Avenue in the 1940s:

Penny Profit (first location – further down the street before second location – where the Paperworks Gallery is today), Evelyn & M's (clothing and bedding), Mr. Harper's tobacco store, Dr. Vonarx (in his own little building), Molly McClaren (notion's store), Herb Hindle (originally a food store – further down the street than the present Hindle's – present Hindle's built in front of the family home), Jack Fletcher (men's wear), Muir's hardware, Black's drugstore, and Madame Louke's 5th Avenue Dress Shop.

Madame Loukes was her grandmother's neighbour; she was always very nice to Joan. Joan's mother, Ruth, purchased her wedding dress from Madame Loukes. Joan also went to Madame Loukes for her wedding outfit.

Ruth married Bert Christian in Powell River in 1931. Ruth and Bert had four children: Joan, David, Beverly, and Fred.

John Fishleigh married Margith Johnson in 1942. They had two daughters, Mavis and Maureen.

William and Arthur Fishleigh never married. Arthur died in 1938. William died in 1973.

Joan recalls, one day a week her grandfather Bill Fishleigh walking the Willingdon Beach trail with a rake and a shovel, fixing all the potholes. It was just something he wanted to do for the community.

In 1947, Emily and Bill Fishleigh moved from the big house in Westview to a little house at Myrtle Point. Bill used to ride into town on his bicycle. However, Emily found it too isolated at Myrtle Point and in 1954, they made a final move to Grief Point.

William (Bill) Fishleigh (born 1878) died in 1970 in Powell River.

In 1972 Emily moved into the Olive Devaud residence.

On June 5, 1979 Emily Louisa Fishleigh celebrated her 100th birthday. She celebrated an amazing life of courage and perseverance – her journey to a new country with three young children, living in the bush in Ucluelet, and camping out in a tent on Michigan (Willingdon) Beach.

Looking Back with Evelyn (Lynne) Taylor

Private Robert Taylor – DCM MM (WWI)
Westview Pioneer 1924-39

Robert Taylor was born in the Orkney Islands, Scotland, in 1890. In 1909 he left the Orkneys as a deckhand; after landing in Seattle, he and other seamen jumped ship. After changing into work clothes, Robert made his way to Canada under an assumed name.

In 1914 the Canadian government declared an amnesty for those living in Canada without official papers. The morning after war was declared, Robert Taylor enlisted in Winnipeg. He spent all four years on the front line, and was awarded two medals: the DCM and the MM for bravery.

DCM (Distinguished Conduct Medal) – for risking his own life to rescue numerous soldiers from gas.

MM (Military Medal) – One night when he was alone on a field by the camp, he saw an enemy soldier disappear into a trench. He called to the soldier to come up and drop his weapons. The soldier did so and was followed by 47 others in file who released their guns and gave themselves up. All Private Robert Taylor was holding that night was a pick axe!

After World War One, Taylor came to Powell River and worked as foreman painter for the **Powell River Company**. He lived in the **Townsite** at the **Rodmay Hotel**.

As a returning WWI veteran, Robert Taylor was granted a piece of land by the government. Robert won the jackpot, approximately **five acres of land on the waterfront in Westview** (2007 – behind Snickers Restaurant, previously the Roxy Theatre).

Robert Taylor married Gladys Rodway in 1921. They had four children: Margaret (1923-), Rodway Robert (1926-), Evelyn Jean (1928-2004), and Elnore Irene (1932-).

Evelyn (Lynne) Taylor in 2002, recalled living in Westview in the 1920s and 30s:

"It was while my father was living in lodgings at the Rodmay Hotel that he met, and soon lost his heart to the striking new Powell River Company secretary, 23-year-old **Gladys Olive Rodway***.*

Gladys was the youngest daughter of eight children born to Vancouver pioneers, Joseph and Margaret Rodway, who in the 1880s had journeyed in covered wagon with four of their children from Fort Gary to Vancouver.

Bob and Gladys were married in her family home on December 14, 1921. After a two-week honeymoon in Victoria and Seattle, they returned to Powell River to take up residence in a Company house near the mill. They lived in this residence for three years before moving to Westview in 1924.

Powell River (Townsite) at that point was a fast-growing company owned town, nestled among the islands and inlets on the beautiful scenic coast of British Columbia. Three short miles down its shoreline lay the elite little dormitory town of **Westview**, a quite memorable spot where we children spent the greater part of our childhood.

Although it had been in operation for a short number of years, the mill was still a fledgling company, having had its beginnings just prior to WWI. It held firmly to its own through both the war and the post-war slump and then, in tune with the times, it picked up the momentum with the world's escalating demand for paper. After that, things ran well for awhile; no one could predict what would soon lie ahead, not only for them, but for the whole world at large (1929-39, the Great Depression).

The Powell River township was surrounded by other little communities like our own (Westview), and like most of our sister districts (Cranberry and Wildwood) we had coped reasonably well throughout the 10-year slump in the 1920s. Though few people escaped a struggle to some degree – and it was known that many found it extremely difficult – the community itself continued to grow and on a whole was able to keep itself afloat.

However, when we were beginning to feel the real impact of the Depression (1930s), it was not so much the lack of work but **a political purge by the mill that put over 200 family men out of a job. This was the never-to-be-forgotten day when life in the town took a dramatic tumble, and an especially black day for our own family, as our father was among the unfortunate whose employment came to an end.** Waves of acrimony, constraint, and distrust were soon dividing up friends, families, and workmates, polarizing those who showed political leanings one way or other, and clouding the skies over a once progressive little town that may otherwise have weathered well through a rough time in history.

It appears that just prior to the 1933 election, the mill workers were approached by a zealous member of a political party, who happened also to be an upstanding member of the Powell River Company. He was soliciting donations from the workers to support the party of his choice for an upcoming election. My father not only refused to give a donation, but admitted at the same time he would be backing the new ultra left-wing

CCF (Co-operative Commonwealth Federation) in sympathy with the workers who wanted to reinstate the union at the mill. Alas, his refusal was a little too vocal; the next day, his card was pulled and he was out.

We were soon to find out that our very best friends did not change, even though in some instances they knew their friendship could have meant an enormous cost to themselves. **Sam Dice**, a father of four who worked as an electrician for the Powell River Company, was openly threatened that if his wife continued to befriend or sympathize with any of our family that they too, could face the axe.

For several years my parents came through by selling off parcels of land. My father was a capable cabinet maker and was able to pick up the odd piece of work, but the payment of taxes was always hard to keep up with. However, we were blessed with a huge vegetable garden, fruit trees, and an ocean of fish. There was never a time we were short of food. My father went fishing every day. My mother canned a lot of salmon he caught. Anything that was not eaten fresh was bottled for the winter.

I remember attending Westview School. A **Mr. Davidson** and a **Miss Cluff** were my teachers. I was always well dressed as my mother was a marvellous sewer – she had a White's sewing machine. Mother could easily turn an old dress into something new. She was able to get the marks off the flour sacks and make them into underwear. Mother was quick with her needle and embroidered our clothes to make them attractive. At a very early age, mother taught us to knit.

Our family had wonderful beach and house parties. Often our close friends, the **Dice family**, joined us. We danced to a wind-up record player, waltz, foxtrot and two-step – all to the same tune! A special musical treat was when our friend **Dudley Sleigh** played his trombone.

We did not have far to go into the outskirts of Westview to find people living in circumstances that were desperately poor. These were down-and-out families who lived almost solely off the land. No electricity, no running water, bare wooden floors (if that), and to whom a single bread pudding would be a special treat.

In July 1939 taxes were again owing on our Westview property. Both my parents were in poor health and my father was too sick to look for work. My mother sold our four-bedroom house for $2,250 - a very low price even in a depression. We were forced to take what we could get, as the authorities threatened foreclosure. **On August 31, 1939 we set sail for New Zealand in search of greener pastures. War was declared on our second day at sea.**

My father, Private Robert Taylor DCM, MM had courageously served Canada in WWI. He fought for freedom, but was denied freedom of free speech during the Depression, by the country he fought for."

Looking Back with Victor Poole

Living in a Canvas Tent at Willingdon (Michigan) Beach 1922-23 & Townsite Memories 1920s

Willingdon Beach became a park in 1927 and it was named after Lord Willingdon, Governor-General of Canada.

Prior to this event, the area had been the booming grounds of the **Michigan & Puget Sound Railway**. Where the beach is today, a rail line snaked along the embankment to the Townsite. The beach was known as **Michigan Beach**.

Herbert Poole arrived in Powell River in **1921** and found work with the **Powell River Company**. His wife, **Laura Kathleen Poole (Large)** and their six children: Grace, Ruth, Dorothy, Victor, Sylvia, and Cecil followed in the spring of 1922. Victor (born 1914) was 8 years-old at the time.

There was no rental accommodation available in the Townsite. They lived for a year in a canvas tent at Michigan Beach before they moved into 400 Maple Avenue. The tent comprised of a wooden frame with canvas stretched across it. The family slept in the tent part. The kitchen was a wooden section added on. Drinking water was brought down, by the children, in a pail from a spring near the intersection at present-day Marine and Alberni. An outhouse was nearby.

Bill Burgess, Dick Woodruff, and **Bert Parry** also lived at Michigan Beach in small houses. Bert Parry did not stay long on the beach; he had a war pension and bought property in Cranberry. He started **Parryville** which comprised of 20 small rental houses (long since demolished – opposite present-day Cranberry Pottery 2007). Bert Parry saw a business opportunity in building rental accommodation in the 1920s in Cranberry – the site being in walking distance of the mill. He also became a real estate agent.

The logging activities of Michigan & Puget Sound Railway had ceased before the arrival of the Pooles, however, the tracks were still there. Residents of Michigan Beach used a small flatcar, which had been left on the tracks, for the transportation of groceries, goods, etc. between the Townsite and Michigan Landing. On their arrival in the Townsite, the Poole family was transported to their canvas tent at Michigan Beach by flatbed – Dad pushing them all the way there!

Groceries were delivered by truck, twice a week, from Powell Stores to the residents at Michigan Landing. If the residents needed groceries on another day, they either walked along the rail tracks or put them on the flatbed and pushed them. It was a courtesy, if you were walking the other way, to push the flatbed back!

Victor and his siblings walked the railroad tracks to attend the first Henderson School in the Townsite (2007 – a playground). They also walked the tracks on Sundays to attend St. John's United Church.

The Powell Stores delivery truck had a dual purpose – besides delivering groceries, it was also used for funerals, with caskets being transported on the flatbed of the truck.

Victor attended the Christmas Tree gift event put on by the Powell River Company; **John MacIntyre** organized the event. His wife played the piano while the children were receiving presents from Santa. This event was first held in Central Hall until Dwight Hall was built in 1927.

Victor watched the building of Dwight Hall. In order to build the foundation, the area had to be levelled, and sand removed by horse and cart. The sand was scooped up, dumped into a cart, and then removed from the site.

Victor enjoyed going to see silent movies at the first Patricia Theatre (near the cenotaph); it was owned by **Bob Scanlon** and **Myron McCleod**. Victor went at least once a week. The show changed twice and sometimes three times a week. The film was accompanied by a fellow playing the piano – he played entirely by ear. The accompanist watched the movie and played something appropriate.

One time an adventurer who had been to China came with a display of pictures in an album. He was also a sharpshooter. The projectionist was asked to go up front and put a clay pipe in his mouth. The sharpshooter then took aim to shoot the pipe out of this fellow's mouth! He missed the first time, but the second shot was on target and the clay pipe was blown apart! It was an exciting event for the young Victor.

The building of the second Patricia Theatre in 1928 was, according to Victor, *"a marvel of the age and time"*. The first theatre had been named in a contest by a Mrs. A. Oliver, in honour of the daughter of the Governor-General of Canada, the Duke of Connaught. Her prize was 100 theatre passes. In 1932, sound equipment was added to the theatre.

The post office was in a shack near the mill. **Jack Banham** was the postmaster. Boxes could be rented in the office.

At age 15, Victor started work in the hardware department of Powell Stores in 1929. **Bert Johnson** was his boss. From this department (all departments were paid by the Powell River Company) Victor progressed to quality pulp testing in the mill laboratory.

In 1942 (WWII), Victor and his brother Cecil joined up. They were stretcher bearers in the Canadian Army. Cecil was a stretcher bearer at the D-Day landings in France.

Victor remembers the 1946 earthquake with everything shaking. The big concern was that it may have wrecked the equipment in the mill, however, everything was okay.

Herbert Poole worked for the Powell River Company until he retired in 1947. The family left their rented accommodations in the Townsite and moved to Westview.

Victor Poole, on his return to Powell River after WWII, returned to work for the Powell River Company. He worked there until he retired in 1976. After the war, he married and lived in a Company house. He bought the house on Larch Avenue, from the Company, when it was put up for sale in 1955.

Looking Back with Larry Burroughs

Bill and Edith Burroughs – living in a cabin at Willingdon Beach (1920s)

Bill Burroughs came on his own, from Saskatchewan, in the early 1920s to get work with the Powell River Company. He then made a second trip, bringing his family out to live in a cabin on Michigan (Willingdon) Beach due to the shortage of rental accommodation in the area. Everyone was moved off by the Powell River Company in 1926. The cabin the Burroughs rented was relocated on the south side of Michigan Market, on Burnaby. The Burroughs family moved to a small shack on Alberni (near Anderson's Men's Wear). They added on and built a house at 6828 Alberni. Bill either walked to work on the railroad track (between the beach and the Townsite) or rode a bicycle.

Bill Burroughs worked for the Powell River Company until he retired at 65; initially, he worked in various departments and, in later years, worked in the electrical department.

4554 Marine Avenue, Westview – built by Norma & Robert Bruce Irvine in the 1930s. Present owners, David & Doreen Mitchell.   Photo: B.A. Lambert

4583 Willingdon Avenue, Westview built by Robert Taylor in the late 1920s. Bertha Tuhten lived here from the late 1930s – 2006..   Photo: B.A. Lambert
Photo insert: Margaret Taylor 1926, boardwalk, Townsite.   Photo: M. Ross

Emily Fishleigh's 98th birthday at the Olive Devaud home, Westview. (L to R) granddaughter Bev Christian/great-granddaughter Cindy Gustafson/Emily Fishleigh/granddaughters Maureen Fishleigh and Joan Wilson.
Powell River News & Town Crier – Glacier Ventures - Powell River Museum

Mrs. Mabel Steeds (2008 – 100 years old), Manson Avenue (near Safeway), Westview. Mrs. Steed kept chickens, goats, and peacocks in central Westview (1940s & 50s). Photo: Mabel Steeds 2007

Looking Back with David Myers

Westview Village (from 1928)

My Aunt Ruth and Uncle Bill Rickson owned 1+ acres on Marine, near the Shell station and the Traveller's hotel. They had the foreshore rights to the property. The Ricksons owned a general store (where the Chinese restaurant is today, opposite the Marine Inn). Inside the store was a post office; Bill Rickson was the postmaster. The post office was moved to a small building beside the Marine Inn at a later date. The garden area at the intersection of Marine and Westview Avenue was given by the Ricksons to the town.

Rickson's store eventually became the first location of Bayer's store, later a real estate office, and today a Chinese restaurant. Bayer's also owned the Beach Gardens drive-in. **Dave Harper** ran the projector and **Maureen Harper** ran the small goodie store on the site.

Lois Price married **Harry Myers** in the late 1930s. They had four children: David, Charles, Robert, and Lynn.

Harry Myers was a school teacher and came to Powell River in 1928 to teach at the second Westview School, it was his first position. He lived in a shack near the school. The shack had a dirt floor and there were drafts from the gaps in the walls. A cowhide was his bedding.

In the late 1930s, **Harry Myers became principal of the second Westview School**. Also on staff were: Miss Atkinson, Bessie Rankin (Bemrose), Mr. Davidson, and Alice Cluff.

David remembers his father getting jobs every summer when school was out. In the 1930s he went logging in the bush; during the war years he was working for Kelly Spruce on the Powell River Company mill site, making parts for mosquito aircraft.

David attended the second Westview School for the first four-and-a-half grades. In 1945 Harry Myers and family made a permanent move to Vancouver.

In 1953 **David Myers**, now a young man came back to Powell River looking for a job with the Powell River Company. He was hired by Chuck Wilcox after receiving a clean bill of health from Dr. Marlatt. David started work on November 27, 1953 on the 4-12 shift as a papermaker. He worked on #7 and #8 paper machines. When he retired in 1992 he was working on #11 machine.

Looking Back! The Vonarx Family

Doreen Hampton (Vonarx)

Dr. Max Vonarx (1892-1956) came to Powell River in 1925 and worked nine years in the Powell River Company laboratory.

In 1933, Dr. Vonarx and family moved to Davenport, Iowa, U.S.A. where Dr. Vonarx attended the Palmer School of Chiropractic. In 1936, he practised as chiropractor in Zurich. In 1937, Dr. Vonarx and family returned to Powell River and he started up as a chiropractor on Marine Avenue in Westview, opposite Black's Drugstore.

In October 1925, Dr. Vonarx married a widow, Emmy Schnewlin (1894–1981) in Vancouver. They had a daughter, Doreen. Emmy had two children from a previous marriage, Betty and Bob.

In 1925 or sooner, the family lived near the beach for a short time, then moved up to a small house, a 45-acre property of stumps and stones on the old Westview road. The property had been previously owned by a Mr. Fraser, a returning WWI soldier.

After a period of time in the U.S. and Switzerland (Dr. Vonarx became accredited during this time as a chiropractor) the family returned to their Westview home in January 1937. Doreen remembers it being very cold, and deep snow was on the ground. The small house was enlarged by Johnson Brothers and a finishing job done by George Hillocks.

Doreen Hampton (nee Vonarx) recalls in 2007 many happy memories of living in the Vonarx home on the old Westview road in Westview:

"Mrs. Hanna was our neighbour across the road. She nursed my mother through chest colds, every spring. She was a great believer in mustard plasters. She also delivered the Lasser baby.

We always celebrate Christmas on the eve of the 24th of December. The Lambert family came up to see us on Christmas Day. Mrs. Gertie Lambert usually brought us an angel food cake made from scratch and a creamy pineapple dessert. Very memorable!

Bob went fishing with the Lambert boys and, much to his chagrin, had to take along little sister who was 11 years younger. While the boys went fishing in the creek, I'd stay with Mrs. Lambert. I was especially intrigued by her root cellar – so full of earthy smells.

During WWII Bob was in the RCAF (Royal Canadian Air Force). He was trained in bases across Canada, and assigned to instruct pilots at the Bombing & Gunnery School, Mossbank, Saskatchewan. That was commensurate to an overseas posting.

Betty was working in Genoa, Italy when war broke out. Dad implored her to get out of there as soon as possible. She did. During the war she worked for the ARP (Air Raid Precautions) in Vancouver, censorship in Ottawa, and British Control Commission in Germany before it became sectored into East and West.

Bob bought his farm in Courtenay in 1940. In 1945 he married Mary Winter, a librarian he met in Saskatoon at an educational course for service personnel. It was love at first sight.

My parents bought a piece of property behind Mr. Byfield's greenhouse on Marine Avenue. Dad hoped to build a new office there; however, heart problems plagued him. He was a great healer but a poor patient.

Mom tutored several people in the French language. Harry Myers, principal of Westview School, was one of them.

The Fuller Brush Man and a piano tuner were always given a snack when they came to our house.

Dad loved Mondays, his day off. He would garden with the help of a Norwegian man from Westview. Asparagus was his chief crop."

Dr. Max Vonarx never returned to Switzerland, however, Mrs. Vonarx made a few visits back to the old country.

Dr. Vonarx loved Canada and his chunk of land! He died in 1956. Emmy Vonarx died in Powell River in 1981.

Looking Back at Tom Fong (1890-1955)

Westview and Paradise Valley Market Gardener (1930s-50s)

Tom Fong was born in China. The year he came to Canada is unknown. Tom Fong was a well-known figure in Westview in the 1930s, 40s and early 50s, selling fresh produce from the back of his truck. He went door-to-door selling vegetables.

Initially, he was growing vegetables on a 10-acre field on Valley Road in Paradise Valley. He used Chinese labour to cultivate it in the 1930s and early 40s. He sold this property in the 1940s. Stuart and Russell Lambert owned "the 10-acre field" until the 1980s when it was re-sold.

In the 1940s Tom Fong leased land from **Alphonse and Olive Devaud** in **Westview**. The vegetables in this location grew earlier than on Valley Road.

I remember Tom Fong of Valley Road. He'd come into town in the 1930s, with his truck, and sell vegetables grown in the field opposite the Henderson farm.

Marion Henderson (Beattie)

I remember Tom Fong. He used to drive around Westview in a van with open sides. The fruit and vegetables were displayed for his customers to see. He would give lychee nuts to the children at Christmastime. In the early 1950s, his son or nephew took over his market garden operation.

Lena Pole

I remember Tom Fong. He employed other Chinese to work as farm labourers on his vegetable garden on Valley Road. They lived on the property and helped clear the land of stumps. He told me he moved his operation to Westview as the vegetables grew earlier there and he could make top dollar being first with his produce.

Russell Lambert

I worked with my cousin, Bill Donkersley, picking up potatoes on Valley Road in the 1930s. Old Walter Lasser had a horse-drawn potato digger and it was our job to pick up the spuds after the plough turned the rows. We did the same job for Tom Fong. We were paid the grand sum of 70 cents an hour!

Don McQuarrie

Tom Fong brought gifts of fruit, nuts, and candied ginger to his neighbours in Paradise Valley at Christmastime.

Stuart Lambert

Looking Back with Myrna Ahern (Goddard)

Westview Village - 1930s & 40s

Mr. and Mrs. George Goddard came to Powell River in **1926**. George Goddard took up a position of pharmacist with the **Powell River Company**. He managed the pharmacy in the **Townsite** until 1965; from 1967-73 he worked there part-time.

The Goddard's, husband and wife, shared the title of **Good Citizen** in 1974.

The Goddard's first lived in **Cranberry** for a few years; with five other couples, they formed the **Cranberry United Church in 1927**. They then moved permanently to **Westview**. George Goddard was also on the building committee for the **Westview United Church**. Miron Goddard was an active member of the United Church Women.

George Goddard travelled to the pharmacy in the Townsite by car; his hours did not fit the bus schedule. He had girls to work for him in the pharmacy who could speak Italian. He made up the prescriptions with a pestle and bowls.

George and Miron Goddard had two children, Myrna and Mavis, born in the Powell River Hospital (Townsite).

Memories of Westview

Myrna Ahern:

"The **Byfields** lived next door to my family on First and Michigan, now called Alberni.

The time came when they needed to look after the commercial greenhouse, on the lower side of Marine, as their parents were too elderly to look after it. So, they moved into the housing that went with the greenhouse. They grew flowers. My happiest days were in that greenhouse (located opposite Whooters – the Alchemist restaurant 2007) with Aunty Byfield. I just adored her and the work that went on there.

Mr. Corbett built boats in a workshop behind the greenhouses. My dad's boat was there; it was clinker built.

On the other side of the greenhouse was the house in which the Van Vleets lived. **Van Vleet** owned the busses; today this building is the Legion.

Most of my clothes were made by Aunty Alsgard. The **Alsgards** had moved from Cranberry to Westview when Mum and Dad met them. They had a waterfront home just along from **Harpers**.

Aunty Alsgard knitted all my clothes for me. One time she came to stay with us to convalesce after being ill.

Harpers lived in the big house with the tennis court next door. I played tennis there in my early teens. In the summer I went swimming at Willingdon Beach. I took Life Saving with Locke.

*I attended the second **Westview School**. The school principal was **Mr. Myers**. **Miss Cluff** was my Grade 3 teacher, she was strict; she was a good teacher.*

*I went to work when I was 15 in June of 1944. I washed dishes and made ice cream for the café run by Mrs. Mary Meillieur. The **Meillieur** Garage was on the corner and right beside it was the shop.*

Grades 10-13, I worked at the Patricia Theatre. I listened to the movies. I had to be in the glass cage at the entrance, however, I cracked the door open to hear the movies. I got to be good at recognizing voices! It cost 48 cents for a ticket for the afternoon performance."

Looking Back with Norene Hamerton (Vincent)

Westview Pioneers: Harry and Vera Vincent (from 1930)

Harry (Henry) Vincent came to work for the Powell River Company in April 1930 as a millwright. He boarded with Mr. and Mrs. Vincent Poole's family in the Townsite. Vera, his wife, came out in August 1930 and the family rented a small house on Crown Avenue, at the base of Valentine Mountain, in Cranberry.

Pat Thompson rented a small house nearby. These houses had no running water, well, electricity, or sewer system. There was an outhouse and water was delivered twice a week. **Vera Vincent thought she had come "to the end of the world".** She shopped at Powell Stores and put orders in through Woodward's catalogue.

In 1931 the Vincents bought half an acre of crown land on First Street (Alberni) and what is now Fernwood Avenue, in Westview.

The Vincents walked back and forth between their Cranberry rental and Westview, while they were building their house. Baby Wilma was pushed in the pram and Norene sat at the end of the wicker pram with her feet dangling.

The house was built of shiplap, tar paper, and wood shingles. The Vincents shared a well with the Fosters. In the late 1930s, a waterline came through. There was an outhouse outside and, inside the house a chamber pot in a closet. The house was heated by a woodstove. In 1932 the Vincents moved in.

There were a few other homes in the area at that time: Reverend and Mrs. Good, Theo Carren, Arvin and Helen Hewett. Theo Carren owned a car and gave Harry

Vincent a ride to the mill in the Townsite. These were the Depression years – the mill workers worked 18 days a month.

In 1940 Harry bought his first car, a second-hand Plymouth from a school teacher who had left the area to go to war.

Nearby were two small ponds which froze in wintertime – one near present-day Abbotsford Street and Manson Avenue, and the other near the pole line. Local children in the area skated on them.

In 1932 Norene walked from First Street to old Westview school (site of the Municipal Hall) to attend Grade 1. Harry Myers was principal and taught Grade 6. Slim Davidson taught Grade 5, Miss Cluff - Grade 4, and Bessie Rankin (Bemrose) - Grade 3.

In Grade 7, Norene boarded the school bus for the old Henderson School in the Townsite. The following teachers taught there: Miss Hanna, Miss Cedar, and Gordon Johnson. Grade 8 was taken at Brooks and Norene graduated in 1946.

Norene recalls, in WWII, the air raids and knitting squares for blankets. Her father, Harry Vincent, was in the ARP and worked in the mill for the war effort.

In the 1940s the Vincent family owned a cabin at Myrtle Point. Other cabin owners were the Alsgards, Grahams, Profitts, and Lawrences.

Norene worked full time for Madame Loukes at the 5th Avenue Dress Shop in Westview from 1946 to 1948. In 1948 Norene took up a new position as secretary at Brooks School in the Townsite.

In July 1950 Norene married Al (Alan) Hamerton.

Looking Back with Margaret Bowes-Ferguson (Mitchell)

Bowes Hardware (1947-76) Marine Avenue, Westview

Margaret Mitchell was born in England in 1918. Her father was in the Canadian Forces in WWI and married her mother over there. The family came to Canada after the war to live in Weyburn, Saskatchewan.

Her father was an accountant and lost his job during the **Great Depression**. In order to make a little money, he played his cornet at the local skating rink for 25 cents a night. Sometimes, during the winter, he went on relief and shovelled the snow off the streets.

Margaret Ferguson:
"I remember one time we had to eat porridge for a week as we had nothing in the house to eat. We survived. We kept happy. I remember sitting, as a small child, on a fence in a dust storm and singing,

> *'Make no sense, sitting on a fence.*
> *All by yourself in a dust storm!'*

I started to play the piano when I was 8 years of age.

My mother died when I was 15. Afterwards, my grandmother looked after us. She had been a teacher. With a wonderful sense of humour, she educated me in arts and music.

The railroad tracks went through Weyburn, and everyday we had young men calling for a meal. My brother Bob "rode the rods" looking for work.

In the late 1930s I used to go by the railroad tracks and shoot gophers with a .22 shotgun for two cents a tail!

*I knew **Tommy Douglas** as a Baptist minister in Weyburn. I took elocution lessons from him. One time, many years later, I took my children to visit him when he was Premier of Saskatchewan. On one occasion, he showed me a picture of my grandfather, who was speaker in the house during the 1920s.*

June 1940 – I moved to Vancouver. I was in the Women's Ambulance core during WWII.

While I was living in Vancouver I had voice lessons.

I used to entertain the troops – *I sang and did comedy acts in the hotels. Later on, after the war, I sang in Theatre Under the Stars in Stanley Park.*

*I first saw my first husband, **Howard Bowes**, on a beach in Vancouver! I showed him my address on a ration book. We went out together and were married in 1945.*

I remember the great celebrations of V-E and V-J days in Vancouver. Everyone was singing, kissing, and hugging each other. There were huge crowds downtown on Granville Street and in the theatre districts.

We came up to Powell River in 1947. Immediately, we started the Bowes Hardware store (purchased from Tunstall). I had never worked in a hardware store before – the first person that came in asked if I had a plum; Bob and I went over and found him a toilet float!

I taught music with a letter of permission at Cranberry and J.P. Dallos Schools. I also gave private lessons in piano and voice. I was an accompanist at the music festival.

My children and grandchildren have carried on my love of music: Jan (flute – 1968 crowned Miss Powell River and Miss PNE – Pacific National Exhibition), David (voice, guitar, and drums – 1967 Grade 6 won $100 for composing best centennial song "A Hundred Years of Travel") and Don (guitar, violin, and voice – started the Sunshine Folk Fest with his wife Carole), Jessica (opera), Katelin (voice), Jennifer (violin, piano & voice), and Charlotte (voice – member of rock band "Sweet Stars").

My first husband died in 1971. I kept the store going with an all-women staff until 1976 when I sold the business.

*My second husband, **Steuart Ferguson**, grew up in Winnipeg, Manitoba. Steuart, as a child, threw snowballs at the engine drivers. The drivers threw coal back! Later, all the kids eagerly collected the coal to take home!"*

Stu Ferguson:

"I came to Powell River in 1954 – there were gravel roads and board sidewalks in the Townsite and on Marine Avenue, Westview. I remember Penny Profit and Buckerfields on Marine Avenue. Ed Dunn was involved in demolishing the building (Buckerfields).

I was involved in coaching soccer when **Mr. Devlin was principal at J.P. Dallos**. The original playing field had a landfill of garbage with a layer of soil put on top (the editor recalls kids calling the school in 1968 J.P. Dump school). Mr. Devlin used to give out chocolate bars to kids for "doing good deeds".

I coached, and later refereed, soccer for many years. My own kids were all involved in soccer. I went with the Powell River United team to Expo 67 in Montreal. Our team won the Expo Cup.

I worked hard to establish the track and field track near Malaspina College.

I am a member of the Powell River Pipe Band and sing with Chor Pacifica."

Margaret Ferguson – Looking Back

Margaret met and shook hands with Queen Elizabeth II when the Queen attended Westview United Church in 1971. Margaret was in charge of the choir and played the organ. The Queen said to her,

"I loved your music."

Looking Back – Madame Loukes

The 5ᵗʰ Avenue Dress Shop, Westview (from 1930s)

Madame Loukes opened a successful and exclusive dress shop on Marine Avenue, Westview, in the 1930s. It was a successful business enterprise during the Great Depression, as the Powell River Company was operating on a four-day week. Social events, such as Old Time Dancing and the annual Papermakers' Ball, were held at Dwight Hall. Madame Loukes sold "top of the line" dresses, bought on buying trips in Vancouver and New York, to the wives and daughters of mill management, professional, and business people in the community. The ladies from Wildwood's House of Ill-Repute (1930s & 40s) visited her shop and ordered beautiful, and very expensive gowns.

"Madame Loukes was Jack's aunt. She came to Powell River to visit friends who owned the Rodmay Hotel. She fell in love with Powell River and came back here to live; married Ed Peacock and had two sons.

Madame had a gift shop before she married Jack's uncle. Dorothy knew her in the 1920s and later, in the 1930s, did alterations and dressmaking for her store. Jack drove his aunt around to all the fashion shows.

The title of "Madame" was bestowed on Mrs. Loukes by the hierarchy of the fashion world. This was a really high honour.

Madame went to a university in the southern states and graduated in fashion."

Dorothy (nee Raye) & Jack Loukes 1987

"I knew Madame Loukes. Her dress shop was across the street when I worked at Hindles (1940s). She was a wonderful, lovely lady. She had a great deal of fashion knowledge.

It was a New York fashion house that gave her the prestigious title of 'Madame'. *My sister, Beatrice, did alterations for her in the 1950s and my niece worked for her in the 1960s."*

Stella Saunders (Hall/Hewson) 2007

"Yes, I remember Madame Loukes (1930s). She owned the 5ᵗʰ Avenue dress shop in Westview. My mother bought clothes from her, and on occasion I went with my mother to her shop. Madame Loukes was dressed in a smock held together with a safety pin.

She had incredible taste in clothes and could have made it anywhere. We liked her.

She would ring my mother, after going on a buying trip to Vancouver and say:

'I have two outfits – you must see them –
come round on Sunday afternoon and try them on.'

She had impeccable taste.
Later on, I remember buying a dress from her before I left for Argentina."

Lorna Falconer 2007

"One time (1940s) Grandma Lloyd and my husband, Albert got together and bought me a dress from Madame Loukes. I once went in on my own and she said:

'I'm sorry I can't help you!'
I was living in Stillwater at that time."

Ina Lloyd (McNair) 2007 – Westview

"I brought bouquets of flowers to Madame Loukes which my mother grew in her garden (1930s & 40s). These were displayed in her window. Madame Loukes was a marvellous lady. I worked for her in my teens after WWII. She was unique. A lot of people did not understand her. She had a great deal of knowledge regarding clothes.
Madame Loukes had the sweetest way of handling the gentlemen when they came to buy something for their women. She treated them like princes, and out came all the best things when she knew the size required by the lady. She really knew what she was doing. She had a large selection of hats and the very best of clothing. She didn't dress well herself in the store. She knew where the money was. If you wanted something worthy – she helped you, her taste was impeccable."

Myrna Ahern (Goddard) 2007

"I never bought anything from Madame Loukes' dress shop (1940s). On one occasion, I went in with a friend and I looked at a lace handkerchief. Madame Loukes did not like anyone touching any of the items in the store, so I got a sharp reprimand:

'If you don't want the goods, don't maul them!'

Mabel Steeds 2007

"I bought my wedding dress from Madame Loukes when I married my husband Peter Leach in 1954."

Shirley Leach (Anderson) 2007

"Madame Loukes had an elite store with high fashion goods in Westview (1950s & 60s). She had no competition in the area. She catered for an exclusive clientele of mill management and professional people.
Local people wanted to dress in elegant clothes for events, such as the Old Time Dance Club and the Papermakers' Ball which were held at Dwight Hall in the Townsite."

Ruby Roscovich 2002

"Madame Loukes was my grandmother's (Emily Louisa Fishleigh) neighbour in Westview (1930s-50s). I lived with my grandmother during the 1940s. Madame Loukes was always very nice to me.

My mother (Ruth Fishleigh) bought her wedding dress from Madame Loukes. I, also, bought my wedding outfit from her."

Joan Wilson 2007

"I came to the Townsite in 1948 and found work with the Powell River Company. The Papermakers' Ball was attended by the Papermakers and those at the top of the social structure: doctors, principals, and teachers.

Two hundred dollar dresses had to be bought from Madame Loukes – only to be worn once – not to be given to charity – no one else had to wear the same dress."

Martin Rossander 2007

"My mother (Astrid Pearson) knew her well. I'd be waiting out in the car for hours while the two of them talked. Mum bought lots of clothes from her. I've donated hats that were bought from Madame Loukes to the museum.

Madame Loukes was usually dressed in old clothes – she wore an old sweater. Boy, when she went out of town, she was dressed to the nines!"

Rudy Pearson 2007

"I owned and ran Rowe's Junior Style Dress Shop in Westview from 1955 to 1973. I travelled to Vancouver twice a year to order stock directly from the factory. Occasionally, I saw Madame Loukes buying for the 5th Avenue Dress Shop. In Vancouver she would look like a million dollars, while in her shop she was often seen with pins in her sweater and stockings rolled down at the ankles."

Faith McGuffie (Rowe) 2002

"I went into Madame Loukes' Dress Shop in the 1950s. I looked around and saw what I thought was a cleaning lady and I asked her,

'Where is the owner of the store?'

She looked at me and said,
'I've nothing here for you!"

Eunice Sawchuk 2007

"I saw a white purse in Madame Loukes' display window in the 1950s. I went into the shop to purchase it. She looked at me and said,

'You can't afford it!'

In the mid 60s I purchased a number of dresses from her shop. In 1972 I bought a stylish short dress, made of wool, from Madame Loukes fro my daughter's November wedding. Her clothing was of good quality and came from New York and Paris.

I remember seeing her once when I was on holiday in Hawaii in the 1960s. The dress she wore on this occasion was quite ordinary. Seemingly, Mrs. Loukes went to Hawaii for a holiday every January and February.

She came from New Orleans, in the American South, to Canada.

In her shop she always wore a grey ragged sweater and black skirt."

Doreen Johnson 2007

"All the girls in the House of Ill-Repute came to Madame Loukes for their clothes which she bought especially for them. One of Jack's jobs was to drive the girls down to the store for their fittings.

The dresses the girls wore were really gowns. The girls had the pick of the stock at Madame Loukes' store. They chose only the very best.

When Jack delivered the clothes back to the House on the hill, Dorothy was allowed to go along for the ride. She had to stay in the car while the goods were being delivered."

Dorothy and Jack Loukes 1987

"My mother (Vera Vincent) bought hats and dresses from Madame Loukes dress shop on Marine Avenue in Westview.

In 1944, starting in Grade 10, I worked after school for Madame Loukes. I was a good sewer and able to do alterations. The dress shop sold dresses, hats, lingerie, and suits for women (matching skirt, jacket, and coat made with good English wool). I worked full time for Madame Loukes from 1946 to 1948.

I remember Madame Loukes as a "nice lady". She worked long hours and kept the store spotless. In the store she dressed in "house dress" style – old clothes and slippers. She was a good business person and was well respected. She drove a black Hudson car and owned a summer home on Savary Island.

When attending the Papermakers' Ball or leaving town on buying trips, she was dressed like a million dollars. She was a "knockout" with a great "hairdo" and earrings, wearing a black suit, jacket, hat, and white gloves.

On one occasion, I accompanied Madame Loukes on a buying trip to Vancouver. We went down on the CPR and stayed at the Georgia Hotel.

We travelled by taxi to the factory area where we were shown samples in the order offices. The materials used at that time were silk, wool, and cotton. Nylon stockings were just coming in after the war. Hats had real feathers."

Norene Hamerton (Vincent) 2008

Grief Point (Interdenominational) Sunday School,
Westview 2008. Insert: 1964 (L to R) Stephens children:
Dan/Sherry (Hawkins)/Patti (Green)
Photos: Sherry Hawkins

Harry and Vera Vincent's new house at Fernwood
Avenue, Westview 1934.   Photo: Hamond album

*April 10, 2008 unveiling of marker for Colonel MacGregor VC (WWI); his sons Don (left) and
James (right) in attendance, Cranberry Cemetery.   Photo: B.A. Lambert*

Powell River Transportation Company bus owned by Felix Van Vleet 1928.
*Insert: Ethel Van Vleet residence 1940s, Westview – first sold privately, then later purchased by the Royal Canadian
Legion #164 and named Alexander House in 1946.   Photos: Powell River Museum*

Looking Back with Marion Gallagher (Braithwaite) (1924-2008)

Memories of Westview Village (from 1943)

Marion Gallagher:

"After attending Normal School in Victoria, I gained my first teaching position in Westview in 1943 I arrived on the Union Steamship. It was quite a contrast teaching in a small town after growing up in the city of Victoria.

*I taught in the **old Westview School**. Alan Holmwood was the principal – he also enrolled a class. Other teachers I taught with, during my three years there, were Betty Anderson (Berger), Lilian Dickson, Ken Bradley, Eleanor Johnston, Miss Burkinshaw, and Alice Cluff.*

The population was increasing so fast, in the Westview area that my second year of teaching was in a church annex! I had a kitchen table for a desk, and I had to climb up onto a sink to reach the blackboard. A pot-bellied stove, which smoked, gave out the only heat in the room. The following year I was glad to return to the "big school".

One field trip I had with my class ended in disaster. I took my class for a walk to Duck Lake, through Paradise Valley. We became lost and could not find our way. We eventually arrived back in Westview at 2 a.m., barefooted. The very next day the inspector arrived in class. I had blood-shot eyes and was wearing bedroom slippers!

I married Bill Gallagher after WWII (during the war he was overseas in the Air Force). We rented to begin with, and then bought a half-finished house in Westview on Manson Avenue near Edgehill for $2,500 in 1950. It seemed a waste of money to pay rent money when we could buy in at the bottom of the market and become homeowners.

*There was a tree stump in the front room! We used everything we could find to finish off the house. **The roofing came from the old wharf and the doors from the hulks in the mill breakwater.** One door had painted on it the instruction to "KICK OUT," while another door instructed, "WHEN IN DANGER PLEASE KICK OUT!"*

From 1956-59 I ran the Edgehill pre-school in my own home on Manson. The children came three days a week from 10 a.m. to 2 p.m.; I charged $4 a month.

*My father-in-law **Bertram Gallagher** built the **Patricia Theatre** in the late 1920s. He put an addition onto the **Rodmay Hotel**. During the Depression years he hauled shingle bolts for the **Powell River Company**. Bertram and **Billy-Goat Smith** were good friends and often had a drink together.*

Looking Back with Shirley Leach (Anderson)

Westview Village (from 1942)

Shirley, as a small child, lived on a float house at Claydon Bay in 1937. Her father was logging in the area. The float house, with Shirley on it, was later towed to Haywire Bay. **From 1937-38 the Andersons lived at Haywire Bay camp on Powell Lake.** From 1941-42, due to the shortage of housing, Shirley and her mother lived on Coburn Street, Cranberry, in the front part of her sister-in-law's house.

Shirley attended Grade 2 at **Cranberry Lake School** in 1942; her teacher was **Bessie Bembrose** and principal, **Mr. Holmwood**. It was wartime and Shirley remembers the sirens going. Following instructions, she ran home as quickly as possible after hearing the sirens.

As a teenager, Shirley skated on Cranberry Lake.

Westview Village

From Cranberry village the Andersons moved to Harvie Avenue in Westview village. **In 1942 they lived in an apartment above Black's Drugstore on Marine Avenue.** The drugstore was adjacent to Madame Louke's dress shop. Later, they moved to 290 Marine Avenue.

In 1945, Douglas James Anderson was born. He attended J.P. Dallos School (Mr. Devlin, principal). He graduated from Max Cameron in 1963. Doug later qualified as a mechanic.

Shirley attended Grades 3-6 in Westview School, Grades 6-7 in the old Henderson School (remembers Miss Cedar), Grades 8-12 in Brooks High School. She graduated in 1952.

In 1954 Shirley married Peter Leach; she bought her **wedding dress at Madame Louke's dress shop**.

From 1960-66 Shirley worked at the **Roxy Theatre** (Westview) and the **Patricia Theatre** (Townsite) in the ticket office. Gordon House and Beryl Goddard also worked at the Patricia.

In 1967 Shirley sold tickets at the **Beach Gardens Drive-In** (Westview). The drive-in was popular, as the entire family could go to the movies. Small children could sleep in the back of the car and a babysitter was not required. The drive-in was also a popular spot for young couples to watch a movie and hold hands at the same time!

Looking Back with Mabel Steeds

Westview Village (from 1942)

At age 99, Mabel Steeds recalls moving into her house at 4589 Joyce Avenue (2007 – near Safeway), Westview Village in 1942.

Mabel Holland married Leslie Steeds at St. Timothy's Anglican Mission in Manitoba in 1930. On the advice of a friend, Leslie Steeds came to Powell River to find work with the Powell River Company. The Steeds came up on the *Princess Mary* and docked at the Townsite.

Mabel:

"The journey along the coast was quite an adventure for this prairie chicken. It was a fantastic trip. We stopped at several places; chairs and even a piano were offloaded."

After docking in the Townsite, they hired a taxi to take them to the nearest hotel. They went a couple of blocks and then the taxi driver deposited them at the only hotel in town – the Rodmay!

They looked around for accommodation – the only place they could find in Westview (after taking another taxi) was "a shabby little place, no bigger than a garage, with a single drop line light in the middle of the building".

Luckily they were able to buy one-third of an acre on Joyce Avenue, "with a shell of building on" from a baker whose business had burned down and who was returning to Vancouver.

"We paid $400 for three lots. Finding that $400 then was like find $4 million today."

The Steeds lived in the front half of the building while Leslie Steeds finished the back. There was running water at the sink and electric light. They had to apply for a telephone. The sewer went in later – Mabel recalls the taxes going up.

The place was heated by a sawdust burner:

"I had never seen anything like it. I hated that monster. We later bought a plain woodstove from Burg & Johnson – all I had to do was put a stick of wood in it. I could cook anything on it."

The house was surrounded by trees. Leslie Steeds built a board fence around their place in order to keep stray dogs out.

Joyce Avenue was a dusty, gravel road and the house was never free of dust. Mabel recalls when Joyce Avenue was finally paved; her two grandsons sat on the kitchen table, looked out of the window and watched the cement mixer mixing cement.

Mabel put in a big garden. The garden grew magnificent strawberries and cabbages. **The Steeds kept goats, chickens, and peacocks on Joyce Avenue in central Westview.**

Leslie Steeds came to find work in the mill, but only worked there one day! He was a slight man and found the work in the mill required a great deal of physical strength. He found work, with **Emil Gordon**, as a carpenter. He helped remodel Emil Gordon's furniture store.

Leslie Steeds enlarged and remodelled the house on Westview Avenue belonging to **Dr. Max Vonarx**, the chiropractor. He also did alterations in Dr. Vonarx's office on Marine Avenue.

The Steeds did not own a car. Mabel walked everywhere. She walked along Joyce to St. David's Anglican Church (2007, 7-11 gas station) and to Marine Avenue to do her shopping. Everything was delivered in those days. Few people had cars. The majority of housewives in the 1940s and 50s did not have the use of a second family car.

For a long time Mabel could not afford to buy the *Powell River News*.

Mabel shopped at Bayer's Store by the wharf:

"You could get anything there, from groceries to socks. They delivered all the orders. Inside the store were post office boxes."

Mabel recalls the post-war boom in Westview:

"With the return of the soldiers Westview developed. Lots of money going to entrepreneurs, buildings going up everywhere – new houses and new stores."

Mabel recalls the following stores on Marine Avenue: Woolworth's Five-and-Dime, Black's drugstore, Faith Rowe's Children's Wear store, Madame Louke's Ladies' Wear, Cant's shoe store, a butcher's shop, Smith's greenhouse, Hindle's, Foodland, and Penny Profit. The wharf end of Marine Avenue was working class. The Hindle's end was posh – people with money lived there.

Mabel bought clothing for her husband Leslie, daughter Jean Lesley and herself through Eaton's catalogue. There was an order office on Marine Avenue.

Mabel never bought anything from **Madame Loukes**. She recalls going in once, with a friend, and looking at a lace handkerchief. Madame Loukes did not like anyone touching the goods so Mabel got a sharp reprimand from Madame Loukes:

"If you don't want the goods, don't maul them!"

It was a treat for the family to go occasionally to the Roxy or Patricia Theatre. If they were going to the Townsite, they'd take the bus or, sometimes get a ride with friends. They always tried to get a back row seat, otherwise, the kids behind pelted the rows in front with popcorn, once the music started.

Dwight Hall was visited for musical events.

Mabel:

"The 1946 earthquake got everyone out of bed. Neighbours on Joyce Avenue were outside in their nightwear. We had a slight crack in our chimney, but everything else was fine apart from some goldfish in a tank — some of the water slopped out and a few fish went with it. A house on the way to Wildwood had a chimney which made half-a-turn."

Mabel remembers a special visit to the Beach Gardens drive-in theatre, in a friend's car in the 1950s. It was a memorable experience to sit out-of-doors, eat popcorn, and watch the big screen.

In the 1950s, Mabel worked for four-and-a-half years for a taxi business (at the wharf) owned by **Phil Nunn**.

In 1971 Mabel was standing at the side of the road on Duncan when **Queen Elizabeth II** came to church at Westview United. She was, according to Mabel, "All fixed up beautifully."

Mabel lived for 65 years in her house on Marine Avenue, Westview. At age 99, she has moved into the Kiwanis Village.

Looking Back with Jean Fiedler (Clayton)

Tip Top Dairy and the Fiedler Stump Ranch in Westview (1940s)

I met my husband, Paul Fiedler, in Vancouver. He initially worked at Canadian Pine Company and then at Boeing's. He had previously worked for the Powell River Company from 1941-42.

In the summer of '46 he worked for **Joe Dorval** at Joe's dairy in Westview. We were married in '46 and on January 19, 1947 we moved to Westview. Joe gave us a cow called the "Schoolmarm" as a wedding present. We eventually sold the cow and Joe told us to keep the money.

I worked as a housekeeper for the Dorval's and Paul herded and milked cows, and sawed wood. In addition to selling milk, Joe sold cordwood and cow manure.

In 1946, Paul helped Joe build the **Tip Top Dairy**. The Dorval dairy farm went all the way up from Marine to Joyce. The width of the farm was from Oliver to Nootka. The farmhouse was located near where the present Lighthouse B&B is today on Marine Avenue – to one side of it, where the grey house is. The barn was behind it, on present-day Gordon.

The cows were milked in the barn. Some were milked by hand, the others by machine. Joe Dorval always stripped every cow, even those milked by machine. The milk was kept in a cold room and put into bottles. Joe washed and filled all the bottles. Joe delivered milk and manure in the same truck – it was called the "honeydew" truck! Sometimes he employed others to drive the truck, including his nephew Pete Peterson. Pete and Jim Woods helped with the general day-to-day running of the farm.

Joe kept about 15 cows. He pastured his cows on the property; he bought feed from United Milling and Buckerfields. Ernie Liebenschel with young Roy, delivered feed to the farm. One time the electricity went off, just before milking time, *"Well,"* says Joe, *"I know where I can get some extra hands!"* and he gets his wife, Alma and yours truly to help out. Of course, the power came on just as we had finished milking all the cows by hand. This was the same night the *Gulf Stream* went on the Rock in a terrible storm in October 1947.

In 1948 we bought four acres in Westview, just off Marine and back to Terrace Street. After Frank was born in 1948, and I was ready to go home from the hospital, **Dr. Marlatt remarked,**

"Well Jean, now you can go back to your stump ranch.!"

In 1949, we subdivided the four acres into lots, the lots sold for $400. On our lot we brought in a 16 X 36 foot trailer, it was a bunkhouse from Northern Construction. In 1954, we added on a 24 X 16 section. **Charlie Parsons**, with his machine, helped with some of the clearing.

One of the lots did not sell right away, so we turned it into a potato patch.

We had piped water from the village, but there was not enough pressure for washing clothes. We used rain water to do the washing. Howard Rowe had a good well and we used to get a couple of buckets from him for drinking water. The village water was of poor quality and not good enough for drinking. There was no sewer connection and dirty water from washing the dishes was just thrown outside.

We had an outhouse; we called it the Paradise Inn! In 1952, Paul put in a septic field. In the 1940s, phones were scarce in Westview. Few people, apart from businesses, installed a phone. We didn't have a phone and had to use someone else's phone if there was an emergency.

There was electricity in the 1940s but not enough voltage for a fridge or any other appliances. In the 1950s the voltage improved and Paul bought me a fridge from Sid Proffit as a wedding anniversary present in 1952.

At one time, our house was listed with three different addresses - between Marine and Terrace. I went to vote one time with my husband and Mrs. Edith Jones was working at the voting office. She asked us, with some amusement, if my husband and I were still living together as we were listed at three different addresses!

Occasionally we shopped at Cranberry. We shopped at Ahola's and Bernier's shoe store. Sometimes, we bought meat at Bosa & Mitchells (now Mitchells).

Most of our shopping was done on Marine Avenue in Westview. I'd shop every two weeks. I'd get the bus to Penny Profit, and then walk all the way back up Marine. I bought groceries at Fairway, Penny Profit and Food Land. They all delivered. I would charge the groceries and pay on payday.

In May of 1949, Paul went back to work for the Powell River Company. He rode his bike between the Townsite and Westview.

In 1955, Paul put in one shift building the Willingdon Arena (now demolished – at present a parking lot). It was all volunteer labour.

Our son, Frank, attended Grief Point school in 1954. To get there, he had to walk up a trail. There were no through roads at that time in the area.

On the 1st of July each year there was a big "do" put on by the Union at Willingdon Beach. Ambrose McKinnon went there with his miniature train. The kids loved to ride on it.

We were both in favour of the amalgamation in 1955 when the Municipality was formed.

Looking Back with Herbert Hindle

Herb Hindle served in the Air Force as a flying instructor during WWII. Soon, after the war, he found himself playing golf on New Year's Day in British Columbia. Originally from the Prairies, Herb felt this was the place to be! He came to Powell River as his aunt and uncle lived on Maple Avenue in the Townsite. His uncle worked as a janitor at Brooks School.

Before starting **Hindle's Gift & Stationery** store in its present location in Westview, Herb owned a grocery store; the first location was the site of the present Bank of Montreal, the second location – opposite the Mexican restaurant on Marine Avenue.

Herb recalls Marine Avenue, in the late 1940s, as a dirt road. Other businesses in the area were owned by Dr. Vonarx, Jack Harper, Frank Haslam, and Madame Loukes. Due to the lack of parking spaces on Marine Avenue, the local business merchants in the 1960s bought the present parking lot by Capriccio Coffee House for their customers. After WWII, Marine Avenue was the heart of the business community in Westview; it was made up of individual-owned businesses.

Looking Back with Stella Saunders (Hall/Hewson) (1914-2008)

Westview Memories

After the union layed off all married women at the store, I went to work for Herb Hindle's grocery store in Westview. The meat market was next door and Bert Oustin (volunteer fireman) when called out, just left everything as it was, to help put out the fire.

Going along Marine Avenue were the following stores in the late 1940s and early 50s: Arena (1955), Muir's Hardware, Penny Profit (2007 – Paperworks Gallery), Fletchers/Anderson's Men's Wear, Herb Hindle's grocery store, Bert Oustin's Meat Market, Bank of Commerce, Harper's wholesale tobacco, Doran's Furniture Store, dress shop, Jimmy Cant's second-hand store, Parker's Garage, Barbroff's bakery, Roxy Theatre, Minerva Kent's Insurance, Foodland (under Foodland was Louise's Café, Profitt's electrical shop, and Hydro office.

On the opposite side of the road in the same time period were the following stores: Buckerfield's (demolished 1980s), Frank Meilleur's Garage (2007 – a parking lot opposite Bank of Montreal), café, dry cleaners, Mrs. Louke's 5th Avenue Dress Shop, Eaton's order office, Black's drugstore with apartments above, Burrel's Grocery store, Faith Rowe's children's clothing, Police Station and News Office.

I remember the **1946 earthquake**. It was early Sunday morning, and we were getting ready to go to church. We all ran outside. There was no damage to the house; however, everything in the medicine cabinet fell out. A chimney in Wildwood turned around. Later in the evening was a small after-shock; it did not do any damage.

In the 1950s and 60s I worked at the following stores in Westview: Eaton's, Mac's café, Bayers (old and new store), Knight News and Isaac's drugstore.

Yes, I knew **Madame Loukes**. Her dress shop was across the street when I worked at Hindle's. She was a wonderful, lovely lady. She had a great deal of fashion knowledge. It was a New York fashion house that gave her the prestigious title of "Madame". My sister, Beatrice did alterations for her in the 1950s; my niece worked for her in the 1960s.

I used to babysit for Jack Pearsall, MP. One time **Pierre Elliot Trudeau** came to Powell River (1970s) and Jack gave me a personal introduction! He said to Trudeau, "This is my friend Stella Saunders." I was so thrilled to meet our Prime Minister.

My husband, Laurie Hewson died in 1972. I have one son, Clifford Lloyd Hewson. In 1974 I married Fred Saunders. We both went to the Old Time Dancing at St. David's Anglican Church hall in Westview (now demolished).

Looking Back with Ruby Roscovich

Westview in the 1950s

Frank and Ruby Roscovich first cast their eyes on Powell River in early July 1951, sailing in on the *Princess Mary* ship from Vancouver Island, at Comox. She was then serving Powell River three times a week from Vancouver and to Comox once a week. It so happened that they were temporarily living in Nanaimo where Frank had found a few weeks' fill-in work there at a sawmill after arriving from Alberta as a refugee from a failing coal field. Steam coal on the railways was gradually being replaced by diesel fuel.

Frank could have been employed at the Port Alberni pulp and paper mill, but housing was not immediately obtainable. So it was on that Monday morning, Ruby placed her finger on the map, saying *"Let's try "Powell River!?!" "There is no road,"* said Frank. Somehow, a phone call was made and it was learned that the *Princess Mary* was to leave Comox on that very day in the early afternoon, after her weekly arrival there; Frank and Ruby were in luck but they had no time to lose, and left by car in haste for Comox. Seatbelts or car seats were unheard of, so Ruby must have tightly held on to almost 3-year-old Glen for that fast trip up the island.

Luckily, the ship was still in port with just enough time to put Frank's car in a sling and it was swung air-bound onto her deck. Eventually, after a scenic cruise, the Powell River coastline came into view; the colourful buildings glowed in the afternoon sunshine in sharp contrast to the coal fields with which Frank and Ruby had left behind in Alberta that spring of 1951.

Landing was made at the Powell River Paper Company dock and Frank's car was lowered down, along with some others. It was learned later, that in January that same year, the Westview dock had been destroyed by fire. Frank immediately checked out the mill for job opportunities. He was hired in the ground wood department, to begin as soon as living arrangements could be found. So he and Ruby scanned the local newspaper, which led them to inspect a place at Mowat Bay, then one across from Cranberry Lake, and finally a small, recently completed house at the top of Cooper Road, which then was a steep, narrow dirt trail, uneven with ruts. At this time of writing, the name is replaced with 'Huntingdon Street', and the hill has been considerably cut down and paved. The builder of this freshly-painted house was found, namely Fred Davenport, and for $6,000 the house became theirs to await their household furnishings which were still in a friend's garage in Vancouver.

Now, it was time to book an overnight stay in the attractive Rodmay Hotel, back above the mill site which kept sounding non-stop, to unaccustomed ears. By early morning, Frank and Ruby sailed to Vancouver on the *Princess Mary*. Arrangements were quickly made in the city for the shipment of their freight, and Frank returned to

Nanaimo to gather their remaining belongings. Meanwhile, Ruby and little Glen boarded *Princess Mary's* next sailing at midnight for Powell River. By early a.m. Frank met them at the Powell River dock. Somehow, he already had the essential items moved into the house, making it liveable for his family. Now they could settle in on Cooper Road. It was not long before another family arrived from the same coal branch as Frank and Ruby had done. They were Bill and Mary Kosterewa with their children, Larry and Jean, ready to make the Powell River mill their new source of livelihood. Bill acquired neighbouring property and immediately began building part of their house-to-be, so with Frank's help it was habitable within a month.

The summer of 1951 experienced a record heat wave, so much so, that the vegetation was tinder dry to the most dangerous level for many weeks. Meanwhile, Ruby was enduring her last weeks of pregnancy. Bill and Mary managed to move into their new building before the Roscovichs number two son, Dale was born. While Ruby was in hospital, the Kosterewas' kept Glen because Frank was on shift work at the mill.

The winter of 1951 was depressing for the Alberta immigrants, because of so much rain in December. They were not used to seeing rain instead of the usual snow on the ground. Ruby was kept busy trying to dry the steady flow of diapers, after washing and then boiling them in the copper boiler. They had to be hung above the kitchen stove to dry. This routine kept the small house in frequent steam baths, as rain continued outdoors. A change from "sunny Alberta"?

A ray of sunshine came to Ruby's door in the form of a nearby neighbour, Vivian Camozzi, bringing a freshly baked loaf of her homemade delicious bread. Nothing could have lifted Ruby's spirits more. Vivian and her husband Syl became lasting friends through this act of kindness.

Later on an acquaintance was made with a pair of bachelor brothers, Fred and Bill Cooper, living across the road, when one of them offered goat's milk to the newcomers. They had a spacious acreage, accommodating assorted fruit trees as well as goats and chickens, and a Doberman hound. The latter could have served to discourage marauding bear.

Bill was slight-of-build with genteel manners, but he let loose a volley of expletives every time this dog unbalanced him with its exuberance. As Fred was the dog's owner, the same explosive outbursts were directed at him also, for his dog. Unlike his trimly dressed brother, Fred's attire appeared casually thrown together, topped with a chewed-up straw hat. He rattled around in a fliver with wobbly fenders, and was rarely accompanied by the more refined brother Bill, who mostly avoided the contraption.

One time later Ruby inadvertently left her garden hat lying about, only to learn that one of the Coopers' goats munched through it. Speaking of gardening, Frank went to work the following spring to dig the ground near the house. He ended up with an empty trench, after hauling away wheelbarrow loads of gravelly deposits, possibly remnants from the Ice Age.

It wasn't long before Frank felt the need to enlarge their small dwelling. After consulting Veteran's Affairs, he was advised to go for their building program instead. Adjoining the present lot was a 2½ acre piece of logged over land which Frank acquired through Veterans Re-establishment Credits and he was launched into house building under their guidance. The basement was dug entirely by hand, after his daily work in the ground wood department at the mill, or after getting up following graveyard shifts. Cement pouring was done by hand with help from Bill Kosterewa, Syl Camozzi and other friends.

At this rate it took many years to fully complete the house, but by the fall of 1953 the Roscovichs hastily moved into the enclosure before much partitioning was done, the reason being that buyers Bob and Betty Smith with son Bobby needed to move into Frank's house on Cooper Road. They had just arrived from Alert Bay where Bob, as a meat cutter, was accepting a new job with Overwaitea in Westview.

Now Frank and Ruby's property faced Manson Avenue. It was a dusty trail bordered with bushy bracken on both sides which brushed the car going along. The front door of the house had to be held in place with a plank, supporting mill canvas as there was no time to properly install it for the time being. For kitchen cupboards, empty explosive boxes from the Sterco coalmine filled the bill. The company, Sterling Collieries, had used them when they had the Roscovich furnishings packed for shipping by rail to Vancouver.

The winter was spent with Frank cutting down trees on his new property to keep fuelling the wood furnace. When Ruby prepared for bed, she frequently warmed her nightgown in the oven of the propane kitchen stove because of the cold drafts in the much larger living space. It was too soon for indoor plumbing as no waterline was yet available, so a well had to be located and dug, with pump installed for the immediate use. The traditional outhouse system was set up, and laundry was possible with the washtub and scrub board. In time when the water line reached the Roscovich house, much jubilation burst forth.

The nearest source of food and other supplies was Bayer's store at the junction of Marine and Westview Avenues. It was a long building, housing a wide range of essential goods, and postal service also. Ruby made one trip to shop at Bayer's store, wheeling Dale in the baby carriage accompanied by 4-year-old Glen trudging beside. Down Cooper hill was rutted and bumpy but good time was made. However, on the way back progress slowed down as it was uphill grade all the way.

On reaching the final climb up Cooper Hill, Glen tired out and clung to the carriage, adding more weight for Ruby to maintain momentum. She had visions of her bread dough beginning to rise out of the bowl onto the stovetop, all the time she endeavoured to reach the top. Needless to say, that was the last such shopping trip. Memory fails to verify the quality of that bread.

As spring came, Ruby would explore the new grounds covered with stumps and logs. These logs had deep crevices, filled with writhing blackish snakes, which gave her the creeps. Friends visiting from Vancouver were fascinated with Roscovich's "snake pit" before these logs became firewood.

By the summer of 1954 the family made a holiday trip back to Alberta, but their departure was not smooth-going as it is at this time of writing. Their car had to go ahead of time by barge service to Vancouver. Then they boarded the Gulf Wing vessel, since the *Princess Mary* no longer came up the coast to Powell River after some twenty years of service.

By this time, number two son, Dale, as a 3-year-old, was never still, but kept wanting to explore every nook and cranny, up and down on this boat. A leash had to be kept on him by his dad, who ended up saying that he walked all the way to Vancouver. It was a relief to resume the holiday journey by car.

The first ferry, *Quillayute,* made its initial run August 21, 1954, some weeks after the Roscovichs' return from Alberta on the Gulf Wing, their one and only such adventure.

By 1955 the focal point in Powell River was the newly-constructed Willingdon arena, and also during the many months previously, as the whole community was involved in many innovative ways of donated efforts. Even women kept up a constant supply of food. Everyone knew Bob Muir, the local hardware merchant who contributed to and supported this project from the very beginning to its completion, as "Mr. Arena". With his unfailing enthusiasm he forged a remarkable community spirit that remains a memorial of him to this day.

It seemed like everyone of all ages took to the ice, many for the first time. Before long, juvenile hockey was on the go, and parents, Ruby and Frank also, followed their games. Glen and Dale often had to play at 6 a.m. before school. Senior hockey was another highlight with packed bleachers with people cheering lustily at every opportunity. An outstanding supporter was Cis Wilcocks, a public-spirited lady, who always kept her knitting needles clacking at different speeds, depending on the intensity of the game.

The community bounded by Cooper Road and Manson Avenue kept opening up with some new developments; streets were renamed alphabetically because of progress, meaning some pioneering ones like Cooper Road were lost. Now Huntingdon Street replaced Cooper Road, and soon afterward those colourful brothers sold out, leaving to parts unknown. New neighbours, like the Kroekers, the Drurrys, the McDonalds, Craigs, Boyds, Fetchkos, and Stagers began to settle in, swelling the number of children in this vicinity. Since the Roscovichs had the most space, they got the bulldozer operator, Frank Best to clear an area big enough for a playground free of stumps. So Glen, Dale, and immediate friends had endless games of "scrub" ball. At other times they played war games in the nearby timber. Frank helped them build a "Fort Dunlop" with rough slabs, the name coming from the use of some rubber tire material for door hinges. This addition injected much drama into their imaginative play.

For a time, in another area, an archaeological dig went on to a depth of two or three feet, through layers of sand and gravel, like river bottom. Their play exploration turned up fossilized clam shells, remnants of some riverbed in ancient times. No wonder that only gravel and grit lay beneath the thin layer of topsoil here. The children also carried on trench "warfare" while this opportunity remained before lawns came into being, ending imaginative play.

Soon Frank became the owner of an open top motorboat, because he could no longer resist the tempting waters of Malaspina Strait and the lure of fishing for salmon. He took Ruby and the boys with him into those wide open spaces for the first time. If the water was smooth as glass, Ruby acquiesced, until some large vessel hove into sight, at which time she would urge Frank to slow down or wait for the "wash" to pass instead of crossing over those turbulent waves. By next summer, Frank came across a second-hand cabin boat, which he remodelled and named *Nosey Gal*. That was the start of many holiday and picnic trips to nearby islands, also recreational fishing.

Gardening expanded on this new property where some areas were not as gravelly. The soil had to be built up with compost, also alder bottom that was brought in by wheelbarrow. Enough vegetables grew, with surplus greens to feed rabbits that were raised in cages. Frank would fill the hoppers at night with carrot tops and thinning and by morning all would be gone.

Rabbit meat was a good substitute for chicken, although Ruby went through a time of mourning before opening the first package of frozen rabbit meat. Afterwards she eventually prepared delicious creamed chicken-like dishes. At a beach picnic one time with the Walter and Frances Johnstone family, she surprised them with this recipe. Frances praised the "creamed chicken", refusing to believe it was rabbit. Finally she said, *"Well, it was good anyway"*.

Economical family entertainment took place at the "drive-in" movie by the Beach Gardens. The Roscovich family joined scores of other like-minded persons for a weekend night out, taking care to unplug the speaker before exiting the field.

Rudy Pearson outside the Pearson residence at 5394 Manson Avenue, Edgehill, Powell River 1970s.
Insert: a very young Rudy Pearson with Grandpa's Austen car (1940s).   Photos: Rudy Pearson

Mrs. Harper standing on the veranda of the Harper residence at 4701 Willingdon Ave, Westview, Powell River
1937. One of the first houses to be built in Westview. Photo: Happy Smith album

Christmas (1950) at the Carlson residence at 1250 Cassiar Street, Edgehill, Powell River. Note the radio and piano
– home entertainment in the 1950s. (L to R) Elsie/Barbara/Mrs. Lois Carlson.   Photo: Elsie Parsons (Carlson)

Lemonade stand by the Bergot farm, Edgehill, Powell River circa 1948
(L to R) Sylvia Bergot/Sharon Brooks/Mrs. Marie Pearson/Mr. Jack Pearson/Madeline Bergot (small child)
Photo: Madeline Alexander album

Zuccato home (near Edgehill Store), Edgehill, Powell River (1942).   Photo: Anita Zuccato

Edgehill Store, Edgehill, Powell River. Originally built and owned by Mrs. Nina Lambert after WWII. Present owners Terry & Jan Boulanger – purchased 1985. A luncheon counter attracts old-time customers.
Photo: Ann Bonkowski 2008

The McGuffie family taken outside the family home (1947) Edgehill, Powell River. In the 1920s the McGuffie family came to live in Edgehill. They lived off the land – kept goats and chickens. Back row: James McGuffie/Allen Allerby/Les Jamieson/Norah McGuffie/Geof McGuffie/Mr. Robert McGuffie/George McGuffie/Margaret McGuffie/Clarence Thomas/Flo Thomas/Hayden Swanson. Middle: Jenny Ellerby/Margaret Ingram/Julia Dykes/Mrs. Nellie McGuffie/Betsy Jamieson/Yvonne McGuffie. Front: Robert Allerby/Raymond Allerby/Judy Dykes/Diane Konings/Vernon Thomas/Lilah Sadler/Allan Jamieson/Lorraine Jamieson/Norma Swanson/Joan Fuller/Donald McGuffie. Photo: Lorraine Jamieson

Looking Back with Lorraine Jamieson

The McGuffie Family – Pioneers in Edgehill (from 1921)

Robert and Nellie McGuffie came to Refuge Cove in 1915 from Victoria. They brought four children with them – two boys and two girls. Six children were later born in Refuge Cove (one died).

At that time, First Nations were fishing from dugout boats. Robert McGuffie learned how to fish from First Nations.

The children attended school in Refuge Cove.

"I remember the McGuffies and the Smiths attending the Refuge Cove school. The school was a one-room building with a woodstove. It opened in 1915 and closed in 1923. The same school building was moved to Galley Bay in 1923."
Kay Dickson (nee Hanson) *Chalkdust & Outhouses* – B.A. Lambert 2000

The McGuffies went by boat, to the store in Lund, for supplies.

In 1921 the McGuffies obtained land by present-day McGuffie Creek in Edgehill. They lived in a tent until the house was built. The family home is still there today. The creek is named McGuffie Creek in honour of this pioneer family.

Betsy McGuffie married Les Jamieson at Cranberry United Church in 1931. They had two children, Allan and Lorraine. The Jamieson family lived in Cranberry.

Looking Back with Rudy Pearson

The Pearsons – Pioneers in Edgehill (from 1925)

Three generations of Pearsons worked for the Powell River Company.

Jacob (Jack) Pearson came to Powell River in 1925. He was the first man to retire from the mill in the early 1930s. There was no pension in those days.

Peter Pearson, Rudy's father, came to Powell River in 1927. He worked in the sulphite division until he retired at age 65. Peter, like the other mill workers, worked part-time during the Depression years. He worked two weeks on and two weeks off. His wife, Astrid Pearson, took in boarders to earn extra cash.

Rudy Pearson worked for the Powell River Company from 1952-54 and 1956-60 with Albert Adams in the cutter division. Rudy, as a volunteer, helped build the Arena.

Rudy Pearson:

My parents, Peter Thoralf Pearson and Astrid Randine Pearson (Rassmussen) were born in Torp, Norway. My father came out to Canada in 1927 and my mother followed him one year later.

My mother was active in Canadian politics. She was a founder member of the CCF in Powell River during the 1930s. The CCF women's group consisted of Gertie Lambert, Mable Olson, Mary Crosby, Alva Forslund, Ruby Hart, Christine Marchant, Elizabeth Cartmel, Hannah Johnson, and Mary Monkhouse.

Astrid Pearson hosted well-known feminists Dorothy Steeves and Grace McInnes in the Pearson home.

Mother entertained friends, **Mary Paul and Ada August from Sliammon**. Baskets were traded when Astrid Pearson served her First Nation's friends tea and sandwiches.

Edgehill has always been the home for the Pearson family. They owned one of the first prefabricated homes to be shipped into the area. Peter Pearson, my father, bought four acres on Manson (Avenue) off John Siguresen in 1925. Jeff Mah has since subdivided this acreage. The Pearson heritage house is presently owned by Barbara Sheriff.

Nearby, in Edgehill, was the MacGregor family. **Edgehill started at MacGregor Avenue.**

Colonel MacGregor lived on Manson and MacGregor Avenue. Jack Pearson had acreage there and sold peat moss to the Powell River Company.

The Pearsons had chickens and cows. I remember one cow, she was called "Bossy" – she was bossy! They raised beautiful raspberries and sold the cream to go with them; people knew and ordered them in advance.

Farms in Edgehill: **Scotts** (Scott's farm) came after the **McIntosh** family. **Brookers** sold to **Bergots**.

Andy Carlson originally owned the property **Jim Devlin** owned by the bird sanctuary at the end of MacGregor Avenue. **Golden Stanley** lived across the lake from our property.

Cranberry Lake School

I started school in 1939. My Grade 1 teacher was Miss Livingstone. Bessie Rankin became Bessie Bemrose; I had her as my teacher for two years. Miss Woodword taught me in Grade 4 and 5. Mr. Devlin was my teacher in Grade 6. I remember the fun we had on sports days.

Lots of things quit because of the war. There were no toys available during WWII. We had blackout etc. and could not show any light. I remember the ration books; Mother traded the liquor coupons for sugar coupons. At school we saved 25 cents to buy Victory stamps.

My parents bought a radio from Emil Gordon, in order to hear the news about the war. Mother was worried about her relatives in German-occupied Norway.

Daily Chores

I had to clean the chickens; my brother Tommy chopped the wood. After school, we changed out of our good clothes to our work clothes before doing the evening chores.

We had a good garden with fruit trees. We kept cows, goats, chickens, and turkeys. Mother canned up to 600 jars a year. Family friends, Hans Johnson and Nils Hansen, went hunting and provided venison for our table. My father liked fishing and brought home lots of fish.

Mother bought our groceries from Woodward's, Powell Stores, and Bosa's (Bosa & Mitchell) in Cranberry. Dad worked for the Company and everybody received a letter encouraging the Powell River Company employees to shop there. Mother put her main order through Woodward's as the Company store charged at least 20 to 30% above other retail stores.

Games

We mostly played war games, shooting at each other. My cousin Walter Carlson went to school with Allan Cramb and Fred Diana. We swam in a mud hole at the lake – it wasn't that great! Nearly every year Cranberry Lake froze over (1940s). We learned to skate on the lake. It was a fun time. We had bonfires.

We used to go to Powell Lake every year and stay with **Art Lyons at Rainbow Lodge** for two weeks.

Mum made sure we got down to the Exhibition (PNE) in Vancouver every year.

Old **Charlie Bark** lived in our cabin free-of-charge. He was a carpenter and did odd jobs around the place.

Mike the Belgian used to come by our place. He was a well-known figure going around town with a dog pulling a cart.

We knew **Clara and Andy Anderson**. Clara was half-sister to our next-door neighbour, **Oren Olson**. Clara used to come over there and visit with her half-brother. I met Andy a couple of times.

Lot 450

I remember the **pest hospital** and a couple of houses on the **old orchard** site. **Mrs. Farley** lived there and later, the **Cattermoles**.

Veteran's Village

I knew **Bill Peebles** and his first wife, Evelyn, and later his second wife, Eva. I used to do their hair.

I remember the old fire station and village office in Cranberry – located where the Cranberry Seniors Centre is today.

I remember the Christmas parties at the hall by Cranberry Lake. There were huge piles of sawdust nearby.

Edgehill Store was built and run by Mrs. Lambert after the war. I knew her very well. Her son, Noel Lambert was my age and we chummed around together. She had been a teacher at Olsen Landing. At one time, I took art lessons with her at the Arts Council. Robin Lambert's son is quite an artist.

Olive Devaud

Mother played cards with her. My grandparents knew Alphonse Devaud really well.

Dwight Hall

Mum went to Dwight Hall when various events were put on there. One time Mum went to an auction there, and bought a beautiful decanter for 50 cents. My grandparents were at the opening of Dwight Hall in 1928.

My parents went **Old Time dancing** at Dwight Hall, Cranberry, Wildwood, and Lund. In those days, they just brought the kids along with them.

To get to the **Townsite** we rode the bus either one way or both ways. If we went one way we saved the five cents and spent it on candy!

We had post box #537 in the Townsite. Post boxes were located in the post office where **Mr. Banham** was the postmaster. We bought postage stamps in Cranberry.

1946 Earthquake

It was a Sunday morning and we were in our pj's. It was a bad one and the earth moved like ocean waves. Afterwards, we found just one small crack in the plaster of the house. Tommy was away, up at Whaletown (Cortez Island) and he thought he heard the sound of a gas washing machine – it was the earthquake, of course!

Hairdressing

I worked at the **Inn** for many years. I retired when the sales tax came in – didn't want to bother with it. I kept on working until I was 70 years of age.

Queen's Visit - 1971

I was there at the United Church when the Queen came. I was standing very close to the Queen. I remember Prince Phillip smiled at me. **Isabel Dawson, MLA** was there to meet the Queen. I had prepared Isabel's hair for this special occasion.

In 1987, Astrid Randine Pearson was honoured by meeting the King and Queen of Norway in Vancouver.

Miron and George Goddard with daughter Myrna Goddard, Westview, 1933..
Photo: Myrna O' Hearne (Goddard)

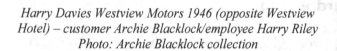

Harry Davies Westview Motors 1946 (opposite Westview Hotel) – customer Archie Blacklock/employee Harry Riley
Photo: Archie Blacklock collection

Second Westview School 1939 (L to R) Harry Myers
(Principal)/ Miss Atkinson/Bessie Rankin (Bemrose)/
Mr. Davidson/ Alice Cluff.
Courtesy of the Powell River Museum

Ben Ogden clearing his corner lot by Abbotsford Street
and Manson Avenue, Powell River 1956.
The family lived in a tent before moving into the
basement of the new house.
Photo: Ben Ogden

Looking Back with Oren Olson

Olsen Valley (1914 – 1920) and Edgehill Pioneer (from 1930s)

Oren Olson:

*"I was just a young boy, 7 years of age, when my family went to homestead in Olsen Valley in 1914. The valley had been burned out in 1912. I had six brothers and sisters: Clara, Tina, Pat, Peggy, Ray, and Bill. The first winter we all lived in one building with one big room. Ray and Bill spent the nights outside in a tent. I attended the first school in Olsen Valley, my father helped build the school. Fifteen children attended the school, including five Olsons. We left Olsen Valley in 1920 and moved to the States. Clara stayed in Olsen Valley and married **Andy Anderson** in 1927.*

*We came back to Powell River in 1927. Andy hired my dad to log the old golf course, by the mill. From 1932-60 Andy and my sister Clara operated the **Lakeview Lumber Company** at Haywire Bay, Powell Lake. During the war years, Andy and Clara shipped sawdust out from their mill. They sold sawdust just as fast as they could make it, as it was dumped in boats and used as ballast. The tanks just ran right over it! After the war they were busy producing lumber for returning servicemen to build new homes.*

*In 1929, I went to work for the **Powell River Company**. I joined the **CCF** in the 1930s. I have been a member of the CCF (NDP) nearly all my life. In 1933, Ernie Blackwell was elected CCF member for the Mackenzie Riding. The Powell River Company manager was furious; over 300 CCF employees were fired before the mill became unionized in 1937. I used to peddle CCF pamphlets around the mill – I was never blacklisted. I used to go around Edgehill, Cranberry, and Haslam Lakes in my car, peddling CCF pamphlets. In 1939, I helped build the **Wildwood Hall** (for CCF functions). I knew **Tommy Lambert** in Paradise Valley; he was a good socialist.*

I was in the Army Reserve during the war. I continued to work at the mill. Women worked in the mill for the duration of the war. The only place they didn't work was on the log boom. The women had to leave when the servicemen came back.

*My wife Mabel was a great support. We used to go over to Texada Island to peddle NDP pamphlets for **Don Lockstead**. When **Dave Barrett** was in Powell River, he always stayed with us in **Edgehill**. Dave told everyone that Mabel was a good cook!*

I finished working in the mill in 1971. I had worked on the log booms for 42 years!"

246

Looking Back with Sylvia Alexander (Bergot)

The Bergot Farm in Edgehill (1944-59)

From 1944-59 the Bergot family owned a 16-acre farm in Edgehill, from MacGregor Avenue almost to Furness Avenue, on Manson Avenue. It was bordering Mrs. May's and the Scott farms. Previously, it had been known as **Brooker's farm**.

Marianne and Raymond Bergot kept horses, cows, pigs, geese, ducks, and turkeys on their farm. There were many different types of fruit plants: gooseberries, red currants, and raspberries. Marianne Bergot sent raspberries to the hospital in the **Townsite**; she rode a horse to ratepayer's meetings in **Westview**.

The Bergots had four children: Sylvia, Marie, Madeline, and Sharlene.

Raymond Bergot worked for the **Powell River Company** and shopped at the Company store in the Townsite.

Raymond died in 1954. In the late 1950s, Marianne Bergot sold some of the lots from the farm property; the remainder she sold to Miles McCleod who later subdivided them.

Mrs. Bergot bought the house which **James MacGregor** had lived in. The house was located on a lot Raymond Bergot had previously sold to James MacGregor in Edgehill.

Don MacGregor's mother taught piano. Sylvia Alexander (nee Bergot) remembers having a piano lesson at the MacGregor house during the 1946 earthquake. Everything in the house started to shake! Don was terrified and ran outside.

Sylvia remembers the following stores in Cranberry: Bosa's store, Dick's dry goods, Wilshire's, and Bernier's shoe store.

Sylvia also remembers **Mrs. Lambert** who built the **Edgehill Store**.

Sylvia attended Grades 1 to 6 at **Cranberry Malaspina School**. Mrs. Lambert (a qualified teacher) was a substitute teacher at the school.

Sylvia attended St. Anne's Academy in Vancouver for Grade 7 and later completed her high school education at Brooks, Powell River.

Looking Back!
John MacGregor   VC MC DCM

Lived in Edgehill – worked for the Powell River Company and started the MacGregor brick factory in Cranberry after WWII

During WWI John (Jock) MacGregor became the most decorated Canadian soldier.

In April 1917, Sergeant MacGregor won his first medal, the Distinguished Conduct Medal (DCM) at Vimy Ridge – he was the first man from his brigade to reach the top of the ridge. Nine months later, in January 1918, he won the Military Cross (MC) for leading a trench raid and capturing prisoners. MacGregor was then promoted to Captain. Later, in the same year, he won the Victoria Cross (VC) when he single-handed attacked three German installations. At the end of WWI, in November 1918, Captain MacGregor was awarded a bar to his Military Cross for capturing two bridges from the retreating German Army.

John MacGregor was born in February 1889 in Cawdor, Scotland. In 1909, he came to Canada as an immigrant.

In 2007, Don MacGregor, his youngest son recalled his father was apprenticed as a young man to a master stonemason and carpenter in Scotland. He joined the reserve army and rode horses in the Garrison Artillery.

John used his skills as a carpenter to find work as he travelled across Canada to British Columbia. He became a trapper in northern B.C., before volunteering to join the Canadian Army in 1918. John was determined to fight for King and Country.

According to his eldest son, Captain James MacGregor, in his book *MacGregor VC*, the skills his father learned as a trapper were put to excellent use on the battlefield in reconnaissance work.

A few years after the war, in 1923, John married Ethel Flower, a nurse he met in Prince Rupert.

It was Ethel who persuaded John to live in Powell River. It was a company town with good housing and employment opportunities for an experienced carpenter. John worked for the Powell River Company for 18 years.

Initially, John came on his own to Powell River and boarded at the Powell River Lodge in the Townsite. In 1924, he bought a five-acre lot in Edgehill. **He chose Edgehill, as the price of land was too expensive in Westview.** There were few families living in the 1920s in this area. The lot John bought was near the Culos' farm and it had an old barn on the property. Nearby, near the lake, was a bog where cranberries could be gathered. John MacGregor dug the foundations, well, and outhouse by hand – a backbreaking job.

After WWII the property was subdivided. The end lot on MacGregor Avenue, by the lake, was first purchased by Andy Carlson, later sold to James Devlin, principal of Cranberry Lake School. The original MacGregor house is still there, at the corner of Manson Avenue and MacGregor Avenue.

In 1939, John MacGregor was presented to King George VI and Queen Elizabeth (the Queen Mother) on their visit to Vancouver, B.C.

In **WWII**, MacGregor was promoted to Major and later Lieutenant-Colonel. He served during WWII in a military camp in Vernon, B.C.

John MacGregor & Son Brick Factory

It was after WWII that John MacGregor started a brick factory in Cranberry Village, Powell River. The idea of making concrete blocks came to him when seeking buildings for army use during the war.

He formed a partnership in October 1946 with his youngest son, Don. James, his eldest son, was working full time for the Powell River Company; however, James, in his spare time, helped out by driving the delivery truck. The site of the brick factory was purchased from Jimmy Ford. A gravel site was leased from the government. From 1947, Don ran the factory because his father was ill with cancer. Don continued to run the factory after his father's death in 1952.

Producing concrete bricks was a successful business venture in postwar Powell River. In order to learn about brick making, John MacGregor had visited a cement brick factory in Seattle, Washington. He built the factory with second-hand materials – using lumber from the Radford chicken houses on the Powell River Company orchard, which was located on Lot 450. The machinery was not available in Canada and had to be imported from the U.S.

The concrete bricks were used in many Powell River foundations and basements, including: the Powell River Arena, the Edgehill Store owned by Mrs. Lambert, and Charlie Parson's house by Cranberry Lake.

Looking Back with Ben Ogden

Memories of Edgehill (from 1948)

Ben bought a half-acre lot in Edgehill in 1948 for $150. He built his own house at, what is today, Abbotsford Street and Manson Avenue. Sometime in the 1950s, Ben bought the acre behind his place as an investment for $250. He later subdivided it.

After WWII, Ben came to find work with the Powell River Company. He was employed with them from 1948-56. He worked in the sawmill, foundry, finishing, and cutter rooms. To begin with he batched in the Townsite before bringing his family to Powell River.

During WWII, Ben had been overseas in the U.K. as a mechanic with the Air Force. It was in England that he first met Bill Gallagher, who was a pilot. What a surprise to meet up with him again, after the war, when Ben came to work for the Powell River Company.

On his return to Canada, in the RMS *Mauretania*, Ben caught a chill when he was on deck during adverse conditions – a gale and intense cold. While heading west in a train, he came down with a fever and ended up in the Air Force hospital in Winnipeg. It was there he met Alberta (known as Poppy), a nurse in the hospital. They corresponded and then Poppy came out to the West Coast for a visit, it was then Ben proposed,

"Poppy, you looked after me while I was in hospital.
Let me spend the rest of my life looking after you!"

Poppy and Ben were married in 1946. They had four children – two girls, Elizabeth and Nancy, and two boys, Tim and Andy. **They lived in a tent** on the half-acre Edgehill property until Ben built the house. A roof was constructed over the tent to keep the rain out. When the house reached lock up stage, the Ogden family moved into the basement until the house was finished. Ben used a Fordson tractor to clear the bush around his place.

In 1948 there was no electricity, no sewer, no water and no phone connection for this area.

The Ogdens were camping in the bush with an outhouse at the back. Abbotsford Street did not exist. Manson Avenue was a gravel road with many potholes. There was no curb or sidewalk. The road only went as far as the park where it met the Paradise Valley logging road. There was no airport and no Duncan Street. A logging road went off into the bush where Edgehill School is today. Behind the Ogden house and adjacent properties was a one-acre pond. Edgehill kids came to skate on the pond in winter.

Looking Back with Elsie Parsons (Carlson)

Memories of Edgehill (1954-73)

Before moving to Edgehill in the mid-1950s we lived in the Townsite and rented from the Powell River Company. My father, Ernie Carlson, worked as a carpenter for the Powell River Company.

My mother, Lois Carlson, shopped at Powell Stores. We went to the library in Dwight Hall. Mother had 100 rose bushes in our garden in the Townsite.

There were six children in our family: Madeline teaching at Refuge Cove; Barbara was married and lived in the States; John, Norma Jean, and Elsie living at home.

We probably moved from the Townsite because we could afford to buy a house at a reasonable cost. **In 1954 we moved to #10 North Lake Road, Edgehill.** We had just over an acre of land. There was a cabin on the property. There was an indoor toilet in the house. We had a coal oil heater in the bathroom – we put our pj's on it to get them warm! My mother pulled stumps and my teenage brother helped her; together they cleared an acre of land.

Parson's Tractor Service and a rock quarry were nearby.

We walked all the way to Cranberry the first year we were in school. Then my sister Madeline bought the kids bikes for Christmas and we were able to cycle all the way. I remember passing Scott's farm.

One time Madeline brought us beautiful Indian sweaters from Refuge Cove, where she taught.

In 1955 I attended Grade 2 in Edgehill School – the first year the school opened. Kids were never driven to school back then. We did all sorts of plays at school.

I remember the first TV we had in the 1950s. It was black-and-white and grainy. The adults watched Tommy Hunter and Lawrence Welk, the kids watched "I Love Lucy".

In the early 1960s, when I was in Grade 7, I worked in **Edgehill Store**; Nora and Dewiss Brown ran the store. They lived in the back of the store with their two sons, Phillip and Neil. Mrs. Lambert (the first owner) lived in the house near the store. Mr. Oxbury brought in the bread. A big, red, Coke truck came in and made deliveries. The store sold tin food, cigarettes, small Coke bottles at 10 cents each, and penny candy. I worked from 6 to 9 p.m. and earned something like 50 to 65 cents an hour. In high school I worked at Woolworth's for about a dollar an hour.

We swam at Dead Dog on Cranberry Lake, just before Charlie Parson's place. There was a small raft there. If the weather was too warm for too long, one could get the Cranberry Lake itch. One time I nearly drowned; I went out on the raft and I fell off – someone had to rescue me! We went skating on the lake at Charlie and Gerri Parson's place.

We also skated at the **Willingdon Arena**. We went to hockey games there and the big Fall Fairs – mother put in baking. We often walked to Willingdon from Edgehill. We roller-skated at Cranberry Arena.

We shopped in Cranberry – the odd time we stopped in at Dick's dry goods, Wilshire's, Jimmy Cant's shoe store, and Ahola's hardware store. As little kids, we shopped in the Townsite when we lived there. Later on, we went to Westview on Marine. On Marine there was Buckerfield's, Marshall Wells, Penny Profit (Paperwork's Gallery), Martis' music shop near Hindles, Bayer's store, and Fairway. My mother worked at Fairway one day a week. She felt she was progressive for her time, working outside the home. She worked in the Avenue Store when we lived in the Townsite.

I remember tasting the first soft ice cream when Super Valu, the first shopping mall, opened up.

The big mall came when I was a teenager; Hudson Bay, Sweet Sixteen, and Woolworth's. As a teenager I went to the **Beach Garden's Drive-In** in Tom's orange-and-white Ferrari.

The Dairy Queen opened up by the bowling alley and then moved further along Marine. I remember Smitty's Pancake House.

After I left Edgehill in the 1970s, my brother John had a cement plant, Powell River Trumix, where Springtime Nursery is today.

I married Tom in 1973 and moved to the Parson's farm at Blue Mountain in Westview.

252

Wildwood District

Tom Higgins holding reins of draft horses (1930s); horses played an important role in clearing the land. In the background is the Higgins' house in Wildwood.   Photo: Brian Crilly collection

1930s boat houses, Powell River. Wildwood bridge in background.   Private collection.

Looking Back with Bessie Banham and Judith Lehay (Banham)

Wildwood District (from 1900)

The smallest of the three outlying districts of Powell River is Wildwood, situated northwest of the river, on a level stretch of land approximately 500 feet above sea level.

In 1900, Jimmy Springer logged Wildwood for the B.C. Timber and Trading Company.

The district was opened up in 1914, when the government subdivided it into 40 acre pre-emptions. The applicants waited in line, on the Vancouver Courthouse steps, 40 days and nights, for the first come-first served and the first served had first choice. Jimmy Springer called the roll call every four hours. At night they slept on the courthouse floor. Those who were absent could get a friend to answer the roll call for him; if no one did, then on reappearance, the unfortunate fellow was sent to the end of the line.

The 13 original lots in the area went to:

Peter Barron, Frank Alfred Smith, George F. Smarje (Smarge), Wilfred Percival Barrett, James A. McGorran (abandoned and taken over by John R. Banham), George R.C. Webb, James J. McKenzie, George "Sunset" Olley, Maud Lane, George William Urquhart (a.k.a Jim Springer), James Thomson, Herbert Thomson, Douglas Flemming (abandoned and taken over by Frances Xavier Joncas 1915).

It was necessary to take up residence on your claim six weeks after it was granted. There had to be some member of the family sleeping on the property ten months out of the year for five years. The pre-emptor had to clear five acres and do improvements to the value of $10 an acre for each acre in the homestead before the "Crown Grant" was given.

The staunch pioneers, fighting their way over fallen trees, logs, and stumps to find their homestead, knew what they were doing when they named the district "Wildwood".

In the early 1930s, when it was suggested that the name be changed to "Arbutus Heights", the pioneers of Wildwood put up a terrific battle. "Wildwood" it was going to remain. It was necessary to add "Heights" to the post office, as there was already a "Wildwood Post Office" in British Columbia. The "Heights" was never added to the district.

Mr. Herb Thomson with his brother Mr. Len Thomson, who acted for their father, Mr. James Thomson after whom the Wildwood School is named, camped on the flats where the Shingle Mill is now located, until they could make a trail to their homesteads.

Mr. George Smarge and Mr. Frank Smith also made trails and followed skid roads out to their new homes. Mr. F. Joncas followed a few weeks later, and the Higgins a year or so later.

Owing to transportation difficulties, most of the cabin homes were made of material available on the claims. The men hewed logs for foundations and beams, while the women slivered off the rough edges and squared the cedar shakes. After crossing the river on rafts; food, furniture, stock, feed, and equipment were packed in. Later, it was hauled with a stone boat and a horse over the rough trails and skid roads. It was surprising how nicely the homes were furnished, although tables, chairs, and other articles of furniture were often homemade. Mrs. Percy Barrett even had a piano that her husband and his brother had carried up the hill, and then transported three miles on a horse-drawn stone boat.

The bridge was built in 1915 and was a wonderful boost for the homesteaders and the few other families who had leased property. The sandy switchback up the side hill was a treacherous piece of road. The drifting sand made a poor roadbed and no amount of cribbing and planking could keep the road from shifting. The sand slipped as a vehicle passed, with the sand from above filling the inside rut and the sand sliding away from the outside rut. Although there was never a serious accident, more than one wagon, and later cars, would settle with the entire road, feet down the bank or have their wheels slide over the edge. There was one cut out. It was located, where, if you were lucky, you could squeeze past without snagging hub caps. Even with the sand hazard, the pioneer women piled their youngsters into buckboards and drove to town or went on horseback.

Wildwood was a bonanza for the woodmen after the bridge was built. Logging companies had no sales for cedar when it was logged over in 1902, so the cedar was felled to get it out of the way, or left standing. Cords of shingle bolts were hauled out with teams. Other wood was plentiful too. Mr. Jacob Andersen cut 200 cords on his two-acre lot in 1919, and with the aid of one block, removed 56 stumps. The Anderson's two acres was across from James Thomson School, to the corner of Highway 101. The stumps in the district were enormous, it costing in those days, approximately $500 to clear one acre.

Conditions were hard until the roads began to take shape. The claim is made that some roads were originally made by cows, following the line of least resistance around the stumps. And then the horse-and-wagon came followed by a Model T Ford, progressively widening these trails into roads. The swamp parts were corduroy. Even now the skids can be seen when you hike through the bush on Lot 450 or down the skid road to Little Sliammon Lake or Three Mile Bay. The children walked to Powell River to school, down the little trail and crossed the river in rowboats, until the bridge was built. Then they went to the top of the hill and down the flight of steps, except the venturesome ones, who insisted on sliding down the grand sandy side hill, on the seats of their trousers.

The homes were widely separated. There were few social functions, as every one was busy clearing and building. In 1916, when the Andersens moved to their new home, their neighbour walked through the trail to tell them how nice and friendly it was to see their light twinkling through the trees.

In 1922 the first one-room schoolhouse was built with an additional room added a year later. Mr. Joncas practically gave the property to the district, and the Powell River Company built the school to relieve the congested condition prevailing in the Henderson School. Miss Florence Lynch, who later married Bill Wellband, was the first teacher. The Wildwood Social Club, the first organization in Wildwood had been formed and they held some parties in the school to raise money for a piano and equipment. The desks were on slats so they could be picked up in units and stacked along the wall.

One chapter in the history of Wildwood could be headed, simply "Cows". The Sliammon Indian Reserve herd romped around the district, terrorizing the settlers and tramping their gardens. The herd contained two frolicsome bulls that were so fierce, it was necessary to keep children off of the roads, even home from school. A tale was told (with many chuckles), of how the bulls put one man going to work, up on top of a convenient stump. His lusty cries for help brought aid only to have his rescuer also stumped. The story goes that they spent one entire night there while the enraged bulls stood guard. Mr. Jack Ellsworth, one of the early settlers, wouldn't say a word about it because the ranchers finally took matters into their own hands and the bulls disappeared. Investigation by the police followed, but not a soul in the entire district knew a single thing about the incident.

Dairy farming was an important industry. Wildwood's herds and the odd family cow foraged the road sides and the old skid roads. Mr. George Ethofer had a smart old bossy cow, famous for its ability to open practically any gate in the district. About 1931, with more families moving into the district and after a lot of investigating and red tape, the "pound law" was enforced with Mr. Fred Erickson named pound keeper. Depicting the spirit of the community, and it still prevails, Mr. C. Zorzi who had a flourishing dairy, after putting up a good fight against the law said, *"It will put me out of business, for I can't afford to buy all the feed for my herd but I'll work for the best interests of Wildwood just the same"*. He was one of the most ardent workers for any worthy cause or improvement to the district. About 1929, the Wildwood Welfare League, incorporated under the Societies Act was formed with Mr. Bert Ward, President, and Mr. Charles Bird, Vice President, and Mrs. J. Banham, Secretary-Treasurer. The League went to work with great enthusiasm. Their first accomplishments were the "pound law" and obtaining a post office in the district.

A few months after it was organized, a committee was appointed to investigate the possibility of installing a water system and an electrical distribution system. Committees were appointed, and by 1931 complete data had been compiled, and it was decided to drop the water question temporarily and concentrate on electricity. The district was incorporated into an improvement district, and eventually three trustees were elected: Mr. Herb Thomson, Chairman; Mr. Jack Banham, and Mr. Paul Kurpil. They worked night after night, getting out figures and estimates, trying to keep the cost to the ratepayers as low as possible. Mr. Thomson measured the roads; Mr. Dick Woodruff and Mr. Jack Banham planned the layout for installation, and Mr. Kurpil investigated the financing. The estimated cost was $10,000. A Vancouver contractor came to their aid by accepting, as part-payment, a portion of the bonds for installation of the line. The remainder were sold to residents of the district, their relatives, and friends. In 1932 the line was completed at a cost of only $9,000.

The North-West Telephone Company installed phones throughout the district. It was a joyful occasion, the dance that celebrated the lights. Electrical equipment salesmen went to town, selling pumps, washers, and household conveniences to eager homemakers. One housewife was elated to have used only 25 "killawacks" (kilowatts) for an entire month!

Mrs. George Beattie organized the Ladies' Aid Society, affiliated with the Powell River St. John's United Church Ladies' Aid, at an early date and held the meetings in her home. After Mrs. Beattie passed away, the ladies until they disbanded still held their meetings in the Beatties' home. The Aid specialized in carding wool, which they made into lovely quilts.

In 1927 the present bridge was built, eliminating the use of the old switchback. Because the new route adds a mile or more to the road, it is regrettable that the old bridge was demolished before the residents could put in a bid to have it left for pedestrian use. At that time Mr. J. Bigold started a bus service which he operated for three years, then sold to Mr. Van Vleet, who in turn sold to Mr. Joe Ward. He operated for only a short time, and then there was no bus or means of transportation, except by private car. In 1933 Mr. Joe Van Es bought his GMC 16-passenger bus and started his much-needed independent business. It soon expanded to a 33-passenger bus and then a 43-passenger bus, but that gave the commuters good service, toughing all of the main roads. The route has been altered and lengthened periodically to cater to the patrons, eventually turning the bus around at Mr. John Gibson's corner.

The water question that had never been completely dropped, came to the fore after an exceptionally dry summer, when wells dried up, adding to two disastrous fires and the fact that the residents of King Avenue, hard pressed for water and tired of waiting for a move from the district, decided to pipe water from a small spring that would only be adequate for their own needs. It seemed a shame to pipe water in for just a few families, so, they were asked to hold their plans while committees went to work in earnest on the water question. All available sources were thoroughly investigated, and it was finally agreed to pipe the water from Powell Lake. The district had water and sewage incorporated into the Light District by the three trustees: Mr. Herb Thomson, Chairman; Mr. Harry Hagan, and Mr. Ed Mannion. Later, Mr. Duncan Gibson went to work with the aid of their hardworking secretary, Mr. J.E. Hanson. With Mr. W. Jamieson as their consulting engineer, they drafted up their specifications. Financing was a big headache, as it was during the war and no assistance was forthcoming from the government.

The estimated cost was $40,000. At a meeting, a ratepayer suggested that if each tax payer bought $300 worth of bonds it could be financed in our little district. When a canvass was made, it was over scribed, so the work was started immediately. To cut down the cost, every Sunday groups of men cleared the pole line and dug the ditch to the lake. Horses were borrowed and poles snaked in. Mr. Hans Rud took over the responsibility of the building of the pump house and installing the pump. Mr. Harry Hagen took charge of the pipes and fittings, while Mr. F. Joncas erected the 50,000 gallon storage tank, and Mr. J. Missio saw that everything was painted. Mr. H. Lacatelli and Mr. A. Bombardir were the only two men on an assigned pay basis, and they had a big job, as there was no assistance for them in extra paid help, owing to the manpower shortage. Mr. H. Thomson was the virtual overseer and Mr. J.E. Hanson was kept at it, keeping supplies rolling in. Most of the householders dug their own ditches, in front of their properties, and all from the road to their homes. Fraternal lodges sent out members to dig ditches for their brothers who were ill or unable to do the jobs themselves. When the water system was put in, there were no houses on the hill above King Avenue. The only house over the hill was the house of "ill repute" at the corner of Chilco Avenue and Lois Street.

Wildwood has always been ready with a helping hand. When it was decided to fix up Sandy Beach (Gibson's Beach) for the children, the Wildwood Welfare League brought it up at a meeting. Volunteers immediately got together and fixed the road, built a bathhouse, and improved the beach so it would be safer and more attractive. Those who could not actually do the work donated money, gas, and lumber. It was rather a shock to find, after only one summer's use, that the bathhouse had been removed, board by board, and the only improvements that could not be carted off remained.

The Wildwood Welfare League became inactive. When the Ratepayers' and Welfare Association were organized, they took over the League's charter and incorporation. One of their first undertakings was improving the "Sunset" playground that has become an up-to-date park at the base of Scout Mountain. An active group of women organized the Wildwood Service Club. Their aim is church and welfare work. The PTA was reorganized. Sunday school was held in the school each Sunday. All social functions were held in the school, which always caused considerable controversy. The school trustees had full power to grant or deny permission for the use of the school. Dances and card parties were the main means of raising money for the community welfare and improvements. For years the League and before that, the Social Club, collected money at Christmastime and had a Christmas tree for the youngsters. Mr. Herb Thomson was usually Santa Claus. One year Mr. Zorzi as Santa thrilled the children by arriving in a sled, complete with sleigh bells on his prancing horse.

The fire that destroyed Sliammon nearly burned Wildwood. Bones of horses, trapped and burned, can still be found on the skid roads in the vicinity. Subsequent fires have touched the fringe of the district, then passed on and burned to the river mouth, causing anxious days and nights. The present fire department is made up of well-trained and conscientious volunteers. One of the original fire chiefs was Pat McCullagh. An ancient but reliable truck was well-equipped and kept in perfect running order. The air raid siren was used for a fire alarm.

Wildwood Stores
The first store in Wildwood was built in 1922 by Dr. Marlatt's father who also built the group of houses on the corner of Sutherland Avenue and LeMay (Lois Street). Mr. Marlatt operated the store until it was purchased by Mr. Leo Walker – about 1925. It was later taken over by Mr. and Mrs. J. Huxter, and then sold to Bell Brothers. Mr. M. MacCartney was also an owner. This store is now an apartment building.

Then a new store was built on the opposite corner by Arnold and Norah McQuarrie. Vito Massullo and Arnold were butchers in the store; Arnold McQuarrie was a fantastic accordion player. In this new building was Bert Torgerson's store, like present "Buck or Two". Bert had a sub-post office. In the same building Margarete Cantryn had a hairdressing salon – there was also a laundry.

The Laundry on Hillcrest Avenue became a bingo hall before it was made into apartments.

About 1925, Paul Kurpil erected a small store on the corner of Sutherland Avenue and Lund Street. He later built a large modern building with attractive living quarters behind the store. It changed hands several times, and then finally burned down. It was a most spectacular fire with the tin goods exploding like machine guns. A couple of years later, a store on LeMay Road (Lois Street), owned by Mr. M. Biden, also burned.

Hanson Brothers ran a very modern general store on the site of Mr. Kurpil's original building. Peter and Carmela Toigo eventually ran the store for years. First Nations from Sliammon used to shop there. Dave Payne used to drive the delivery truck for the Toigo's. The Wallaces operated the store after the Toigos. This building is now the **Red Lion Pub**.

The corner across from the Top of the Hill Grocery, with the new solid board fence, was the location of Ritchie's house and repair shop. Old-timers still call the corner, "Ritchie's Corner".

Mr. Bombardir and Mr. Wolford had plumbing shops.

The area where the **Tide's Trailer Park** is now was once known as the **China Block**. There were a bunch of rental houses there. It was owned by **Sing Lee** and the property ran right along King Avenue. Wildwood has beautiful soil, and in the early years most of the vegetables for Powell River were grown here. One time I took some beautiful apples home; my mother said they were from the remaining apple trees from the Chinese gardens. I had been in the bush behind Beattie's, towards Scout Mountain.

Wildwood Dairies

There were several prosperous dairies over the years; they delivered milk in Wildwood and other areas of the town.

Claudio and Maria Zorzi ran a dairy in Wildwood (moved there in 1917) on Lois Street. Their daughter Carmella delivered milk, butter, eggs, and chickens in a Model A truck. On the Zorzi property was a small building, close to the road (it is still there); this was a butcher's shop (from 1931) run by Claudio and his son, Sergio. Sergio left Wildwood in 1937 and went back east.

As a kid, when I walked to school and came around the corner out of the bush, this little building (the butcher shop) would have a chimney fire.

After the deaths of her son Peter (a talented accordionist – well known in the Italian community) in 1944, and her husband Claudio in 1945, Maria sold the dairy to **Gino Pitton**. The Pittons ran this Wildwood dairy in the 1950s.

In my time, **Jane and May McMahon** looked after the McMahon's Dairy on McMahon Avenue. Jane looked after the delivery of the milk; May was a registered nurse.

There was the **Lewis Dairy** run by the Lewis family. At one time there were ponies on the property for kids to ride.

Also the **Smith's Goat Dairy** at the corner of Smarge Avenue and Taku Street.

Wildwood residents will just about try anything – barnyards boast cows, goats, chickens, pigs, and turkeys; the Birds and Johnsons tried raising Chinchilla rabbits and the Banhams had a flourishing wormery that supplied lake fishermen with bait.

Wildwood Motors

Wildwood Motors is one of the oldest and most established businesses in Wildwood. It was started in 1926 by Sam Sasko and purchased by Harold Ford in 1946. In 1946, just three employees worked there.

In 1986, Don Ford was President and Sales Manager; he had the Nissan dealership. Other employees of Wildwood Motors, at this time, were: Robert Ford (General and Sales Manager), Dennis O'Malley (Parts Manager), Glenn Hartley (Assistant Parts & Service Manager), Joe Pisaila (mechanic), George Ferreira (mechanic), Ken Jenkins (mechanic), Chris Jones (mechanic's helper), and Bev Keddy (front end attendant). Andy Crawford eventually bought into the business.

Wildwood Churches

Eddy Erickson had a garage in the building that is now the **Apollo Apartments** on Lund Street. Prior to it becoming an apartment block, the garage was bought from the Shell Oil Company in 1951, and immediately converted into the Wildwood Pentecostal Tabernacle. The Reverend John York (the cowboy minister) started the church.

The first meetings of the Pentecostal Church in Wildwood were held in 1950 in the CCF Hall at the corner of Fraser Street and Sutherland Avenue (now apartments). Later, they rented the house at 6564 Sutherland Avenue and used the living room and front bedroom for the church and Sunday school before moving into Lund Street.

Following **Reverend John York**, the following ministers served in the Tabernacle in the 1950s: Reverend G. Kosner, Mr. Gordon Falconer, Reverend L. Blackmore, Reverend Forsberg, and the Reverend C. Preston. By 1960 the Pentecostal Church had 75 members.

The United Church had a small building at the bottom of Duncan Gibson's property on Nass Street (after WWII). Marlene Gustafson played the organ.

In 1947 the Catholic Church built St. Gerard's Catholic Church on the corner of King Avenue and Lois Street.

WWII

Besides putting in a water system with a shortage of much needed manpower, the little District of Wildwood did its bit for the war.

There was hardly a home that did not have one member or more away. The six sons from the John Gibson home set the record for one family in the Powell River District. Ten local boys gave their lives: Lucien Brooks, Ronny Baker, Willie Ditloff, George Ethofer, Dick Keaist, Aldo Bortolussi, Bill and Bud Daubner, John Bell, and Gus Eckman.

Organizations such as the ARP, under Mr. Jack Banham; the Red Cross; Mrs. C. Bird and first aid station; Mrs. Jessie Brown all kept the district regimented.

After WWII, a number of Dutch families came to Wildwood. The area they settled in was called Little Holland. **Mr. and Mrs. DeGroot** had one of the show places of the district with their rows and rows of colourful tulips imported from Holland. Painted over their door were the words, "A Labour Alcratte", Latin for "Labour Created". These words, "Labour Created" could well be painted on an arch over the road to the entrance of Wildwood, for practically all the homes were hewn out of the wilderness by their owners.

Mr. H. Boettger had a "Lilliputian" garden that the adults, as well as the children, loved to admire. He took the little tots by the hand and led them around the winding miniature roads, past mountains to a lake where small statues and benches had taken on a very realistic atmosphere. Everyone watched, with anticipation, as the miniature train weaved its way around the yard and through the mountain tunnels.

Looking Back with Arline Dear (Sing)

The Sing Family – Wildwood Village 1919-68

The Sing family lived in Wildwood from 1919 to 1968. George Sing was the last member to live there.

In the early years, Wildwood families had to rely on individual wells for water. It was a long time before a water system came to Wildwood.

Arline started school at age 7. She attended the first Wildwood school from 1926 to 1933. Arline recalls the following teachers: a Miss Beattie and a Mr. Buckpitt.

Arline and her brother Paul were athletic and participated in interschool sports. Paul excelled in the pole vault and Arline in the high jump. In the schoolyard, Arline remembers playing baseball and softball.

At Halloween, pranks were played. Arline will never forget, on one Halloween night some pranksters hanging a gate from the school flagpole!

Left: Bird residence, Lois Street, Wildwood District 1920s. Far right: Duncan Bird (WWII)
Photo: Duncan Bird

The Bortolussi family, King Avenue, Wildwood District 1920s.
(L to R) Marino & Amabile Bortolussi/Gino/Nellie/Aldo/Leah/Leo.
Insert: (L to R) Sergeant Geno Bortolussi (winner of sprint championship – Canadian Army overseas)/Sergeant
Aldo Bortolussi (killed on bombing raid over Germany).   Photos: Nellie Hunter (Bortolussi)

The Beattie family (from Wildwood) on a day trip to Lund 1964. Lund hotel in background.
(L to R) Mrs. Grace Beattie (Pember)/Joan/Douglas/Mr. Horace Beattie.   Photo: Grace Beattie

The Rud family home, Nass Street, Wildwood District 1940s. In 1926 Hans Rud bought two acres of land in
Wildwood for $250. He moved the old wharfinger's office to Wildwood and converted it into a house. In the late
1930s he built a new home for his wife Thora and their seven children: Paul, Louise, Elmer, Edwin, Walter, John,
and Margaret. Insert: Ed Rud 1930s   Photos: Ed Rud

Looking Back with Brian Crilly

The Higgins Family – Wildwood from 1915

"*My grandparents* **Tom and May Higgins** *were early homesteaders in Wildwood. Tom and May came from the Ottawa Valley. As a young boy, Tom had been indentured as an apprentice in filing saws.*

Tom was employed by the Powell River Company. He came in 1913 and worked on the dam. He worked for the company until the late 1930s.

At first, the Higgins family lived in the Townsite for two years. In 1915 they took up a pre-emption in Wildwood. It was a large acreage between Atlin and Chilco Avenues. While the house was being built **the family lived in a tent**.

Tom had teams of horses which he rented out. One horse was called "Paddy" – he had an unusual habit – he would lie on his back to be shoed!

After the death of Tom, May sold the main house to Dick Jacobs and she continued to live on the same property, in what had been a small rental house."

Looking Back with Don McQuarrie

The McQuarrie Family – Townsite, Wildwood & Paradise Valley

The McQuarrie family came to Powell River in 1918. Frank (Francis) (1871-1944) and Honor Hope McQuarrie (1875-1973) had four children: Christina (Clayton-Price), Elizabeth (Forset), Arnold, and Charles. In 1926 Dad (Arnold) married **Nora Patrick**; Charles (Bud) married **Iris Henderson**.

The McQuarries lived on Maple Avenue in the **Townsite**; before coming to Powell River, they lived in Sechelt. My grandpa was a logger and road builder there. My dad greased skids on the skid roads with bear grease – so the logs would slide easier as the oxen pulled them out of the woods.

Dad got a job with the **Powell River Company,** by answering an ad in the **Vancouver Sun** for a teamster. He was signed up by **Emil Gordon**. Dad played the accordion. He became a member of the first 25 year-club of the Powell River Company.

In the 1920s my grandpa, my dad, and my Uncle Bud all worked in the Powell River Company General Store.

My grandparents moved to **Paradise Valley** in the early 1930s. My grandfather, at this time, was building roads for the government. **Fred Salt had a blacksmith's shop on the property.**

My parents, **Arnold and Nora McQuarrie**, ran a store in **Wildwood** from 1942 to 1962. The meat counter was looked after by my dad and **Vito Massullo**.

Looking Back with Horace Beattie (1913-2008)

Wildwood Village (from 1917)

My father, George Beattie came to the Townsite in 1912. Dad and a brother-in-law helped build the first Henderson School which opened in 1913.

My father worked full time for the **Powell River Company** during the Great Depression. He and a Mr. Schram maintained and operated the sluice gates for the dam.

My family lived in the Townsite before we moved to a three-acre lot in Wildwood in 1917. I was just 4-years-old at the time (born 1913).

The Beattie family comprised of Mrs. Jessie Beattie (George's mother), George, and Belle Beattie and their three children: Dorothy, Alice, and Horace.

The pioneers called the area Wildwood. Back in those days Wildwood was pretty wild. A couple of fires had gone through, including the Sliammon fire, and there were black spars everywhere. The spars were really dangerous, especially for children walking the trails on windy days. During the Depression, men on relief were allowed to come in to cut down the spars for cordwood.

There was a post office in Bells' store. Bell Brothers had to use the name "Wildwood Heights" as a postal address because there was another Wildwood. When Charlie Bell sold out, there was no more post office.

Wildwood hill – the whole bank was pure white sand. We never came down the steps when we attended the old Henderson School. We slid down the hill and then emptied out the sand when we reached the playground.

My father **George Beattie, Frank Smith, and Harry Thomson** were all school trustees. They pushed for a school in Wildwood and finally got a one-room school in 1923. My first teacher at the Wildwood school was Miss Florence Lynch; the second one was Mr. Buckpitt.

Wildwood was shingle bolted out before we moved in. The Italians moved in at the same time as we did. We dug our own ditches.

Mother had a huge garden. Mother canned a lot of the fruit. Dad dug a huge hole and covered it with canvas – we stored winter vegetables in it.

Sing Lee had a vegetable garden on King Avenue. The property behind us was owned by Chinese; they grew a lot of vegetables. Chinese gave up gardening after WWII.

My mother bought a lot of salmon from **Sliammon First Nations**. Sometimes she paid 50 cents a fish, other times she traded clothes and food. She also traded for baskets and trays. Mother canned most of the salmon.

Once in a while my father hitched up the wagon and we drove to Sliammon and visited with **Mr. Basil Nicholson**, the school teacher and government agent there. The Nicholson boys attended the first Wildwood school.

We shopped at the Company store; for awhile Sing Lee had a store in the Townsite before moving to the Shingle Mill. My mother also ordered from the catalogue. Mill management did not like this, but could not stop it as the orders came in at the government wharf. Eventually, they went out of the grocery business.

We had Jig suppers in Wildwood – we ate corn beef and cabbage like Maggie and Jig in the comic strips. The money raised was used for the school.

Where the water tank is now – it used to be a cat house (1930s & 1940s).

Joe Van Es had a bus service – used to take the bus to work and back again.

Volunteers got together and built the first fire truck; there was a public library above the fire hall.

There were dances at the school house and Wildwood Hall. I was just a young boy when I learned, with my sister, to dance. At first no one outside Wildwood was allowed to attend the dances.

I knew **Rod LeMay**; he came to Powell River in 1907. I visited his studio in Lutsville. On one occasion Rod LeMay had made a bust of **Doctor Marlatt**; it looked exactly like him.

Andersens had a commercial greenhouse (from 1928), sold a lot of things; at the corner of Sutherland and Lund highway.

I started working for the Powell River Company in 1933. I earned 27 cents an hour to start with. I worked in the Powell River mill for 38 years as a papermaker. From 1933 on, a number of men were fired at the mill for their political views – some supported the CCF. They fired too many, so they had to hire some of them back. In 1937 the mill was unionized.

Wildwood is a country area where people enjoy living. It has very good soil; from King Avenue back, gets a bit lighter but where we are it is very good.

There used to be a lot of dairies in Wildwood. During the Depression the following dairies operated: the Pocock, Rockwell, Zorzi, Furness, and Pitton dairies. They sold milk around Powell River (Townsite) for 20 cents a quart. Cattle roamed at will – we fenced our yard to keep them out. Later, the pound law came in.

We had Cole oil lamps and an outdoor toilet. We had a grease trap; later, the sewer system did away with all that.

There was a Full Gospel Tabernacle – not sure how long it lasted; located where the apartments are now.

Nobody had a car for a long time in Wildwood. Later on (1920s & 1930s) there were one or two cars in Wildwood.

I've been to Italian Hall for a couple of wedding receptions. Wildwood Hall is now a private residence.

After I married in 1948, I moved in the little house on my parents' property. After my father died, we moved into the big house. We rented the little house out for a few years. We kept a couple of cows, chickens, and pigs.

I worked in the mill during WWII. The women liked working there – they had a steady job and got good pay.

After WWII more folks started to move into Wildwood.

It was a big mistake in 1955 when Wildwood joined the Municipality. We had money in the bank. A lot of people didn't vote; I was wishing afterwards I had driven people around to get the vote in. I voted against it. We haven't gained anything by joining the Municipality.

After the amalgamation the Municipality stole Wildwood's Christmas lights!

Looking Back with Ingrid Cowie (Andersen)

Andersen's - First Commercial Greenhouse in Wildwood (from 1926)

The Andersen family came to the Powell River **Townsite** in **1918**. **Jacob Andersen had a job with the Powell River Company.** Initially, they lived in a rented company house; however, in **1919 the Andersens started a farm in Wildwood.**

Memories of Wildwood

Dad worked for the company for 16 years before he was purged in the early 1930s. **Our entire family was blacklisted; this included my brothers Paul and Einar.** Eventually, Einar got a job on the tugs. One young man who was staying with us tried to get a job in the mill. He was told, if he wanted a job at the mill, to get his trunk out of the Andersens!

In 1926, my father built a big greenhouse on our property. Initially, he ran the nursery as a sideline but, after he was purged, he worked full time with the business. We had nursery stock, fruit trees, etc. My mother, **Karen Andersen** also worked in the greenhouse – planting seeds and caring for the plants. Dad had a Ford truck and delivered all the orders.

The greenhouse was heated by hot water; the boiler was fed with four foot logs. **Hans Rud** pumped the system. There was a water tank near the greenhouse which collected all the rain water.

Before electricity came to Wildwood, the well had to be pumped by hand – 100 pulls a day to get sufficient water. When electricity came in 1932, my father bought an electric pump.

Everyone in Wildwood bought plug-in radios when electricity came to Wildwood. We could have more than one radio in different rooms! One had to pay a licence fee for every radio owned and operated. A white van used to go around the village and word soon got out to hide the radios!

We now had electric light. I remember a special ceremony with my mother when we dumped the coal oil lamps over an embankment!

The Sing family owned the farm from Columbia to Lund Street. Chinese labourers worked on the farm. One time **Sam Sing** went on a visit to China. At Mother's request, he brought back a beautiful piece of silk to sew with. Mother used flour sacks to make clothes. When I was about 10, she made me an outfit, a top and bottom, out of two flour sacks.

Japanese children from the Shingle Mill attended Wildwood School prior to 1942. Wildwood pioneers, in the early years, used to row across the river. A bridge was put in so that the Shingle Mill could get its product (shingles) out to the dock to be sent to Vancouver.

First Nations from Sliammon came to Wildwood with fresh fish in a bucket. We were always told, *"Caught this morning!"* The fish were 25 cents each. On one occasion, I traded a good coat for a beautiful basket. On another occasion, I traded a gooseberry bush for a basket.

The cows in Wildwood had to be fenced out of the Wildwood properties. They roamed around the village. The cow herd from Sliammon also wandered around Wildwood. One time the Sliammon bull treed two men overnight. Pretty soon after that incident, the bull mysteriously disappeared.

Wildwood School

I first attended the old Henderson School before the one-room school in Wildwood was built. The janitor at the school used to raise the flag 10 minutes before school started, so we all knew we had just 10 minutes to get there when we saw the flag go up. If we were in a hurry to get there on time, we would just slide all the way down the sandy slope and end up tramping sand into the classroom. I attended old Henderson School from 1920-24. The last year at Henderson, all the Wildwood students were put into the basement. We were then in the same class with our brothers and sisters.

In 1924 we moved to the new one-room school in Wildwood. There were six grades in the one room. We had different teachers every year until Mr. Buckpitt came and he stayed for a few years. I remember the Nicholson boys in my class, Basil and Babe.

The school had no electricity or running water. Water was brought in a bucket from my place, the Andersen's. It was kept in an enamel container with a tap. We all drank out of it from the same cup! Near the school were two outhouses, one for the boys and one for the girls.

There was no real playing space for the children. The school was surrounded by stump piles. We played Anti-anti-I-over, Hide-and-Seek, Scrub, and Red Rover. A memorable trip was to Sliammon for a picnic on the beach there. I remember having races on the lawn in front of the Nicholson place; Mr. Nicholson was the teacher and government agent at Sliammon.

I graduated from Brooks in 1931 and then went to Normal School to train as a teacher. I taught at Galley Bay School from 1933-34. After the school closed at the end of the school year, I obtained a teaching position at Wildwood in 1934. Thus, I was now teacher in the school where I had been a student!

I taught at Wildwood School, now a four-room school from 1934 to 1937. Mr. Dawson was the principal and taught Grades 5 and 6. Bessie Bemrose taught Grades 3 and 4, and I taught Grades 1 and 2. The extra room was used as an activity room. In 1937 I married and left the school.

I was asked to teach again at Wildwood School during the war years (WWII) from 1942 to 1946 and was principal from 1945 to 1946. By then, there was running water and electricity. The children saved their pennies to buy war bonds. They bought stamps with their money. It entailed a great deal of book work to keep track of their savings. There were Red Cross sales to raise money for the war effort. I recall two of the principals: John Lidstone and Mr. Devlin. Mr. Devlin later became the principal at J.P. Dallos. Edna Freeman, Miss Kennedy, and Mr. Dupe also taught at Wildwood.

Looking Back with David Myers

Wildwood – the Price Family (from 1920s)

David **Myers** has happy memories of visiting his maternal grandparents, **Mr. and Mrs. Hedley Price** (Ma and Pa Price) in the **Wildwood** home. The house was located between the fire station and the old Wildwood Hall (now a residence) on a large 20-acre lot. The Prices kept cows and chickens. They had lots of fruit trees on their property.

David recalls sleeping over at his grandparents' place and waking to the smell of propane and oatmeal porridge.

Prior to moving to Wildwood, during the 1920s, Pa Price had worked in the limestone quarry at Blubber Bay on Texada Island. During the 1930s, he worked on the roads in Wildwood.

Ma and Pa Price had 13 children. Lois Price (David's mother) was the second eldest of the girls, born on Texada Island in 1908. At age 18, Lois worked in the Townsite Post Office.

Ruth Price, the eldest girl, married Bill Rickson and they lived in Wildwood. Before and after the war, Bill drove bus in Westview. During the war he was a driver for the military in the Canadian Armed Forces.

Looking Back with Duncan & Peggy Bird

Memories of Wildwood:
Duncan Bird (from 1926) Peggy Bird (from 1945)

Duncan Bird:

My dad bought our property in Wildwood in 1923 and we moved up in 1926. The old house was here; an Italian family had lived in it. To get to his property my father walked up all the steps on the Wildwood hill. I was just 6 years-old when I came to Wildwood. The area had all been burned off, all the way from Lund.

My dad worked as a wharfinger for the Powell River Company.

My mother shopped at the Company Store. It cost my mother 25 cents for a taxi from Powell Stores to Wildwood.

Wildwood School

There was a great big stove in the school. All the wood was brought in by hand; the kids passed it along – like a huge conveyor belt.

Some of the kids went to school in bare feet. It was the Depression years. I went to school with Nellie Hunter (nee Bortolussi). In my class was a Japanese girl. Her mother used to cut my hair at the Shingle Mill for 25 cents.

One time the principal took us down the road – there was a cow in a ditch and he showed us how the cow chewed its cud. We took up tree samples and had them growing on the window sills. The principal was very keen on nature and taught us a lot.

Joe Bigold started a bus here in 1930; it was taken over by Joe Van Es. Charlie Bigold grew up in Wildwood. He worked in the mill, then quit and worked for himself – he went logging. Charlie worked on Wildwood's first fire truck.

I attended Henderson School at one time. The Wildwood kids went on the school bus. Old Joe Van Es was the bus driver. He was a character – wouldn't stand any rowdiness. Any backchat from the kids and he'd stop the bus at the bottom of the Wildwood hill and dump the troublemakers off!

Goats

Nellie and Hubert Smith kept goats. Their goats got into Daubner's greenhouse and chewed up all the tomato plants. Hubert was a bus driver on the Westview run.

Hubert Smith had goats. He drove the bus for people out at Lund. He worked for Van Es. One time he came home late and left the bus door open. The next morning the alarm clock went off and he went to pick the bus up in a hurry. He got on the bus and was all the way down the Wildwood hill – and then he discovered his goats were in the back of the bus! Of course, he had to turn around and take them back to his place.

Wildwood – electricity

Before we had electricity we had kerosene lamps in Wildwood.

Wildwood pioneers organized for electricity at the Wildwood School. They hand dug all the post holes for the electricity. People had to go up the poles and put up all the wiring. This was the first precious thing that came to Wildwood.

People started putting in electrical things – like washing machines, electric stoves, and heaters. The lights came first, and then folks started thinking of pumping water up the hill later.

Wildwood – water system

Water came from One Mile Bay (as kids we used to swim down there). Carpenters covered the pipes up in box and filled it full of sawdust to prevent freezing in areas where they could not bury it. The water still comes from One Mile Bay. We put a big tank on the top of the hill.

Water system – it was most important for our community. Wildwood folks got rid of their wells. A lot of people had outside toilets. They had to put in a sewer line as well as a water line – and a discharge line. Up on the top road, the houses there still have septic tanks.

Wildwood Stores

There was a post office in Bell's store. First owner, before the Bells' was Jimmy Huckster. Martin McCartney was in charge of the Bell store in 1945. Carmella Toigo (nee Zorzi) worked as a helper for a short time. When the store finished, the post office finished. We now get door-to-door delivery.

McQuarries had a store on Sutherland and Lois. Mr. Zorzi had a butcher shop, Jack Evoy was the butcher – made the best sausages I ever tasted – never had any as good since.

Mrs. Toigo owned the store on the corner where the pub is today.

Once a week Nelson's Dry Cleaners picked up and dropped off items in Wildwood.

Pitton family ran a dairy and farm; for years they delivered milk around the district. It was taken over by the Lewis family.

McMahon had a farm and they delivered milk around Wildwood.

Erickson's had a dairy. Ed Erickson made his deliveries on a bike. Sometimes the milk froze, and the cream was pushed off the top of the bottle. If there was sufficient extra cream at Christmastime, it was left on the doorstep as a present.

Sing Lee used to pump water from a spring that Duncan's dad witched on the now Clancy property.

At one time there were no numbers on the houses in Wildwood. Then somebody came in (-here today and gone tomorrow) and made a survey. That's how we got the names and numbers we have today. Lois Street was originally LeMay Road.

Gibson's Beach (Sandy Beach)

Gibson's Beach was originally called Sandy Beach.

Ken Gibson worked in the mill and when he passed away; his ashes were placed by one of the big maple trees on Sandy Beach. It then became known as Gibson's Beach.

Wildwood Hall

We went to dances there. It's next to the old fire hall. Lots of meetings and dances held there. That property has since been sold and made into a nice house.

Wildwood cattle

I remember when the cattle roamed around Wildwood. My dad had a gate at the front of our yard, put a chain in there. A cow belonging to Tonny Ethofer managed to get in. She was right there in the garden eating Dad's corn.

The cows just wandered around Wildwood.

First Nations had cows and they used to come up to Wildwood and grazed on top of the Wildwood hill. The kids were afraid of the Sliammon bull.

Then they (First Nations) took the cattle over to Harwood Island. There were cattle over there for years, but eventually they all got shot.

Joncas lived in a log cabin across from the Wildwood garage; he had 80 acres. He worked as a blacksmith in the mill. He was an interesting old fellow.

Valentine – he got fired from the mill. His wife ran a little store and made a lot of baking. She went door-to-door; she bottled fruit and only got 10 cents a bottle. She made root beer and ginger beer. He went fishing.

Herb Thomson had a lot to do for Wildwood. We would not have the park up here today if it hadn't been for Herb.

Salmon went up the stream to Nellie Smith's, almost extinct now. Salmon also went up Sliammon Creek.

Postscript: After World War II: Duncan & Peggy Bird

Peggy came out as a war bride to Wildwood. During the war, Peggy had corresponded with Duncan Bird who was in the Navy.

Peggy met Duncan for the first time after the war was over. Duncan had been demobbed and they met at the railway station in Edmonton. Duncan was en route to Vancouver – final destination, Powell River.

They continued with their correspondence and Peggy came out to Vancouver. They kept on meeting and finally Duncan proposed, words to the effect,

"It was expensive to keep on meeting – we might as well get married!"

Duncan's mother subdivided the Bird property in Wildwood and gave one lot to her son. Duncan began building their present house in 1945.

1946 earthquake – the newlyweds were still in bed. Peggy recalls the perfume bottles rattling on the dressing table. Neighbours told them they had missed all the excitement; the road rolling in waves and chimneys turning around.

Duncan and Peggy's five children attended Wildwood School. Peggy belonged to the Wildwood PTA and became a grandma to generations of students. One time Peggy moved the picture of the Queen to a new location in the school. One little boy, looking up at the Queen, made the comment,

"Oh good, we now have a picture of Mrs. Bird in the school!"

Duncan and Peggy belonged to the Goat Club. Other members were Herb and Nellie Smith, Bob and Freda Stutt, and the Moores. One time they made a float for

Labour Day – all the kids dressed up. The Wildwood Goat Club float won $100 for first prize!

The Birds kept chickens, goats, and at one time chinchillas. The chinchillas were sold as a quick rich scheme – never did work out.

Looking Back!

Powell River was a wonderful place to bring up a family – lots of freedom. Remember Joe Van Es who drove the bus – he smoked cigars. He was a good man – stopped at the house with Christmas parcels instead of the bus stop.

Looking back – the biggest change is the mill economy in the town. At one time over 2,000 employees, today just a few hundred.

Looking Back with Ed Rud

The Rud Family of Wildwood (from 1926)

Hans Rud was originally from Norway. After learning the steel trade in Norway, he immigrated to the U.S.A.

In 1916 he came to Canada to install a sawmill near Prince George. After installing a big flume in Chase and working in the Beaver Cove pulp mill, he came to Powell River in 1923 to put the felt washers on the old paper machines in the mill. Hans liked it so much in Powell River, he decided to stay. **In 1926 Hans Rud bought property in Wildwood** – at the same time he bought a Fordson tractor to clear the land.

He moved the wharfinger's office from the old wharf and converted it into a house for his family on the Wildwood property. When his sons were old enough to use a hammer and saw, Hans tore down the old house and built a big, new house. The chimney was built of stones from a nearby island. Teak, from the warships in the breakwater, was used to trim the hardwood floors. The main room was "as large as a ballroom".

Hans worked hard for the Wildwood improvement district. He was one of a dedicated group of pioneers who pushed for electricity and water.

Hans and Thora Rud had seven children: Paul, Louise, Elmer, Edwin, Walter, John, and Margaret.

Walter, Elmer, and Edwin went into the logging business. Walter owned his own outfit. Elmer and Edwin went into business together at Sullivan Bay. Hans was always there to help with advice and the repair of the machinery.

Ed Rud:

*"My father was a millwright for the Powell River Company from 1922-50. He got 80 cents an hour. Our family lived at 220 Oak Street in the **Townsite**, before buying land in **Wildwood**. He paid $250 for two acres on Nass Street. There were lots of stumps – took lots of stumping powder to clear the land. We used a 24-horse power tractor in the clearing.*

*I remember the **Great Depression**. Everybody was in the same boat. We got $30 for a cow. One year we had 15-16 pigs. It was a gravy train (in the Powell River area).*

Tough times when the papermakers got the boot in the 1933-34 purge. Some stayed here; some went fishing, most got back in.

Story went around here that New Zealand and Australia wouldn't buy the paper if the mill didn't get unionized – they bought quite a bit of it.

War (WWII) changed everything – people went to work in the shipyards. Couldn't pull those tricks off anymore (intimidation and firing without due reason by management).

*There were three or four dairies in Wildwood. Old **Pitton** had a few cows. He had 15-18 milking cows. He bought most of their feed; it came up on the Union Steamship.*

There was no pound law, cows just roamed and the bull went all over – even to Lund. The pound law came in - $5 if your cow got into someone else's yard!

***Mary Masales'** father had a cow that got loose and headed down the road (from Southview) to Wildwood. The **Sliammon cows** – 16 of them – would get loose and come all the way to Wildwood. They'd eat the feed at the side of the road.*

Mum shopped at Powell Stores when we lived in the Townsite. In Wildwood, Mum shopped at Kurpil's. Kurpil's had a truck – they delivered orders.

Huxtor's had a corner store; sold out to McQuarries. Walker ran a store for Emil Gordon. Huxtor bought off Emil Gordon. Bells took over after Huxtor's.

Bell's store had a post office. Dad picked up the mail at the Townsite.

Mother made clothes; she had a sewing machine. She also bought clothes through Eaton's – they came through the mail.

Sliammon (First Nations) came round trading for clothes. They sold fish and clams for old clothes and cash. Had it pretty tough – not allowed to have a fishing licence. Pretty rotten system we had.

Old-timers have all died off. Old **Jameson** had the Shingle Mill – he was a character and-a-half. Called him Doc Jameson – didn't know if he was a doctor. Yes, they cut a lot of shingles down there (Shingle Mill). I went to school with Japanese kids (from the Shingle Mill).

Chinese at Wildwood, Grief Point, and Paradise Valley. **Sing Lee** owned property in Wildwood; today it is the Tide's Trailer Park.

1932-33 got electricity in Wildwood. Gas lamps were always going haywire – not as good as they are today. Had to strike a match to see if it was burning. We wired our house.

We had a water system (1945) and a well – lots of water, good water. We had an outhouse and septic tank for a short time. People bought water bonds, yes, we bought them.

Then Municipality took over (1955) and dissolved it (Wildwood District). **Herb Thomson** didn't want to join Westview. He wrote letters to Victoria. Herb was boss of Public Works (1930s), the road gang – the relief gang. He took over after **McQuarries**.

Cat house (House of Ill-Repute) was still there (1930s & 1940s).

I was a logger. I worked nine months in the mill – couldn't stand that place. We had our own gypo outfit. I was called up in 1944 but I got a deferment. My brother was in the Army and he got out in 1946. We both worked in the woods – bought a machine and started our own gypo (logging) outfit. We quit in 1973.

Mum (born 1889) died in 1981 when she was 92 years of age.

Everything changed after WWII – more houses. Westview changed the names of the streets."

Higgins family, Wildwood 1937.
(L to R) Eileen/Mildred/Norma Higgins.
Front: unknown boy.
Photo: Brian Crilly

Wildwood Hall, Wildwood, Powell River 1990.
The hall was built in 1930s by a group of CCF (NDP)
volunteers. It was a popular spot for Saturday night
dances with a live five-piece band. 1962 – sold. 1976 –
purchased through the sale of bonds by the
Commonwealth Holdings Society. Today it is a private
residence. (L to R) Laura Russell/Ernie Hunter/
Rommi Kliauga/Nina McLeod.
Photo: Private collection

Pioneers Golden Jubilee 1960
(L to R) Mr. & Mrs. Art Johnson/Mr. & Mrs. Hazelton/Bessie Banham.
Bessie Banham – Wildwood resident – writer – historian.
Powell River News and Town Crier photo. Courtesy of Glacier Ventures. Photo: Powell River Museum

The Smarge family: Townsite – Cranberry – Wildwood pioneers.
Photo: George & Agnes Smarge with their children Louise and Charlotte, Wildwood 1916. 1910 George Smarge hired by the Powell River Company. 1911 the Smarge family lived at 160 Maple Avenue. Louise Smarge was the first child to be born in the Company Townsite. Photo: Private collection

Looking Back with Jack Banham

Memories of Wildwood (from 1920s)

Jack Banham (2008):

My parents, **Jack and Bessie Banham** were married in 1922. They probably got the **Wildwood** property around that time. They built the house in 1925. My paternal grandparents never lived in Wildwood.

My mother, Bessie Banham, was well known for her interest in the history of the community. She wrote many historical articles for the ***Powell River News***. Bessie was involved in Wildwood's community affairs; she was secretary – treasurer of the Wildwood Welfare League, a trustee of the Wildwood Light District and a charter member of the Wildwood PTA. In 1961, **Bessie Banham received the Good Citizen Award**.

We kept cows, pigs, ducks, and chickens. We rarely bought milk from the dairies. Mother was really into birds - she raised bantams, geese, guinea fowl, chickens, and turkeys. She had a .22 gun; she was always taking a pot-shot at something in the yard.

During the 1930s, **Jimmy McEndoe** came out one time and wanted fish worms for the guests at **Rainbow Lodge**. My sister and I dug some up and put them in a tobacco tin – he paid us two bits! My mother thought it looked pretty easy money, so she had places all over the yard where she fed the worms. She then dug them up and put them into butter boxes and **Jack Wilson** would take them up the lake if there was a pretty big party at the lodge.

Gino Pitton delivered milk to the **Rodmay Hotel** for many years. He gave up farming in the 1950s. For three years he worked in Powell Stores; he was quite elderly at the time. The old man subdivided the original 40 acres and gave his kids a chunk.

I grew up here and went to school in Wildwood. I chummed with **Ed Rud** when we were kids; we hiked together. He went into logging.

I shall always remember how the school bus driver, **Joe Van Es**, used to get mad at the kids on the school bus. Often, he would stop the bus at the top of the Wildwood hill and give a speech. One time the kids really wound him up and he deliberately missed a few stops, and when we reached the top of the hill the kids were shouting, *"Speech! Speech!"* He left all the kids off at Bell's store. He lost his licence for awhile and had to hire drivers. **Bigold** was the driver before Joe Van Es.

As a kid, I had a paper route in Wildwood and the Shingle Mill – knew every family in the late 1930s.

Airplanes were a real novelty in the mid-1930s. If we heard a plane coming into Powell Lake, all the kids would tear down Wildwood hill to see it.

Herb Thomson owned the homestead from the school to Lois Street. He sold a big chunk, facing Lois Street, to **Dr. Marlatt**.

Pittons lived up the street; owned the top corner. They bought off Marlatt. They had a dairy there until they became too old to handle it.

The trailer park on Wildwood hill – **Tommy Higgins** lived there. He had a wood business and a whole bunch of rental houses.

The other trailer park is on property owned by **Sing Lee**. It was originally a big garden all along King Avenue and way up to Columbia Street. All the workers were Chinese in the 1930s, until the start of WWII. They used to go around the Townsite selling vegetables. Before the Wildwood water system came in, Sing Lee had a good well. This area was called the "China Block". A number of houses were rented on the property.

1920s – Wildwood was fenced in – before my time. **First Nations** had lots of cattle which roamed around Wildwood. They used to roam around our fields. My mother and sister used to hide in the house. Erickson was pound keeper.

Lewis Dairy – bought milk to the mill in the late 1950s. **Wolfy Gibson** drove the mill truck. When brass was being poured, the workmen were given milk. Otherwise, the men could get the shakes from the fumes. The milk stopped the shakes.

Zorzi had a farm; he had quite a garden. He had a butcher's shop at the house.

The **Pickerleys** lived at the blueberry farm.

The **Price** house was between the Wildwood Hall and the fire hall. Price was a good carpenter – he and Thomson built the first Wildwood Bridge. You can still see the original bridge when the lake is low.

The Gibson's lived nearby. **Gibson's Beach was named after Kenny Gibson** – he was a city councillor. It was originally called **Sandy Beach**.

Dance hall (Wildwood Hall) was the original **CCF Hall**. It was built on donations.

The post office was named "Wildwood Heights" because another post office was named "Wildwood". ONLY the post office was named Wildwood Heights. Charlie Bell ran the post office. Nice logo of a bell on the store.

1932 – Electrical system came in. Thomson had meetings down at my dad's place – where to put the poles and transfers in. My dad involved every housewife in the push for an electrical system.

Remember one time, in the early 1930s, my father was asked to do an electrical job at the cat house. He didn't want to be seen going in and creating the wrong impression, so I was brought along and left outside. Anyways, I was given a dog. It was always a joke in the family where the dog had come from!

Never went to the Papermaker's Ball at Dwight Hall.

Late 1940s – knew **Nick Hudemka**. He was a trapper, quite a guy, had a cabin on Second Narrows and at the Head of the Lake.

In the early 1950s I towed a scow to **Rainbow Lodge**. They were getting some high profile guests and needed extra beds.

Rod LeMay was a great friend of my mother's (early Townsite years). He had a photo studio near the golf course. One time, I was in hospital and Rod LeMay was in too. He was old, old, old. He was bedridden. Mum brought him a bottle of beer.

I was in the merchant navy during WWII. I married **Irene Pitton** in 1950. Her family owned the **Wildwood Dairy**. Irene recalls washing hundreds of milk bottles in the dairy.

1955 Amalgamation of Townsite & Villages

Westview was up to its neck in debt. Wildwood and Cranberry had money in the bank!

*Charles Rushant, Powell Lake with catch of the day -
1930s. Powell Lake, close to the Townsite, has been a
favourite recreational playground for Powell River
residents for many generations.
Photo: Herbert Rushant*

*Irene and Bert Pritchard, Powell Lake 1919.
Photo: Carol Pritchard*

Looking Back in Wildwood

The Cat House on the Hill (1930s & 40s)

Old-timers from the 1930s and 40s recall stories about Wildwood's famous "cat house" – the House of Ill-Repute. The ladies on the hill visited Madame Loukes 5th Avenue Dress Shop and ordered beautiful (and very expensive) gowns.

Frank Haslam 2008 (age 103):

"I delivered coal up there one morning and was told to come back in the afternoon! Of course, the ladies were asleep.

Dr. Marlatt occasionally went up there, during the day, to give the ladies a medical checkup. The madam in charge was called May. There were four or five ladies living there."

Eunice Sawchuk (2008):

"Sometime in the late 1950s, my husband bought a house in Wildwood. We were informed later, after the sale, that it was the "cat house"! The house had a large entrance hall and main room plus nine small bedrooms. The kitchen wasn't up to much. In the basement, hams and meat were hanging up. There were also bottles of whiskey and homemade Italian wine. We never lived in the "cat house". We later resold it."

Roy Leibenschel (2007):

"I used to make deliveries to the "cat house" in Wildwood during the 1930s and 40s. One time I left my cap there. My parents got a phone call regarding the cap – I had some explaining to do! There was a "cat house" in Cranberry during the 1930s on Drake Street. It was a little house behind Joe Derton's poolroom."

Duncan Bird (Wildwood 2007):

"It came up at a meeting (1930s) regarding putting the lights as far as the "cat house". One Wildwood pioneer, an Englishman, said:

'I'll go back to England if you give them lights up there!'

Herb Thomson replied,

'We need those girls a lot more than we need you!'

Electricity went to the "cat house" and the Englishman went back to England.

During WWII big freighters and tugs came to Powell River (Townsite) from all over the world. Sometimes, crew members took a taxi ride up the Wildwood hill to visit the "cat house"."

Angelina MacMillan (Piccoli) – 1987:

Looking back at Emil Gordon's laundry at the Shingle Mill (1920s):
"There was a sorter when the clothes came in. You could only have whites with whites. Then there was a bag that was taboo and that came from a special house in Wildwood (the "cat house") and no one was allowed to touch that bag and it was put in the wash by itself!"

Powell River Old-Timer (2008):

"One elderly lady I knew referred to the House of Ill-Repute as the House of Joy!"

Dorothy Loukes (nee Raye) and Jack Loukes (1987):

(Madame Loukes was Jack's aunt by marriage. Dorothy did alterations and dressmaking for Madame Loukes in the 1930s).

"All the girls in the House of Ill-Repute came to Madame Loukes for their clothes, which she bought especially for them. One of Jack's jobs was to drive the girls down to the store (5th Avenue Dress Shop on Marine Avenue) for their fittings.

The dresses that the girls on the hill wore were really gowns. The girls had the pick of the stock at Madame Loukes store. They chose only the very best and only had the best of makeup from the drugstore.

When Jack delivered the clothes back to the House (of Ill-repute), Dorothy was allowed to go along for the ride but she was not allowed in the house! She had to stay in the car.

They were all lovely girls, but the one that was having her 21st birthday (on one special occasion) was the most beautiful girl that Dorothy had ever seen. The "madam," of the house on the hill, was a very gentle lady."

Looking Back!
Vito Massullo – Wildwood from 1933

Vito was born in Italy in 1925. He was only 8 years-old when he came to Canada with his mother in 1933. He was unable to speak English, but very quickly became fluent when first attending Lund School in 1933, and later James Thomson School in Wildwood.

Vito's father, Michele (Mike) Massullo was born in Italy in 1905, and died in Powell River in 1976 at the age of 71. His mother, Emilia was born in Italy in 1907, and died at age 84 in 1991 in Powell River. Vito has two younger siblings, Jim and Mary.

Mike Massullo came on his own to Powell River in 1933, a few months before his wife and son. He rented a place at the Shingle Mill and worked in the grinder room at the mill. He worked there until he retired from the **Powell River Company**.

The family initially lived at Lund because relatives were living there (DeVitos). They then moved to Wildwood. His father had help building a house at 5868 Nass Street. The family kept goats, sheep, and rabbits. Vito remembers drinking goat's milk. The family put in a large garden. Every year they made wine; it was stored in a 60-gallon barrel. Sometimes, the family raised a calf for beef. In the fall, Vito liked to go moose hunting in the Interior. He cut and wrapped his own meat.

As a young boy in the 1930s, Vito worked at Bell's store delivering groceries. He remembers delivering groceries to Rod LeMay – Vito remembers "he was not young".

Vito attended and graduated from Brooks School in the Townsite. He remembers taking the bus driven by Van Es.

During the "Dirty Thirties" Herb Thomson was in charge of highways in Wildwood. Vito worked for him, digging ditches – his only aid was a shovel! Vito worked on the Wildwood water line in 1942, digging ditches from Powell Lake to where the large storage tanks are located in Wildwood.

Vito worked as an extra hand, scything the hay at McMahon's farm in Wildwood. The hay was brought to the barn by horse and wagon. It was left loose and not put into bales.

Vito became a logger. He owned timber rights in Okeover Arm; he knew old man **D'Angio**.

Looking Back with Nellie Hunter (Bortolussi)

Wildwood Pioneers – the Bortolussi Family (from 1933)

Marino Bortolussi came to Canada in 1920 and his first job was building the Canadian railroad. His second job was working in the Alberta coal mines at Brûlé. When the mine closed down, he came to Powell River and worked in the **Shingle Mill** for **Doc Jameson**.

Marino and Amabile Bortolussi had five children: Gino, Nellie, Aldo, Leah, and Leo. When the family first came to Powell River they rented a house at the Shingle Mill. **From 1931-32 they lived in a house on Riverside.**

In 1933, Marino bought a one-acre lot with a house and three two-roomed rentals, in Wildwood, for a cost of $1,000. The rentals had no running water or light and the rent varied from $3 - $5 a month. Water came from a well and there was an outdoor toilet.

The family kept a cow, goats, and chickens and grew their own vegetables.

Marino belonged to the **Italian Hall Society**. In the 1930s and 40s Nellie recalls attending picnics at Myrtle Point with the Society. They brought their own food and played bocce.

Nellie attended Wildwood and Henderson schools. After completing Grade 8, Nellie was needed at home to help with the family. A neighbour, Fred Brooks, used to pick up grocery orders through Woodward's department store from the wharf.

Prior to WWII, **Gino and Aldo Bortolussi** were well-known lacrosse players. **Gino and Leah Bortolussi** played softball after the war. Gino was also a well-known sprinter. During WWII, Gino represented the Canadian Armed Forces in 100-yard sprint relays. In 1942 & 1943 he was Canadian Army sprint champion. In 1949, an All-Star selection for track-and-field included Gino Bortolussi.

Aldo Bortolussi was an air tail gunner in WWII and was shot down over Germany.

During WWII, Nellie worked at **McCartney's General Store** in Wildwood. Because of the war, the shelves were not well stocked; items such as sugar and butter were hidden away, out of sight. These items could only be purchased with coupons from a ration book. **Mr. Evoy** also worked at the store as a butcher.

Not too far down the street from the Bortolussi family was the house **Rod LeMay** lived in. He was a well-known photographer. Nellie remembers him as a "gentleman".

In 1941, Nellie married Gordon (Dint) Hunter. She bought her wedding dress at **Madame Louke's exclusive dress shop in Westview.** At the time of the sale Madame Loukes was wearing slippers. She looked at Nellie and said, *"I've just got the dress for you!"*

Dint Hunter came to Powell River in 1934 and worked for the Powell River Company. Prior to that, from 1931-33, he had worked in the shipyards in North Vancouver, making masts for sailing ships. In 1933 Dint worked in the kitchen, washing dishes on the CPR boat going to Alaska.

Before and after WWII, Dint worked as a pulp tester for the Powell River Company. He also worked in maintenance after the war; he retired in 1973. From age 60-65 he worked as security guard at the mill.

During the 1930s, Dint played for the Company baseball team. For every home run he made he was promised a dollar by Ketchum! Dint was also an outstanding back (defender) on the Powell River soccer field. During his years working for the Powell River Company he was a volunteer for the Company fire hall.

Dint was an aircraft technician for the Canadian Armed Forces in Burma during WWII.

In 1949, Dint bought a one-acre lot in Wildwood for $400. He later subdivided. One lot was later sold on to Paddy Behan for $400. Dint spent three years building his house and the total cost came to $8,000.

Dint volunteered to work for the **Wildwood fire hall** and in 1973, when he retired, he was **fire chief**.

Looking Back!

Dancing, prior to the war, was held at the Beach Gardens dance hall. On one memorable occasion, Nellie and Dint won the first prize for dancing the Lambeth Walk. They also enjoyed the shows at the Patricia Theatre and attended dances at Dwight Hall.

The Behan residence at the Shingle Mill 1940s.
Insert: Pat Behan (1907-1968) on the Michigan & Puget Sound railroad tracks between the Townsite and Michigan
Landing (Willingdon Beach Trail) 1920s.   Photos: Monica Pagani (Behan)

The Behan family, Shingle Mill 1942
Rear: Mrs. Marion Behan (Sheard) holding baby Tony. Middle: Tommy, Joe, Katherine (Kay)
Front: Monica, Jerry, Dorothy.   Photo: Monica Pagani (Behan)

Sing Lee store, Shingle Mill 1930s. Standing outside the store: Kay Behan/store employee called "cook" – also a butcher/Lil Bourassa
Photo: Monica Pagani (Behan)

Bert Frederick (Roy Leibenschel's cousin) delivering ice to the Sing Lee store 1937.
Photo: Roy Leibenschel

Looking Back with Daniel (Dan) Behan

The Behan Family – Galley Bay - Shingle Mill and Wildwood

Dan Behan, born in Powell River in 1943, recalls the Behan family coming to British Columbia nearly nine decades ago.

In the early 1920s, Dan's father, Patrick (Pat) Behan (1907-1968) travelled by train from Quyon, Québec to the British Columbia coast along with his siblings: Agnes, Rose, Viola (Vi), Merlin, James (Jimmy), Earl, and Dorothy accompanied by their father, Jeremiah Behan. Pat was 13 years of age at the time. Jeremiah's wife, Ellen, had tragically died during the birth of their youngest child, Eddy. Eddy was to stay in Québec and would join his siblings and father years later.

Jeremiah had contact with a brother-in-law named Ed Paquette, married to his sister, Susan. Ed Paquette had a logging outfit up near Galley Bay, outside of Okeover Arm. Jeremiah settled his family at Galley Bay. He and his sons went to work in the woods with their Uncle Ed. With time, they were able to grow vegetables in their own garden and hunt for deer and other game. It is possible that supplies were also brought up to the family from Lund. While the boys worked, the girls took care of the home and all of the chores that came along with that.

After Ed Paquette's death, Jeremiah may have stayed in Galley Bay forever. But the girls, desiring a social life, persuaded him to move into Wildwood. They crowded into a small house near property owned by Jimmy Behan. The girls, Agnes (McCullough), Rose (Flemming, Crosby) and Vi (Lee) soon married local boys.

Just prior to leaving the Galley Bay area, Dan's father Pat was injured in a logging accident. He was taken from Galley Bay down to the hospital in Powell River for treatment. Tragically, he lost a foot. He was 16 years of age. It was 1923. He never returned to Galley Bay. The accident did not deter him from working. He worked as a truck driver for Jameson at the Shingle Mill, and later for Goffin Logging Company. He also worked at the Powell River mill for a short time.

In 1927, Pat married Marion Sheard (1903-1987). Marion had come from Vancouver to visit two brothers who were working for City Transfer. Marion, originally from England, worked as a teacher for a short time in Porcupine Hills, Alberta. Pat and Marion moved into the Wildwood area, near where Pat's father, Jeremiah and the rest of the children had originally settled after coming from Galley Bay. They lived in Wildwood for a few years but moved down to the Shingle Mill because the rent was much more affordable. They had 12 children: Theresa (Bourassa), Mary, Paddy (P.J.), Tommy, Kathleen (Squizzato), Monica (Martin), Joe, Jeremiah (Jerry), Dorothy (Thiesen), Anthony, Daniel (Dan), and Yvonne (Morrissey). Initially, the family lived on the upper road, later moving to the big house down by the water. The boys slept upstairs, the girls slept downstairs. The children attended school in Wildwood and would later go to Brooks School.

Living at the Shingle Mill, Dan remembers playing "peggy leggy" with his friends; all that was required were two sticks and a scratch hole in a small trench. Dan also recalls losing a very close young friend. At just 8 years of age, Dan's friend Wayne Body had fallen into the lake right in front of their home. Dan's brother, Jerry, dove into the lake and pulled Wayne out. Though he tried, he was unable to revive him. The Shingle Mill was a close knit community. The entire village was in mourning.

At the Shingle Mill, the Behans had Japanese and Chinese neighbours (they worked at the Shingle Mill for Doc Jameson). The Japanese were moved out after the events at Pearl Harbour. After the war, families from Holland moved into the Shingle Mill area – The Mayenburgs, DeGroots, Stroomers, and others.

Marion shopped for 90% of her basic groceries at the Shingle Mill, at the Sing Lee store. The rest she purchased at the Company store in the Townsite. Mom (Marion) was always at the stove. She was a beautiful cook. She would often send meals along to other families who were even less fortunate than her own. Marion would help young mothers with their first children. Many would go to her for advice about their crying or ill babies. Marion was able to purchase a Singer Sewing Machine which she had to pay $3 per month for. She was known to sew swimsuits for children who did not own one.

The eldest sister, Theresa, was required to leave school at the age of 14 to help her mother with the rest of the family. Theresa also worked at the Shingle Mill. This was demanding, physical work. Her brother, Paddy, was also required to leave school to help support the family. Younger children did whatever they could to make a little bit of money, from babysitting to selling bottles. Some worked in the Shingle Mill, picking up shingle bolts for which they received 10 cents a piece.

Theresa was able to save enough money to purchase a piano. Extra posts had to be placed under the front stairs of the veranda to keep it from falling through the floor. Many songs were sung to entertain aunts and uncles. A few of the older boys scraped enough money together to buy the first family car, a Model A Ford. Paddy went to get his learner's licence and was told by the provincial policeman, "I've seen you driving all over the place for a couple of years; it's about time you got your licence!"

Kathleen, the third eldest daughter, had a job at the Sing Lee store. One of her jobs was to fill orders for Billy-Goat Smith. His orders were pretty general. Although, on one occasion his order included a request for a pair of gum boots, anything from size 9 to 12.

One evening Dan's father, Pat, was up at One Mile Bay, visiting his dear friend Lionel Battergil. Of course, they were having a few drinks; Billy-Goat Smith was there too. Billy Goat was a pretty "shifty" character, and in the middle of the night he took off in his boat without saying a word to his drinking buddies, and headed back to his own cabin at the head of Powell Lake.

Dan recalls the time when Billy-Goat was brought out by float plane after he died in May 1958. Sergeant Rothwell and Bertram Wilson (the game warden) towed the body on a float behind the plane, down the lake. It was too decomposed and smelly to be placed inside the plane.

Pat also knew Nick Hudemka. Nick was a well-known Powell Lake character. He lived in his float cabin at Second Narrows, near Rainbow Lodge, from 1938 to 1976. He had a trapline for nine miles to Joan Lake. Nick loved women and often bought them chocolates. Nick took a fancy to Kathleen Behan and told Pat that he wanted to marry her! Kathleen had other ideas and chose her own beau!

In 1952 the Powell River Company gave notice to all the families living at the Shingle Mill – saying they were going to raise the lake level and that the houses were a fire hazard. The houses (many of them shacks) were imploded, then bulldozed down. Tommy, the second eldest boy, was able to buy one of the houses for $150. He dismantled the house and transported the lumber, piece by piece, up to a small lot that he had purchased in Wildwood. Pat and Marion and five of their children moved back to the area in Wildwood where they had previously lived.

In June 1953, the Shingle Mill was demolished. Dan remembers helping other kids to dismantle it. The timber was used to build the Willingdon Beach Arena. The kids were promised a free skating ticket at the new arena for their help – Dan does not recall ever receiving one!

Dan worked in the Powell River mill for 32 years, the first 12 years in the finishing room, and the remainder as a millwright. His brother Tony also worked in the mill, in the grinder room for 14 years. The older brothers had gone into logging; however, Tommy and Joe did work for a short time at the Powell River Company. Kathleen and Monica worked, at one time, in the Powell River Company offices. The two sisters rented rooms in the back corner of old Doctor Henderson's house in the Townsite.

People from many walks of life had come to live at the Shingle Mill. It was a thriving community that has left many with wonderful memories!

Contributions also made by
Theresa Bourassa, Paddy Behan, Tommy Behan, Monica Martin, and Yvonne Morrissey.

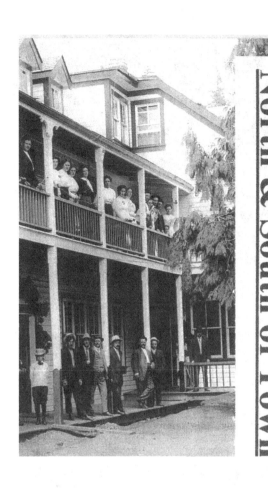

Malaspina Hotel, Lund 1913
Extreme right balcony: Mrs. Ida Thulin .
Extreme right ground level: Fred Thulin
Photo: Thulin album

Ida and Fred Thulin – wedding day 1908
Photo: Thulin album

Since 1891!

Lund Hotel

AND

Thulin Trading

COMPANY

Aerial photo of Lund hotel and harbour 1954. High ground rear: Lund School and Thulin barn.
Photo: Thulin album

Finn Bay 1912. Photographer: Rod LeMay Courtesy of the Powell River Museum
Insert: (Left) Adele Gustafson and her son Neil Gustafson. (Right) Alex and Adele Gustafson 1931 wedding -
Finn Bay farm.   Photos: Gustafson album

Looking Back with Ruby Victoria Thulin (Johnson) 1914-1996

Lund – The Thulin Brothers (from 1889)

Before the Powell River Company began building their pulp and paper mill in the Townsite in 1910, the Thulin brothers, Fred and Charles, had built a hotel at Lund in 1891-2, and obtained a licence to operate it in 1894.

Both brothers started building in Campbell River in 1904. In 1927, they divided the two businesses; Fred stayed in Lund while Charles moved to Campbell River.

In 1900, Fred married **Vira May Palmer**. They had three children: Oscar, Clarence, and Harold. After the marriage broke up, Fred married **Ida Emilia** in 1908. They had three children: Holger, Ethel, and Gerald.

In 1935 Fred Thulin died and his sons Holger and Gerald took over the management of the Lund hotel. After Holger Thulin died in 1954, Gerald, his wife Ruby, and their two sons carried on the family business in the 1950s.

Ruby Victoria Thulin (Johnson) – from a handwritten account – family archives
*"**Frederick (Fred) Gottfried Thulin** was born in Sweden on January 1, 1873. He came to America in 1889 and came to Vancouver on the 8th of March the same year.*

Almost immediately he left for Pendrell Sound to join his brother Charles where he was hand logging; they made up booms of logs which they shipped to Vancouver and sold to the highest bidder. With the money they made they bought the place called "Hole in the Wall" which they renamed Lund, after an old university city in Sweden in the province of Shini (Scania). They wanted the place to have a Swedish name and one that was easy for all to say and to spell.

At Lund they cleared the land and built a workshop. They worked long hours selling logs and wood to the tugs that came up and down the coast. They built a wharf and waterworks and sold water to the boats that called in. This was their hardest time, but also the most interesting time. They were soon able to purchase better machinery so they could do more extensive logging. By this time, more settlers had arrived and they needed a post office. They had the first post office north of Gibsons Landing. Beside the post office they had a general store beside the hotel. The Thulins also had a small shipyard at Lund where they built several tugboats and smaller craft.

***Charles and Maria Thulin left Lund and moved to Campbell River** where he started a business and a hotel; he owned 2,500 acres. He owned three hotels; one was the famous Willows, known to tourists from far and near. Charles built the dock, a drugstore, and the hotel, also the post office where he was postmaster for 30 years. They also had a shoe factory, a service station, and last but not least, a big farm where they had livestock etc."*

Looking Back with Adele Gustafson (Goski)
(1913-2008)

Finn Bay – Lund (1913-31), Wildwood (1931-46) and Edgehill (1946-2008)

Oscar William Goski (1884-1966) emigrated from **Finland** to Canada in 1910. He came as a skilled goldsmith, however, in order to make a living he logged and worked on the railroad to Prince Rupert. He later went into fishing.

His wife, Anna, and 2-year-old son 'Ahti' came out the following year. Adele and her twin sister, Helgi, were born in Comox in 1913. **The family settled in Finn Bay, Lund the following year.**

Tragically, Anna died in 1920 when the twins were 8 years of age. Her gravesite is on the Goski farm. Oscar, for a while, looked after the young children; later, Tati (aunty) Alma Salminen (from Finland) became housekeeper for the Goski family. Tati lived on the farm until her death and was buried there.

Ahti, Adele's brother, went to Russia in 1933 at the age of 18. Initially, he taught fishing; later, he worked as a tanker trucker driver delivering milk. In 1973, he came back to Canada for a six-month visit.

Oscar Goski obtained land from **John Hendrickson**; he was leader of the Finnish community at Lund and was the registered owner of pre-emption 1615 (160 acres) now known as **Baggie Bottoms** farm area.

By deed of sale, John Hendrickson sold a portion of his property (approximately 22 acres) to Oscar Goski on March 17, 1918. This property was legally surveyed in 1931 and formed Lot A & B, Plan 6365.

Hendrickson then sold Lot B along with the remainder of Lot 1615 to **Matt Nystrom** on November 26, 1931.

John Hendrickson died in December 1931 and his grave is located on the Nystrom property.

Matt Nystrom sold Lot 1615 and Lot B to **Violet Cummings**, in September 1935. Violet sold the remainder of Lot 1615 and Lot B to **John and May Elsworth** on May 12, 1938. The Ellsworth's sold Lot 1615 to **Bourassa Bros. Logging** and Mrs. Elsworth retained Lot B. Mrs. Elsworth sold Lot B to **Joan and Courtney Cressy**. Bourassa Brothers sold Lot 1615 to **David and Norma Butterfield**.

The Goski farm was originally 22 acres in size, today it is 18 acres and owned by the four children of **Neil Gustafson** (grandson of Oscar Goski). The property name "Annala" commemorates the many Anna's (neighbours, friends and family) associated with the history of the property.

Adele recalled John Hendrickson as a generous man and a good fisherman. His home was the gathering place for many Finnish newcomers in the area. It served as their initial home until they secured property to build their own homes.

The sauna was a necessity for the Finns and had other uses than bathing. Women often gave birth in the sauna; it also functioned as a distillery for making spirits.

The **Thulins** ran Lund store and delivered winter feed for the animals and basic household supplies, such as flour, sugar, and salt. They delivered by horse and wagon, on a logging trail, to the Goski farm.

Adele attended the Lund school with her twin sister. **Faith Rowe** (McGuffie) attended the same class. **Mr. Dippie**, the well-known Lund artist, worked at the Lund store. He was generous and nice. He had no hair on his head. He lived in a cabin on a beach near Sorensens. Adele sometimes bought five cents worth of candy at the store and Mr. Dippie generously filled a bag full of candies. On occasion, Dippie walked about the one mile from the Lund store to the Goski farm for supper.

In 1931, at age 18, Adele married **Alex Gustafson**. From 1931 to 1946 they rented a house, opposite the Wildwood school, from **Herbert Forslund**. They bought all they needed in Wildwood stores, owned by Kirpils, Bells, and McQuarries, with the exception of clothing, which was purchased in the Townsite. They kept cows and pigs.

Alex Gustafson worked in the grinder room (devil's hole) at the Powell River pulp and paper mill from 1930 to 1974. If the family could afford to go out they went to the Patricia Theatre in the Townsite (possibly once a month). It cost five cents on the bus to get there and five cents for the return journey. A special treat was ice cream after the show. Adele and Alex attended the Papermakers' Ball on New Year's Eve. Her sister Helgi, an excellent seamstress, made beautiful gowns for Adele.

In 1946, Alex Gustafson built a house in Edgehill. According to Adele, "they were living in the bush".

Looking Back with Adele Gustafson (Goski)

Memories of Finn Bay, Lund (1920s)

Finn Bay, as far back as I can remember, which is about 60 years and even prior to that, has provided a harbour for the fishermen of the B.C. coast. Bad weather was not always the only reason boats stopped there. It was a stopover for the fishermen from the Fraser River, Vancouver, and Gibsons area going north for the annual sockeye salmon runs at River's and other inlets. Many stopped just to rest overnight; others who had friends in the area would stop and visit before continuing on their way. On their return journey back home, many would stop again.

Tourists vacationing along the coast in their yachts, would often drop anchor in the Bay and stay awhile. We used to call them the "idle rich" and were suspicious of how they made their wealth.

Most of the people who settled in the Bay or the surrounding area were immigrants from Finland. Consequently, the name became Finn Bay. Most of them had learned a trade in their native homeland, but likely the lack of knowing the English language or that there was not enough demand to follow their own trade, they took to fishing for making a living. They felt they were their own bosses, and that it was a free life. No matter how you look at it, they did have to work.

They built homes, some right in the Bay and others not too far away, so as to be near as possible to where their boats were moored. There they raised their families and most remained for life. Some of the best and prosperous fishermen on the coast are native sons of Finn Bay where they learned the fundamentals of fishing right in its waters.

Many single fellows lived right on their boats, keeping Finn Bay as their home base; leaving only as different fishing seasons demanded and returning again to winter there; to them Finn Bay was home. Ill health forced some of them to leave because they couldn't cope under such conditions any longer. Few were fortunate to stay all their lives, dying right on their boats.

There were no disagreements over where each one should moor his boat. The ones who came first, chose their spot, anchored a buoy to tie to and that was their place until they chose to leave of their own accord. When anyone left his place, another took over, according to mutual agreement by everyone concerned.

The west side of the Bay was the side which was more protected from the weather, and so was favoured for anchorage and keeping live bait boxes sunk and tied.

Nets and fishing gear not in use were stored until needed, in the net houses which dotted the shores of the Bay. Most of them were shared by more than one. The one my dad kept his gear in was shared by three others. The dry docks, where boats were pulled up at high tide or painting was done by the fishermen, many who donated their labour when needed, were used by all. There was a blacksmith shop and a boat shop, at the head of the Bay, owned by **Andy Miettinen**, the father of a family that has lived in the Bay unto the second and third generation. In this shop he built many boats for himself and for his sons when they grew old enough to go fishing on their own. There was also a boat shop on the island at the mouth of the Bay (Sevilla). Wherever there are Finns there is also a sauna for every family. Finn Bay boasted of at least three, where many people enjoyed a real Finn steam bath and afterwards, the hospitality of the family over coffee or a meal. At times, these sauna parties became quite loud with raised voices, so more than steam in the head was suspected.

Some of the fishermen who kept their boats in Finn Bay lived a distance of a mile or two away on places that, in those days, we used to call stump ranches; my Dad was one of them. Many is the time I remember when in the middle of the "wee hours of the night" because the southeast wind had started to blow, he would arise and walk to the Bay by lantern light to check the boat. This happened often to the Lund fishermen who kept their boats there, when the westerly wind blew. They would have to move their boats to Finn Bay because it was a better shelter than the open Lund harbour which was unprotected by any breakwater then.

Each spring, the herring run in the Bay provided its people with food and bait for catching of larger fish such as cod. The herring were kept alive in live boxes, sunk in the water from which they were later scooped out by dip nets, into live boxes on boats and used when fishing for cod, from the several banks which were not too far away.

It seemed we ate herring for days, so I was always glad when the run was over; although I liked the taste of them, I hated the bones which stuck in your throat. There was also a time in the spring when the spring salmon were plentiful, and as we got older, we would hand troll for them around the mouth of the Bay during the Easter school holidays. Some of the boys who had energy enough to get up early for the morning bite, and again fished at night, made themselves a fair amount of pocket money.

I have pleasant memories of the summers at Finn Bay. The men, having gone to Rivers Inlet or whatever fishing they did up north, left the Bay empty of the regular boats and the women and kids to their own resources. Before leaving, the family men, who kept a cow or two, cut the hay that grew on their places. If the haying time happened to be rainy, the men often had to leave to get to the opening of the sockeye season before they had time to dry and store the hay for winter use. This often left some of it, if not all, for the women and kids to take care of. Happy was the day when the last of it was carried and stored in the hay barn.

It was then we could have some time for leisure, such as going down to the Bay to swim. Nudity was a culture not unknown to people even then, so we kids did our share of skinny dipping and sunbathing nude on the hot rocks at the head of the Bay, defiantly, even if there happened to be a yacht at anchor. If they didn't like it, they could very well leave we agreed. It was our beach!

When the men were away, Mrs. Miettinen would often set out a net to catch fresh fish for eating and sometimes some unwanted dogfish went into the net. She would tie a pair of them with a rope round their tails to a rowboat and have them tow us kids, zigzagging around the Bay. This to us, was a thrill equalling the terror movie *Jaws* of today.

Yes, Finn Bay offered us a wide choice of things to do. Often we would pick clams, which were plentiful at the beach, and cook them right there on an open fire in an empty coal oil tin and have a clam feast. Fishing for rock cod off the floats was fun. They were good for eating, too. Chasing us girls with a crab or a snake was a delight the boys enjoyed. They would daunt us to put a live crab in our mouths. I never dared to, but my sister thought nothing of it, so it left me to be the brunt of their teasing because they got a charge out of me.

The beach at the Bay was clean and unpolluted, but very rocky. To clear it, a raft was built from logs with planks nailed on top for a platform. At low tide the raft was loaded and as the tide came in, it was towed away and the rocks dumped close to where they were later used for building dry-docks, breakwaters, and as footing for walks around the Bay. This left the beach more attractive and easier for us to swim at, especially before we could swim well enough to venture into deeper water. I remember one time, us kids volunteered to load the raft by ourselves. So, all the time while the tide was out, we carried and loaded the rocks. But, as the tide came in and refloated the raft, it tipped and all the rocks, to our dismay, dumped back unto the beach. It was a lesson for us to load more evenly next time.

At least once in the summer, including the women folk, we managed to go for a picnic, usually not any further than to the island at the mouth of the Bay. Winds would whip up, even in the summer, suddenly, and as we depended on oar power alone, we were reluctant to venture far.

It was when the men folk were home that we would go to the surrounding islands on picnics. The first of May, which is an international labour day in commemoration of when the eight-hour workday was gained by workers, was observed by all the Finn Bay people. It was then, every year that we all would go by boatloads to usually Hernando Island, where there were wide beaches and grassy banks for us to run around on. While the women cooked and laid out the food, we would explore the island. The men would have a tug-of-war and other showings of strength. A singsong of politically-inspired songs was usually joined in by all. A strange feeling of pride would swell in my chest as I listened to words such as *"Workers of the world unite, you have nothing to lose but your chains".*

It was a great disappointment to us children when the weather was bad, and it was often so, and we would have to settle for the Ragged Islands to have our picnic at, and even sometimes, just the field in Finn Bay. Nothing, however, would keep us from going somewhere, for it was an event we looked forward to for a long time.

Visiting other Finn families living outside of the Bay was something we did in groups while the men were there too. They in return visited us. So, the summer would go by all too quickly, with the men returning and once again, we would settle back to a more male-dominated lifestyle.

When the men arrived home, they rested and relaxed for a day or two. The saunas were heated, for a much-needed bath was welcomed to wash away the grime which had accumulated while they were away. There were no bathing facilities on the boats then. I don't know if the fish canneries provided any either.

Next on the program was fall fishing, so their rest had to be cut short, to prepare for it. Nets had to be hung with float and lead lines, and if they had been used before, holes which had been torn in the web had to be mended. Toba and Bute Inlets were where the Finn Bay fishermen usually went for the fall fishing, some often came home on the weekends, especially if they fished at Toba.

After the fall fishing, many fished for cod again until the end of the year when a closed season ended fishing for a couple of months. Work, however, did not cease. It was then when work around home had to be done. Firewood was cut for the ever-hungry kitchen stove, gardens were dug in readiness for spring sowing and the manure was hauled out of the barn and spread on the hay fields. When the closed season ended, it was back to fishing again for cod, and later in the spring, trolling for salmon and coho and then again back up north for the sockeye run.

It was in this fashion that life went on year-to-year for the fisher folk of Finn Bay. Later on, when the children were older and more independent, the older men stayed around home and fished in local waters only, for they could get by on a smaller income as the family got smaller. For many of them years of fishing in cold, damp weather in poorly heated boats, had left aching limbs and poor health.

Sometimes tragedy would strike and shock the little community of the sea, claiming one of its fishermen and leaving a family without a provider. Silently, they would be mourned and life would go on.

Floating school, Deep Bay, Desolation Sound 1929
Left window: Irene Anderson/Pearl Anderson/Right
window: unknown.. Deck (L to R) Mildred
Palmer/Lloyd Anderson/teacher Eleanor Lusk/Julie
Anderson/Bill Palmer/Patricia Palmer
Photo: Eleanor Anderson (Lusk)

Okeover Inlet 1933
Kit Phillips (Palmer)/Mrs. Sarah Palmer/Nel Fletcher
(Palmer)/Leone Couling (Palmer)
Photo: Eleanor Anderson

Goski sauna, Finn Bay, Lund 2004
Insert: Helji and Adele Goski (twins), Goski farm, Finn Bay 1929.   Photo: Gustafson album

The Mace house, Savary Island – Mrs. Laura Mace at entrance 1930s. Bill Mace worked from 1912 on Savary
Island, building and fixing summer cottages. Insert: Irene Farnden (1909-2008) and baby Joan Farnden
(McDonald) Savary Island 1933.   Photos: Irene Farnden (Mace)

305

Looking Back! With William Peebles

Homesteading in Lund (from 1916)

The Peebles family came to Lund in 1916 and homesteaded 160 acres; their Lund property went down to what is known as Second Bay.

Alice and William Stanley Peebles were married on December 12, 1902. They lived in the Cariboo – young Bill was born in Quesnel. William Stanley worked in the Barkerville gold mines.

Young William was one of seven children. His siblings were: Jack, Allie, George, Marge, Millie, and Iris.

William fished with the famous Lund artist, John Sidney Dippie. Mr. Dippie lived from 1910-1950 in a tent at Second Bay, near the Peebles property.

Besides homesteading 160 acres, Alice and William were fish buyers. They picked up salmon and cod from fishermen in their own boat called the *Dollarette*. When the fish packers came to Lund, they went out of this business venture.

William Peebles (1913-2007) - **The Great Depression**

"I was just a kid in 1929, and I worked for Fred Flander and Eddie Moyer who were in the fish buying business.

I came home to Lund in 1930 and my mother told me there was no money in Lund - my father was not working and there was no money coming in. I would have to leave home to find work.

I left Lund in 1930 – there was nothing there for me. There was no work in Lund during the Depression.

I went to work with my brother for the Harbour Towing Company on the Fraser River...

During the Depression, my father also had to leave Lund to find work in the Cariboo. He owned, with John Peebles, the Beaver Pass Roadhouse in Barkerville, he also panned for gold in the Dragon Creek Placer Mine. Dad came home to Lund for the winter months.

During the Depression, my mother was left on her own in Lund with my sisters, Millie and Iris. She kept the farm going while Dad was away in the Cariboo. There was a cow and chickens on the farm and a dog named Sport.

Mum was an excellent shot with a rifle. The ducks used to come on the swamp in front of our place and Mum used to shoot them. After plucking them, she roasted the birds. Later, she stuffed flour sacks with feathers from the ducks to make pillows.

In 1937 my mother died. In 1939, my father sold the homestead and moved to Vancouver."

WWII

"I went to North Africa, chasing Rommel; then I was nine months in Italy, and then I came back to England. I wanted in the worst way to go over to France, but they wouldn't let me because of my eyesight.

The food was terrible overseas. Sometimes, we had mutton four times a day – you could almost taste the wool in it!

Altogether, I was in the army for five-and-a-half years. I was discharged in December 1945. I came back to Powell River."

The circumstances regarding his leaving Powell River for the war were related by William Peebles with quiet humour:

"In 1940 I went to Powell River to find work. I went to see my sister, Iris, who was living on Willow Avenue in the Townsite. She said, 'Whatever you do, don't join the army; don't join the forces at all! Go down to the mill and Chuck Wilcocks will give you a job.'

So I did, I got a job that night in the wood room on graveyard shift. Next morning, everyone is joining up around me. I knew these fellows and they said, 'Why don't you come too?' So I said, 'Okay, I'll come!' So I only worked the one night at the mill before I joined up."

William Peebles worked the one shift at the mill before he joined up. The Powell River Company kept its promise and hired all its former employees back after the war, including William Peebles, a man who worked one shift before joining up!

From 1946 - 2000 William (Bill) lived in Cranberry in one of the Veterans' homes built on land donated by the Powell River Company. From 2000–2007 William lived on Tatlow Street, Cranberry with his wife, Sylvia (Keets).

Looking Back with Moyra Palm (Palmer), Bessie Banham, and Charlie Fletcher:

The Palmer Family of Theodosia Inlet (from 1900)

Moyra Palm (Palmer) 2000:

*"**The Palmer family pioneered in this area before the turn of the century.** My great-grandfather, **Jim Palmer**, and his son **Will Palmer**, came from Oregon in 1898. They trapped in the Gordon Pasha Lakes and then sold furs at Frolander Bay.*

Jim and Will went to Van Anda, Texada Island, where they cut cordwood for the steamboats from 1899-1900. It was in Van Anda that they met Fred Thulin (who was there for business reasons). Fred Thulin, wanting to meet the requirements for a school at Lund, encouraged Jim and Will to go back to the States and bring the family to the area. Ironically, he forgot to ask how old their children were! In fact some of the children were in their teens.

The younger children: Inez, Irene, Nellie, and Kit were some of the first students at Lund School. The oldest daughter, Vira May, 16 years of age, married Fred Thulin in 1900.

The Palmer family homesteaded in Theodosia Inlet in the early 1900s."

Bessie Banham (1940s):

"With the arrival of the Palmer family, there were enough children for a school (at Lund), and a Miss Cameron of Vancouver arrived to teach a handful of children.

*In 1900 Mr. Palmer took up 160 acres on the Theodosia River, at the head of the arm, next to the 40-acre reservation held by the **Sliammon people**. The family lived on a houseboat until the home was completed in 1904. Once a month, in the family rowboat equipped with a sail, they made a trip to Lund for provisions.*

Forty acres were cleared and the ranch gradually became a farm, stocked with animals, including a herd of purebred Polled-Angus cattle that sometimes numbered more than 110 head. These were slaughtered there and sold to stores and camps in the vicinity."

Charlie Fletcher (2000):

*"**I was born in Theodosia Inlet in 1910.** My mother was a **Palmer** and we lived in a house on the Palmer homestead. **Will Palmer** was my uncle.*

*I was the first white baby to be born in Theodosia Inlet. Members of the **First Nations** came to see me after I was born. I was passed from person to person. I made cooing sounds as babies do; they named me "Amahoo", meaning Pigeon."*

Looking Back with Eleanor Anderson (Lusk)

Palmer's Logging Camp at Desolation Sound & Toba Inlet (1929-31)

Eleanor taught at Deep Bay (Tenedos Bay), Desolation Sound, and Salmon Bay (Brem Bay) in Toba Inlet from 1929 to 1932 at a logging camp owned by **Will Palmer**.

"I graduated from Normal School during the Great Depression. I wrote over 100 applications before securing a job at Palmer's Logging Camp in Deep Cove, Desolation Sound.

At the age of 18, September 1929, I boarded the Union Steamship at 9 a.m. and began a life completely different from anything I had ever imagined. Although the camp was only a few miles north of Powell River, it was 2:30 a.m. the next morning before we finally arrived. Will Palmer came out in a boat to meet the steamship.

The next morning, Mrs. Palmer offered to take me around to meet my pupils. She neglected to tell me we would have to walk on boom sticks, some under water!

The schoolhouse wasn't quite ready, and we held classes in Palmer's large dining room. My salary was $96 a month. I paid $20 a month for room and board and I sent $35 home to my parents.

In the winter we skated on nearby lakes. The young people, at weekends, attended dances at Cortez Island, Bliss Landing, and Lund. As we went by boat, we had to have some daylight to come home in; so we danced the night away and often stopped in Galley Bay on our way home to drop off the Galley Bay schoolteacher and have breakfast!

During the third year of teaching, I had a unique experience. The whole camp was moved on floats from Deep Bay, Desolation Sound, to Salmon Bay in Toba Inlet. As we were being towed I taught school on the float! The children were excited and my lessons had many interruptions, as we dashed to the windows to see the sights.

There was a First Nations Reserve at Salmon Bay and a few of their children attended my school.

Toba Inlet was quite beautiful. I watched the men catch steelhead salmon at Salmon River. A walk I loved in the winter was across the beach, through the snow, on clear, starlit nights.

When I finished my third year of teaching, I was engaged to Jim Anderson, nephew of Will Palmer. That was the end of my teaching career for many years. It was 1957 before I taught again, this time in Grief Point School at Westview, Powell River. In 1967 I taught music at the elementary level throughout the district at Henderson, Cranberry Lake, Grief Point, Kelly Creek, and Lund."

In 1932 Eleanor married **Jim Anderson, nephew of Will Palmer**.

The Andersons and Palmers

Will and Mildred Palmer came to Lund with their family in 1900. The Palmers had five children, four girls and one boy. Bill, the only son, took up pre-emptions with his father in Theodosia Inlet.

From 1899 to 1900, Louie Anderson and Bill Palmer logged on **Savary Island**. Later on, Louie logged with George Ashworth, Bill Mace, Ashton Spilsbury, and Harry Keefer.

Louie Anderson married Bill's sister, Irene Palmer. **Louie and Irene Anderson made Savary Island their home.** After Louie died, his widow married George Short.

Irene Palmer's sister May (Vira) married **Fred Thulin of Lund**.

Jim Anderson (born 1903) was the eldest son of Louie and Irene Anderson. His siblings were Andre (?), Terry (1906), Sylvia (1908), Pearl (1910), Lloyd (1922), and Julia (1927).

All the Anderson boys were interested in logging, boats, and fishing. Jim and Terry built the *Sylpene* in the 1920s on Savary Island and named the boat after their mother, Irene and two sisters, Sylvia and Pearl.

Jim Anderson was a friend of **Jim Spilsbury**. Jim was the son of Ashton and Alice Spilsbury; the couple made their first excursion to Savary Island for their honeymoon in 1898.

Jim Anderson knew **Andy Anderson**, as they were both in the lumber industry. Jim logged and towed logs to the **Anderson sawmill at Haywire Bay**.

Looking Back with Gerry Bleiler

Memories of the Bleiler Farm at Lund (1940s)

In 1939, my uncles Ted and Clarence Bleiler became joint owners of the Peebles farm, situated one mile north of the community of Lund. William Peebles had obtained the land by homesteading 160 acres in 1916. He finally decided to put the farm up for sale because his wife Alice had died in 1937, and his children had moved away either to get married or find work (Great Depression era).

In 1949, Clarence bought his brother Ted's share of the farm and moved onto the land with his wife Helene, and sons Dwight and George. This arrangement suited Ted as he wanted to go back into teaching – he had been offered a position at Fort Simpson in the N.W.T. Clarence farmed the property for 20 years and then sold out and moved into Westview in 1969.

Ted and his wife Almuth, farmed at Lund for 10 years. This covers the period during which Ted and Almuth, now deceased, lived and farmed the property.

Between 1940 and 1945, Gerry Bleiler lived at the farm almost every year during summer holidays. During 1946-47 Gerry lived full time with Uncle Ted and Aunt Almuth and with their newly adopted children, Douglas and Noel Bleiler (ex-Wickman). The three children, now in Ted and Almuth Bleiler's household, rode the school bus into Powell River's Brooks High School every day, helped with work around the farm, took piano lessons, and generally enjoyed life as a family unit. Gerry has wonderful memories of his visits and life spent on the farm as a young man growing up. Gerry is the son of William Bleiler, who was also a brother to Ted and Clarence.

****

We flashback to the year 1941; Uncle Ted and Almuth have now been relocated from the Yukon for a year or so, purchased an interest in a farm, and Ted has been teaching at the Lund school. There, he taught grades 1 to 7. Gerry spent part of his Grade 2 in his uncle's classroom that year. After the school day and during summer holidays, Uncle Ted could be found toiling on the farm.

In order to meet expenses and pay for improvements, Uncle Ted took a second job during the summer. He worked for the **Thulin Brothers** in the general store situated across the road from the Lund Hotel. He worked as a clerk and warehouseman. Aunt Almuth also had a job working for **Gerald and Holger Thulin** in the coffee shop, which was attached to the store but situated on the dock, where the Union and Gulf steamships tied up – i.e. *Lady Cynthia, Gulf Steam* (which sank on Dinner Rock), and the *Gulf Wing*.

The farm consisted primarily of the farmhouse with an orchard, a large garden, woodlot, and several outbuildings made out of lodge poles and shakes. Buildings included: a workshop, blacksmith, feed house, barn, and three chicken houses. The wonderful red fertile soil made the garden very productive. As a young boy, the task of weeding rows seemed endless. In those summer months, the orchard was filled with succulent fruits. Red and yellow cherries were first to appear, followed by apples, pears, and peaches.

Ted and Almuth kept cows – "Bessie" and "Cathy". Cathy was raised for beef. Bessie was milked in the barn and the warm milk was taken to Almuth in the farmhouse, where the milk was strained through cheesecloth and allowed to settle. The "blue" milk was separated from the cream, which was saved to be made into butter. Because there was no refrigeration, the cream milk and butter were kept cool in the creek and dealt with before souring. Drinking water came from a well.

The Bleilers had a clever dog called Pal. At 5 o'clock Jens Sorensen blew a whistle at his machine shop in Lund, which was a mile away from the farm. Pal could hear the whistle and without fail, herded Bessie into the barn to be milked.

The Lund farm was labour intensive – there were always chores to do: inevitable housework and cooking; chickens and ducks to feed and water; cows to feed and milk; the garden to dig, weed, and harvest; fruit to pick; canning and preserving; water to haul in buckets from the well and creek; and trees to fell, limb, cut into rounds, haul from the wood yard; firewood and kindling to chop in the woodshed; chicken houses and barn to clean and provision with hay. There were eggs to collect, clean, grade, candle, and deliver; ducks, chickens and beef to kill, clean, butcher, and deliver.

Uncle Ted had a good business raising and marketing chickens and selling eggs to butcher shops and the hospital. There were sheds for chicks, for the laying hens, and one for fryers. Every two weeks, 288 eggs were sold to the Powell River hospital. In order to keep the eggs fresh after collection and before delivery, they were kept in a crock full of "icing glass" because the farm did not have electricity for a refrigeration unit. Fryers were pre-sold, fresh-killed, plucked, cleaned and immediately delivered to the hospital and stores in town. Once laying hens became unproductive these were identified, killed, and Aunt Almuth canned the meat for home consumption.

Uncle Ted had two vehicles. He owned a 1929 Erskine (made by Studebaker) and a Model T truck. The Erskine was a cute little two-seater coupe with a rumble seat. Gerry enjoyed riding in the rumble seat, except when it was rainy. The Model T Ford truck was included as part of the farm purchase. It was always parked near the blacksmith shed and only used on the farm property to move wood, feed, and other heavy things.

On occasional Saturday nights (perhaps once a month) Uncle Ted, Aunt Almuth, and Gerry would dress up and drive the 15 miles into town to deliver the eggs and fryers, have a meal at the **Rodmay Hotel**, and then stay to watch a movie at the **Patricia Theatre**. On these days, the chickens and eggs rode in the rumble seat going into town and Gerry squeezed into the front seat of the Erskine with the adults. He rode in the rumble seat on the way back to the farm. Gerry remembers how Uncle Ted bought everyone a milkshake after the show.

Sunday night was a special night for radio shows. William Peebles had left several battery radios behind when he sold the place. These were cobbled together into one working radio. The radio ran on dry cell batteries, and as soon as the favourite programmes were finished, the radio was promptly shut off to preserve the battery. Batteries were expensive things and a luxury that could be ill-afforded.

Ted played the violin and there was a gramophone with records to provide music. The Bleilers had a piano in the living room, and after doing daily chores Gerry practiced for an hour in order to be ready for the next lesson.

****

It seems most kids who grew up in the Lund area had access to one kind of boat or another. Most were rowboats, because few could afford engines or gasoline. Gerry would row Ted's engine-equipped Newfoundland style dory around the bay. Later, as he gained experience, he was allowed to use its Briggs and Stratton 5 horsepower engine. He would jig for lingcod. Sometimes, Gerry went fishing for salmon with **Mr. Sorensen** in his west coast troller. Gerry also went rowing, sailing, and fishing with **Mr. Dippie**. They would often tandem-row his clinker boat over to Savary Island. If the wind was right, Mr. Dippie would rig a bedsheet sail to come home. There were times when they dug for clams on the beautiful sandy beaches of the island.

Picnics were held at Savary Island in the summertime. Most of the citizenry of the Lund community would go over in the various fishing and pleasure boats owned by fishermen, loggers, and private individuals. The **Gustafsons, the Miettinens, Janzens, Thulins,** et al from Lund, Finn Bay, and surrounding areas would find their way across the two miles of ocean to **Savary Island**. The Bleilers usually went over in the Sorenson's boat. Potato salad and produce of all kinds from all the farms around would be served. Marshmallows and wieners were roasted on the beach. The sun would shine on the shallow sandy beach and when the tide was out, shallow pools of warm water remained for the people to languish in. There were no picnic tables – people sat on driftwood logs and ate on their laps. Oh what fun!!

****

Mr. Dippie was often invited to the Bleiler farm for Sunday dinner. Gerry would often visit Mr. Dippie and get further instruction in art at Mr. Dippie's home. Mr. Dippie lived in a tent on the beach in the early 1940s, but as time went by, the tent became a shack as driftwood replaced the rotting canvas material.

Mr. Dippie, known as "Dippie" to everyone, spent much of his time drawing and painting. He did black-and-white sketches in pencil and painted on fungus, seashells, and canvas. His paintings and sketches looked like photographs. Dippie was a man who lived a solitary life – he was probably the world's first hippie!

In 1941 Gerry helped Uncle Ted install a direct current lighting plant for electricity on the farm. Later, a dam was built on the creek (about a city block away) and a water line was constructed out of woodstove pipe to bring water directly into the house. This made things a lot easier for Aunt Almuth. With a good supply of water and electricity for lights on hand, life became a lot more civilized. Uncle Ted bought Aunt Almuth a Briggs and Stratton engine washing machine, which was kick-started with a pedal. Prior to this, washing was done with a washing machine, which was drum-shaped and with an agitator that looked like a milking stool. This machine was hand cranked to operate the "stool".

Until 1944, baths were a weekly affair. Water was heated on the woodstove in a copper container and poured directly into the bathtub. Cold water was added to get the temperature right. Everyone bathed in the same water and more water was heated on the stove to keep the temperature up for the next person. During the summer, when the water was not too cold, we all bathed in the creek, or swam in the ocean. These were the days of spit baths, running shoes, and toe-jam.

When economic times were right, Uncle Ted and Gerry dug a huge hole in the ground and put in a septic field. Then a toilet and washstand were installed in the room where the bathtub was located. Aunt Almuth was delighted to have indoor plumbing. No more trips to the outhouse or spit bathing from a basin!

1940 to 1946 was the span in which the greatest development took place; water was piped into the house, electricity was added. The house itself was expanded and enlarged, the bathroom and hot water installed.

Looking Back with the D'Angio Family

Okeover Pioneers (from 1914)

John (Giovanni) D'Angio (Sr.) and his brother Ralph (Raffaelle) D'Angio, originally from Italy, pre-empted land at Okeover in 1914; John had 65 acres with 700 feet of waterfront and Ralph with 40 acres behind him.

In 1918, John D'Angio (1887-1962) married Catherine O'Callaghan (1891-1949) in Vancouver. The newlywed couple first lived in a gas boat, tied up near the mill breakwater. Later, they moved to Bon Ton Apartments. John (Junior) was born in 1921 in St. Luke's Hospital.

Ralph stayed on at Okeover to clear his pre-emption. In December 1921 a tragedy occurred when Ralph was shot dead by a crazy Swede, Alec Johnson. After this horrific event John (Senior) and family went to live permanently in Okeover. John kept his job at the mill and walked the 15 miles, back and forth on the trail, through Southview to the Townsite.

Augustine Hodgson (D'Angio) 2002
"There were seven children in our family. We lived in Okeover Inlet. It was pretty isolated. The nearest store was five miles away in Lund. My father John D'Angio worked away, logging and trapping. **In 1910 he worked for the Powell River Company in the Townsite.**"

Elio Cossarin 2008
"John D'Angio worked for the Powell River Company in the 1920s. It was a long walk from the Townsite to Okeover; on occasion, he slept overnight in the mill!"

Mary Nassichuk (D'Angio) 2000
"My mother was born in England and raised in a convent. She was invited to Vancouver by her brother. One day, she saw an advert in the paper, put in by my father John D'Angio; it said he wanted to contact a good Catholic girl. My mother answered it and my father proposed after they met.
She really had no idea she was going to live in relative isolation, on a homestead at Okeover. My father just said he had a nice house near Lund. What a shock for her when she discovered the "nice house" had a dirt floor!"

Augustine Hodgson (D'Angio) 2002
"Mother was a marvellous cook and manager. Mother canned vegetables, fruit, and goat meat for the winter months. She made a lot of clothes for our family. The flour and sugar bags were put to good use and made into children's underwear. Mother was a great knitter and lace maker."

Mary Nassichuk (D'Angio) 2000

"On our homestead we had goats and chickens. All the children would take it in turn to milk the goats. My mother made cheese from the goat's milk."

Augustine Hodgson (D'Angio) 2002

"The Okeover school was kept open in the 1930s because we had seven children in the family. One time our goats got into the school, chewed up the exercise books and drank the ink! After the school closed in 1939, my sister Nellie attended the Lund school for five years to get her Grade 8. She then finished her schooling at Brooks in the Townsite."

Gerry Bleiler 2007

"My aunt and uncle, Ted and Almuth Bleiler, took in a boarder by the name of Nellie D'Angio. Her parents' farm at Okeover was just too far away from Lund for her to walk to school, so she stayed with my aunt and uncle on the Bleiler farm near Lund during the school week. She was one of Uncle Ted's students at Lund School until she had to go to Powell River (Townsite) for the senior grades.

Mr. D'Angio was born in Italy and a great lover and keeper of goats. Every Saturday you could see him and his missus riding down to Lund in their 1920-something Chevrolet Roadster. They always stopped to talk and when the conversation was over; Mr. D'Angio put the car in gear and the axle took a quarter turn before the spokes in the wheel caught up with the rim."

Barbara Ann Lambert 2008

"I met John D'Angio (Junior) (1921-1995) and Honey (Belinda) D'Angio in the 1970s. They were living in **Douglas Bay** where I had bought recreational property from **Pearl and Tom Lang**. I'd walk along the beach and visit in their home. Honey, just like her name, was a honey. She worked for the Lang Bay Community – running the whist game at Lang Bay Hall for many decades. At potluck lunches, Honey always provided the dessert – her most famous dessert had a green peppermint filling with a cream topping, called "Sex in a Pan"!

The D'Angio basement and yard was full of birds and animals carved by John with his chainsaw. A large figure (the logger-thinker) carved by John, stands over his grave in the Kelly Creek cemetery.

In 1983, I visited with my husband Stuart, the D'Angios. We went to see a dead wolf which John had shot. A pack of wolves had moved into Paradise Valley – attacking goats and horses. John, an experienced hunter and trapper, had been asked to move them out. After he shot one from the pack, the rest left the area."

Looking Back with Nancy Crowther (1923-1989)

Cougar Queen of Okeover Arm

Nancy Crowther lived in a log cabin in Okeover Arm. Nancy and her parents bought the land, 135 acres, in 1927 for $10. They split old logs on the property in order to build their cabin. They kept goats, geese, and chickens and planted a large orchard.

Nancy:
"We earned our living digging clams. We couldn't afford shoes, so we wrapped cloth around our feet. We could use it to walk on barnacles. We used a spade; we didn't know about rakes.

Mother used to pack supplies in from Powell River when Dad was working. She might have 20 pounds of rolled oats, plus cans of milk, plus other stuff – all the way from Powell River (Townsite)."

As a young 13 year-old teenager, when walking back on the trail from Lund with her partially-sighted father, she shot her first cougar with a .22 calibre rifle. They had found a fresh cougar kill and her father was afraid that it would kill their goats if not destroyed. After her father died, Nancy looked after her elderly mother for many years. Nancy continued to hunt and kill cougars in the Okeover Arm area in order to protect her livestock; hence the name, given to her by neighbours, "Cougar Queen of Okeover Arm".

Okeover was isolated with trails linking it to Lund and the Townsite. Nancy and a few other children in the area took correspondence courses for their elementary education. Nancy remembered going down on the beach to complete her lessons:

"I could watch the ants and crows and the things that were going on, and they were far more important to me than the lessons at that time."

Nancy remembers her dresses being made out of flour sacks during the Dirty Thirties. It was hard to make a living back then:

"We were mighty glad when a logging camp moved into the area, because they would buy bread and eggs. The tourist was a gold mine."

During WWII Nancy worked in the mill, capping and sheet-laying. She walked the six hours back and forth to Okeover – always on the lookout for a cougar! By 1964 Nancy Crowther – Cougar Queen of Okeover Arm – had 12 cougar kills.

William (Bill) Peebles visiting the old Peebles farmhouse at Lund 1990.
Photo: Bill Peebles collection

Bleiler farm 1954 (originally the Peebles property). Rear: Clarence Bleiler
Front: George Bleiler/Mrs. Helen Bleiler with Teresa Bleiler/Aunt Almuth Bleiler/Dwight Bleiler/Jasper – dog.
Photo: Bleiler album

Powell home, Southview, Powell River 1937
(L to R) Mrs. George Powell/Mary Powell/George Powell/Eunice Wilshire/Cecil Hollands.
Photo: Mary Masales (Powell)

Lund/Southview old-timers:
Len Emmonds (1928-2008)/Mary Masales (Powell) – born Powell River 1921.   Photo: B.A. Lambert 2000

Looking Back with Len Emmonds (1928-2008)

Southview and Lund (1930s & 40s)

Southview School

I attended the second Southview School with my sister Doreen. It was a one-room school with no electricity or running water. Water was brought in a pail from Southview Creek. Wood was dropped off on the road for the wood heater. As soon as the wood was dumped, the teacher ordered the kids outside to pack it around to the back of the school. The little ones would take the smaller pieces and the bigger kids, the bigger chunks of wood. The centre of the road was cleared first, in case anyone wanted to drive to Lund or Wildwood.

After the second Southview School closed (1941), we were driven to Lund for six months by my father in a car with a rumble seat. After that, the school board paid my father $40 a month to drive a van with the Southview children to Wildwood school. I then attended old Henderson School a year before graduating from Brooks in 1945.

Trapping

In the 1940s, I was trapping from Powell River to Sarah Point. Trapping was a good living; I trapped otter, red squirrel, mink, weasel, and coon. Otter skins were valued at $30 and red squirrels at $1 a piece. After WWII, I bought property adjacent to my father's place. In order to pay for the land, I worked for the **Powell River Company**, building #8 machine.

Trapper: Harry Gothard (1875-1968)

I met Harry when I was trapping. He came to live in Southview after he sold his place in Olsen Valley in the 1940s. In 1945 Harry came to live at **Emmonds Beach**; he was 70 years of age and received the old age pension. He built himself a shack and lived there until the 1960s. After that he reluctantly moved to an apartment in Vancouver. His old shack has been moved to a different location on the Emmonds Beach property and is now used as a workshop.

Lund Artist: John Sidney Dippie (1875-1950)

He was known to everyone as Dippie, Mr. Dippie, or Dippie Dippie. He was a fantastic artist. He made pencil sketches of tugboats – they were exact replicas.

I met him at the Lund store which was run by the **Thulin Brothers**. He lived in a tent at Second Bay; it had a canvas roof and the sides were built up with wood.

He used to row down to Emmonds Beach to do some fishing. I met him occasionally, when I was out fishing.

Looking Back with Mary Masales (Powell)

Memories of Southview (1920s & 30s), Townsite, Savary Island and Lund (1940s)

George Powell came to Powell River in 1909. In 1910, he worked as a surveyor for the Powell River Company. Later, he helped build the dam and then worked in the grinder room until the mid 1930s. In the late 1930s (Great Depression), he was on relief. George was married to Maude Powell (Winters). They had three children: Mary, George, and Art. They lived in Southview (between Wildwood and Lund). **It was George Powell who named the area "Southview" because the area pointed south**.

"Only four of us left, that lived in Southview and were born there. I was born in Powell River in 1921." Mary Masales (June 2007)

There was no Powell River when he (George Powell) came here. He worked as surveyor for the Powell River mill. Dad helped build that dam, the dam that is here today. He then went to work in the mill, in the grinder room.

He walked every day, a trail to Southview, to get home. He went up and down the Wildwood hill – just a trail in those days. We'd take our boat from Southview to get groceries from the company store. It was an open boat and we only went in good weather.

I can remember the road going through in the early 1930s – seeing the big donkey pulling the big logs out of the Southview Road. After the road went through, Dad used to pack the groceries all the way from Powell River (Townsite) to Southview on his back. It would take him two hours.

Annie Rondine, her dad looked after the horses. **This country was logged with horses, no machinery was used. Some of those skid roads are here today.** One time the forest ranger, Sid Riley, picked me up and took me up to Scuttle Bay; a fellow was logging there, I showed him the location – he scratched the dirt and there was this old skid road – it still had tar on it!

The Japanese logged for shingle bolts in the Southview area. They built a flume, dammed up Plummer Creek. We walked it many times when we were kids – we went down the creek fishing. They logged with horses. The shingles were put into the water. They had a big dam there on the creek. When it was full of shingle bolts, they let them out, down a long flume, into the ocean. They left Southview area in the mid-1920s. By the time I went to school in 1924, they had all gone. The flume fell down a long time ago.

First and Second Southview Schools (1924-1941)

I attended the first Southview School in 1924; the school was on the Southview Road by the Fulton's place. I was only 3 (years-old) at the time, but I was needed to bring the number up to 10. The teachers were: Miss Puttman, Miss Green, and Miss Ada Doherty. The school closed in 1927. It burned down in 1929.

After the first Southview School closed down, I walked with my brother, George, to Wildwood School. In 1933, the second Southview School opened by Southview Road. The school closed in 1941. Lillian Russell and Zella Stacey taught there. I left the second Southview School after completing Grade 8. My brother George had a ride to Lund School in the Emmond's van.

Southview Residents (1920s & 30s)

Jim Sumner lived in Southview valley; he was a bachelor. The Neaves were the next ones down the line. They had a little farm up there. When they cleared the land, they fenced it with rocks. All the rocks they took off the ground, they made into fences. Not there today. Those rock fences stayed there for years, and years, and years.

The Hultons were next to the Neaves, then the Wasps, George Wasp and his wife – they had one son.

Next Sumners, brother to Jim Sumner; then our place, the Powells. All up on that side of the road.

Cooks and Grangers were on the top side – big acres of land. They had it all cleared and sometimes my dad's cows wandered up there. I can remember the old chicken house with wire around the chicken house. The grouse used to pick the bugs off the apple trees in the fall.

On the water side were the Bays, Brays, and Meads. Mrs. Anderson had a daughter, Margie Anderson. Meads had a daughter, Ruby Meads. I went to school with Margie Anderson, Ruby Meads, Nicholson boys (Mr. Nicholson was the school teacher and government agent at Sliammon), Annie Rondine, Enid Fulton, Jimmy and Roy Sumner and one more.

Southview Dairy (1920s)

Meads had a dairy; they had three or four cows. I have some milk tokens somewhere. They were made of metal – on them it said "Southview Dairy". Old Mead had a fire truck. He used to go into town (Townsite) and sell milk. Meads used to live up Southview Road and then moved down to where Rogers are today. Old Mead sold milk, eggs, and vegetables.

Scuttle Bay Mink Farm (1930s)

There used to be a mink farm there. One time Jim Sumner, he took us fishing down this creek. Old Jim said, *"Let's go down to the old bridge."* We got up to the old skid road and walked down. All of a sudden this big black lab jumped out of the bush; he made all sort of a racket and scared the life out of us.

Here was a fellow digging a well – he came and introduced himself to us. We were just kids then (1930s). *"What are you doing? Why are you digging a well?"* Old Jim asked him. He said, *"I'm going to start a mink farm!"* His name was **John Wilde**. After he got going, he had over a thousand mink; when they had their young, no one could go near their place. He used to sell the pelts. Later, he built a farm in Scuttle Bay. There was a skid road to Scuttle Bay; he tore the skids out and made a road to Scuttle Bay.

My dad loved fish – 3 times a day, 365 days a year. Old John Wilde set night lines for fish to feed his mink. He said to my dad, *"Send the kids down to Scuttle Bay to get some fish."*

We saw this dot in the distance, way out in the chuck, past the point. Finally, it came around the point into Scuttle Bay. This fellow jumped out of this boat – we saw it was old John. He was pulling on something – it was a skate fish, weighed over 800 pounds! He hung onto it until the tide went out. He sent George up to the truck to get the saw and an axe. As he was cutting it up, George and I were running across the beach with the pieces. Finally, we got it all done. Two days later, he got another one – this one was 700 pounds. You never know what is in the ocean.

Old Dick McGuiness caught a halibut over 200 pounds. I saw it with my own eyes – I was working in the café at Lund at that time.

Fishing in a dug-out canoe

We (Mary and George) had real dugout canoes made by old **Chief Tom at Sliammon**. Chief Tom and my father were real good friends. He thought the world of us kids. We used to walk to Sliammon and go fishing there.

Old Jim Sumner used to go to Stuart Island in the summer time fishing; he had a little cabin up there. We just begged Mum and Dad to go with him; it took a lot of persuasion. We had to come back in time to pick the cherries.

We were up there for two weeks. Jim brought us back to the rapids and set us on our way. He told us to stay out in mid-channel. We rowed from Stuart Island to Sarah Point; it was the time the big fire was going in Campbell River (1938). We put our bedding onto the beach. Our hands were so sore from rowing; we just threw the rope out with a rock on the line to hold it. We went to sleep. When we woke up, the boat was floating and the sun was shining. A tug was going by, thought we'd get a tow home, but he was only going to the Ragged Islands. Then we had to row home; it was a long trip. We were just kids and we rowed the whole way. We got home in time to pick cherries.

Great Depression

There was no work in Lund during the Depression – maybe a little fishing. My dad was on relief (late 1930s). He put a big garden in.

We had to weed the garden before we were allowed to go fishing. We'd take just one canoe. We usually fished for salmon. Mum canned a lot of salmon and Dad smoked the salmon and herring. **The salmon was our winter food**; Mum used the salmon for fish loaf, patties, and chowder soup. There were plenty of fish in the 1930s.

In wintertime, when the tide was low at night, we went out clam digging by the light of the moon. We took home a bucket of clams, between the two of us. Mum made delicious clam chowder soup.

We had chickens and our own eggs in spring and summer. Mum put eggs down in water-glass in big crocks for winter use. Usually, for Sunday lunch, Mum roasted a chicken.

We always had a cow and a calf. The cow was butchered in the fall and Mum canned the meat.

Southview Fire – July 26, 1938

It started on the beach near Lund; came almost to Southview, then all the way back. It didn't come as far as our place; it came to the bottom of the hill. Mum had all the bedding rolled up – they were scared if the wind came up it would take us all down along the line. It was a good size fire – George was water boy on the fire. We got some rain and that put it out.

Working for a Living

I left school in 1934, after I finished Grade 8 at the second Southview School. The only job for young girls in Powell River (Townsite) was housework. My first job was for a policeman – I got $10 a month! I also worked for a dentist in Southview for a year then a short time for Dr. and Mrs. Lyons. I could only stick it at Dr. Lyon's place for a week then I asked him to take me home.

It was difficult finding work in Powell River, so in 1939 I went over to join a girlfriend in Nanaimo, and stayed there doing housework for a year before coming back to Powell River.

Housewife

In 1940, during the war, I married **Bill Masales**. We first lived in **Riverside**, Powell River, as my husband had a job in the mill. **We rented half a house. Houses were split between two families, as there was not enough housing for everyone.**

Just before the birth of our first child in 1940, we moved to **Olsen Valley**. My husband was hauling shingle bolts for Grafton to the Shingle Mill. Olsen Valley was a nice place, lots of farms and fruit trees. We then moved to **Wildwood** and rented a house there for a few years. In 1945, we moved to Savary Island for one year.

Savary Island 1945

We lived in a house near the wharf. My husband Bill worked for **Bill Mace** as a carpenter on the island. My Bill was a jack-of-all-trades; he fixed summer houses for summer visitors from Vancouver – anything needed doing, he fixed it.

Only the Maces, Keefers, and Spilsburys were living year-round on Savary Island. The Mace's daughter-in-law ran the only store on the island. She sold basic supplies and ran the post office. Most residents ordered supplies through Woodward's and had them delivered by Union Steamship. I bought shoes and clothes at the Powell River Company store in the Townsite.

During the summer the island was full of visitors. The Union Steamship came up three times a week to Savary Island. The entire island was crawling with visitors. Some lived in cabins; some had tents on the beach. It was part of my Bill's job to meet the boat with Mace's big truck to pick up the visitors and their belongings. At the end of the summer he would do the return trip to the dock. One old girl was fond of my Bill. She wanted to pack a lunch and take him with her for the day. She wanted to steal my husband!

Working at Lund

I worked at Lund. Put five years in at Lund for the Thulins in the late 1940s. I cooked in the café; just one girl to the shift. $1.28 when I first started. Not much money in those days. Washed dishes, made pies, did everything.

There were two families of the Thulins; Holger married to Grace, and Gerald Thulin married to Ruby Johnson.

When I went to work for them, Grace was in the office; Holger had passed away. Grace Thulin, Gerald and Ruby Thulin, and the girl on shift did everything.

I was cook, bottle washer, and jack-of-all-trades. It was terrible in summer. It was a panic.

Tourists were going to Savary Island. We got them all. Kids from Squirrel Cove going to school in Sechelt; they were holy terrors – they were either coming or going. A few loggers, not that many fishermen – they went north.

One boat couldn't take all the tourists – used to hang around the hotel.

First shift started at 7 a.m. to 2 p.m., then another from 2 p.m. to 7 p.m. Then at the weekend we changed around.

After working for the Thulins, I shucked oysters for 15 years. I worked for the Hampsons. When the season was over, my hand was hard as a rock. I was the fastest shucker on the B.C. coast! In 1958, we moved to my present home (between Southview and Lund).

Looking Back

I knew Elmer Rud when we grew up as kids together. I knew all the Ruds. When we had the little schoolhouse down here at Southview, we had dances in it. The old folks and the Meads had a whist drive in their house. We played cards before the dance. Elmer played the guitar and someone played an accordion. One of the Gibson boys played too.

We had many a party at the Rud house in Wildwood. Yes, I knew them all. We were the best of friends. The Rud boys went gypo logging.

In the late 1930s, I used to go to dances at Lund. My brother, George, worked for the forestry in the summer and had a room at the weekends at Lund. Every Saturday night they had a dance at the hotel. We usually danced to a gramophone.

We had a lot of fun – the kids never got drunk.

Parsons' farm, Claridge Road, Blue Mountain, Powell River 1950. Originally the Mohr farm, Freeda Parsons bought the farm from her father, Garfield Scott Mohr in 1949. (L to R) Freeda Parsons (Mohr)/Garfield Scott Mohr. Photo: Freeda Parsons

Insert: John D'Angio – logger – carver – hunter. Well known "old-timer" from Douglas Bay (property purchased from the Stanleys 1940s – original owners Donkersley family). Gravesite at Holy Cross Cemetery, Kelly Creek, Powell River. Carving by John D'Angio. Photos: Private collection

Herbert Padgett and his son Rex, with their dogs Laddie and Nellie – cougar hunting. Paradise Valley. The government paid a $40 bounty for a cougar kill.   Powell River Digester 1930

Myrtle Grove Dairy (old Lambert farm), Paradise Valley. 1926-1936 largest goat dairy in the Dominion of Canada with 80 milking goats – owners Tom and Gertie Lambert.
Photo: Tom Lambert bucket-feeding kid goats 1932.   Gertie Lambert collection

Looking Back with Freeda Parsons (Mohr)

Memories of Blue Mountain Farm (from 1931) and Working for Boeing in WWII

In 1930 my dad, **George Mohr** (1880-1967), heard about the Powell River mill using steam in the plant and that they were hiring people. In the 1920s my dad had worked on a steam threshing machine in Alberta. My dad thought he would take a chance, bring his family to Powell River and seek employment in the mill.

I was only 10 years-old when my family moved to the B.C. coast. **Dad got a job in 1930 as a carpenter with the Powell River Company.** First, we lived in **Wildwood**, then by the **Shingle Mill**, finally we moved to the **Blue Mountain area** where Dad purchased acreage for a farm (near Blue Mountain Trailer Court). Dad decided to leave the mill and work full time on the farm.

Blue Mountain Farm

During the Great Depression, my dad cut and delivered cordwood for the **Powell River Company**. Prices were low and he received $2-$3 for a cord of wood.

Ready cash was hard to come by, so we bartered farm produce around the town. We'd take butter into the store and trade it off. I remember taking chickens to Nixon the dentist.

I walked down a trail to the second Westview School with the Bauman girls and the Lambert boys. The other kids called us the "Valley Rats" – the name came from a comic strip called the "River Rats".

Water was carried up in buckets from the creek. It was hard work on washing day, carrying up bucket after bucket. It was Walter, my husband that brought water to the house, after the war. Mum (Bessie Mohr 1891-1940) never had running water.

World War II – Working for Boeing

I went to work in the mill in 1942. **The mill was hiring women as so many men had volunteered to join up.** We wore white coveralls. We also wore hairnets and caps. I worked for Boeing at the mill. I learned how to rivet; I had no previous experience. The female employees had an onsite male supervisor. Every so often, a lady supervisor from Boeing in Vancouver came up to Powell River to check how the girls were doing. We had a good time at the mill.

I met my husband **Walter Parsons** at the mill. We were married in 1944 and we moved onto the farm with our two children, Tom and John, in 1949. Pat, Allen, Fred, and Lucy were born on the farm. Tom married Elsie Carlson in 1967.

Looking Back – the Padgett Family

Pioneers in Paradise Valley

Padgett Road, in Paradise Valley, is named after **Herbert and Pattie Padgett** who came to **homestead** the area near **Myrtle Point in 1919.**

Herbert (1880-1952) and Pattie Padgett (188_?–1948) were born in Yorkshire, England. They came to Canada in 1904 and pioneered on Cortez and Texada Islands before moving to the Myrtle Point area. Rex Padgett (1908-1982) was born in Vancouver and Roy Padgett (1913-1990) was born in Van Anda on Texada Island.

Herbert was known as a "gentleman farmer"; he had received a good education in England. The Padgett and Lambert families met as pioneers on Cortez Island. It was Herbert Padgett that urged his friend, John Lambert (also born in Yorkshire) to take up the last pre-emption in Paradise Valley in 1923. When the Padgetts sold up and left Cortez Island for Van Anda, they sold their goat herd to Tom Lambert. In 1926, when Tom came down from Cortez to join his father, John, he brought the goat herd with him.

Pattie Padgett was interested in photography. She developed negatives on glass.

Herbert Padgett built an old horse and wagon trail from the original logging railroad track in Paradise Valley. He had a great interest in motorcars and owned the first car in the Myrtle Point area.

Rex and Roy Padgett attended the one-room school at Myrtle Point – sometimes arriving on horseback.

After the fire went through Paradise Valley in 1918, wolves and cougars were a problem. The government paid a $40 bounty for cougars. During the Depression years, Herbert and his two sons, Rex and Roy, and their two dogs, Laddie and Nellie, went cougar hunting. The cougar meat was given to Chinese families living in the area.

The Padgetts kept sheep and goats. Herb Padgett hunted for deer and shot blue grouse, both were plentiful in the area. The Padgetts put in a huge garden and a large, productive orchard.

Barbara Lambert (2008):
"I remember in the 1970s and 80s, every spring, Roy Padgett came to the Lambert farm for goat manure for his garden at Myrtle Point. A few months later, he returned with a gift of gigantic stalks of rhubarb."

Looking Back with Barbara Lambert

The Old Lambert Farm in Paradise Valley (from 1923)

The Lambert family homesteaded on Cortez Island from 1907 to 1923. In 1923 John Lambert, at the urging of his friend Herbert Padgett, applied for and received the last pre-emption on the coast in the valley near Myrtle Point. John's son, Tom, purchased an adjacent lot to his father's in 1926. Tom brought his wife, Gertie, and his two sons, Stuart and Russell, down to the valley in the same year.

In 1930 Tom named the valley, "Paradise Valley". It had been burned out in 1918 and it was full of charred stumps. It looked like Hell, so, tongue-in-cheek, Tom named the valley "Paradise".

Tom and Gertie saw a very good business opportunity in opening up a goat dairy business, in the late 1920s, not too far from the Powell River Townsite. The goat dairy was called Myrtle Grove after Tom's youngest sister, Myrtle, who had died as a young child in a Toronto orphanage. All Tom's goats were certified; a goat with a good pedigree was worth as much as $100, and this was in the Great Depression.

With over 80 milking goats, the Myrtle Grove goat ranch was the largest goat dairy in the Dominion of Canada. Gertie herded the goats all over the valley to find forage; she could not sit down without getting charcoal on her skirts! Stuart and Russell milked the goats twice a day – before and after school.

Tom first delivered the milk in a Model T Ford. In 1928 he bought the first manufactured panel truck in the Powell River area. In the 1930s he bought and paid cash for a new Chevy Standard panel truck. His business was a success, as goat's milk was TB (tuberculosis) free, unlike cow's milk at this time (before pasteurization).

In 1932 the famous **Billy-Goat Smith** came down to the Myrtle Grove Goat Dairy, from Powell Lake, and bought two does for $60. He stayed for supper and Stuart Lambert recalled, years later, how nervous Billy-Goat was if anyone tried to walk behind him while he was eating his supper – perhaps the rumours were true that he had murdered someone in the States before becoming a hermit up Powell Lake!?!

In the late 1930s the goat dairy business came to an end, due to the length of the Great Depression, the Powell River Company operating part time, and competition from other dairies. While the sale of goat's milk dropped off, there was a good market for the sale of milking does throughout the Powell River area and other coastal settlements. In the following decades, the Lambert family kept goats for their own use. The goats were often found wandering in the ditches adjacent to Padgett Road.

Looking Back with Bertie van der Mark

The Open Air Market in Paradise Valley (1987-1998)

The Open Air Market started July 11, 1987 at the Farmers' Institute feed store (closed 1996) on Claridge Road. The following year the market was moved to the Safeway Mall, however, this did not work out and they moved back to Claridge Road.

In 1991 the vendors resurrected the Agricultural Association and obtained permission to build stalls etc. and operate out of the Exhibition Grounds in Paradise Valley.

In the 1980s, a Farmer's Day, organized by the Farmers' Institute, was held each fall.

In 1995, a mini one-day Fall Fair was held at the Exhibition Grounds. The Agricultural Association organized it. The mini Fall Fair was well supported and highly successful. Previously, a Fall Fair had been held, for many years, at the old Willingdon Arena, and later, at the Powell River Complex.

The Paradise Valley Fall Fair has become a successful two-day event each year. The atmosphere is reminiscent of an old-fashioned country fair.

The Trail Riders' Association holds a breed show, on the Exhibition Grounds, on the same days and dates as the Fall Fair.

Part of the ambience of the weekend market (Saturday a.m. and Sunday p.m.) is a place to meet people and relax to the wonderful music played, on a voluntary basis, by local musicians. Initially, the musical entertainment was provided by members of the Enjoyment Band, under the direction of Martin Rossander. Other musicians now come, on a regular basis, to entertain a successful Open Air Market.

The Market celebrates July 1st, Canada Day, with a special celebration of Canada's heritage. All the stall owners wear colourful costumes. Music, singing, and folk dancing are part of the celebrations.

In 1997, the Open Air Market, on the Paradise Valley Exhibition Grounds, celebrated its 10th anniversary with the cutting of an extra-large cake.

In 1998, an enlarged and improved bandstand has been built, with voluntary labour, for the musicians to perform on.

Looking Back with Mary Gwilliams (nee Nassichuk)

Homesteading in Kelly Creek (from 1924)

Settlement came to the Kelly Creek area in 1924, when a large group of Austrian settlers came via Saskatchewan to seek the sunshine of the Sunshine Coast. Many left when poor economic times hit in 1926. A few stayed on, including the Zilnics, Martiniuks, Nassichuks, and Gurlics. The families worked hard on the land, which was burned and bare due to forest fires. Forty-acre blocks of land were originally purchased in 1924 for $2.50 an acre.

Mary Gwilliams:

My parents, John and Dora Nassichuk, homesteaded an 80-acre property at Kelly Creek in 1924; that was the same year I was born. At first, we lived in a little log house, by Wolfsohn Creek, until my father built the house on our property.

We were always clearing stump piles. Blasting powder was used to get the tree stumps out. It was hard labour and all the kids had to help.

On the farm we had pigs, geese, cattle, and two horses. My father worked for the highways department, digging ditches, etc. Often he would get up at 4 a.m. and walk to work at Stillwater.

My mother was up at 4 a.m. to do the big hand wash for a family of 12 children. Doing the wash for that many children took all day. She had to wash diapers everyday. Her work never ended.

We had a root house in our basement. We kept the root vegetables and all the canning down there. My mother would put up half-gallon jars. This was the only practical size for our large family. She would put up dill pickles and sauerkraut. We would make jam from the small wild strawberries growing in the area. It would take the kids all day to pick 10 pounds of strawberries for making jam. My, they did taste good!

We had our own chickens, and Mum used two dozen eggs every day!

Someone would call at our house, about three times a year, to take an order for basic supplies to be brought up by the Union Steamship to either Lang Bay or Stillwater. Sometimes it was too rough for the boat to dock at Lang Bay. My father would hitch the horses to the wagon, to meet the boat. Our typical order for four month's supplies consisted of:

2 100-pound sacks of sugar
3 or 4 100-pound sacks of flour
1 or 2 100-pound sacks of rice
4-5 boxes of canned Pacific (condensed) milk

Looking Back with Woodrow (Woody) Runnells

Memories of Stillwater (from 1920)

Woody Runnells:

"I have lived in Stillwater most of my life. I have never been interested in a direct road from Stillwater to Vancouver. Too much traffic. We do all right the way we are.

*My father, **Wes Runnells**, was born in the State of Maine, U.S.A. in 1883. He heard about Stillwater from a timber cruiser who got acquainted with him in Seattle. He heard the pay was good. Dad came up here in the fall of 1919 and worked for Brooks, Scanlon and O'Brien as boom man until 1928.*

I was born in the State of Maine. I came up to Stillwater with my mother and sister Phyllis in the spring of 1920. We came up from Vancouver on the old Union Steamship to Stillwater. There were about five or six families and bachelors living there at that time. There was a store and post office at the hotel in Stillwater. Could get groceries there. Used to keep lots of corned beef – it was popular with the bachelors. No farming except at the McRae estate – cattle and sheep.

I was 17 when I got my first job greasing skids for McNair. It was just for the summer months. Grease was needed on the skid roads – teams of horses went over them with shingle bolts. Chinese used to load them (shingle bolts) on their backs and bring them out of the woods. They cut most of the bolts. Next job was punching bolts up a jack hammer – then onto a flat car on the railroad. They were loaded up, dumped in the salt chuck, and towed to Vancouver, up Burrard Inlet to the mill for making shakes.

(Steam) donkeys originally burned wood but later converted to oil. Steam pressure was 100-200 pounds; it would take an hour to get the steam up – loci a bit longer. Fires got started by donkeys. When there was a fire at Stillwater, everyone ran for the saltwater.

In 1933 I got a job with the Stillwater railroad. My first job was firing the loci – we used oil. In 1937 the Stillwater school was built and the kids used to come down to wave to me when I came down with a load.

There were few homesteaders up by Lewis Lake – Golden Stanley, Pallisers, and the Dukes. The train crossed Copenhagen to Horseshoe Valley. The settlers came out by walking on the line or by hitching a ride with a loci or by speeder. They ordered freight by Woodward's and we dropped it by the railroad track."

Looking Back with Ted Lloyd

Stillwater Memories (from 1937)

I worked in the woods all my adult life.

We moved out from Manitoba in the late 1930s – it was a cultural shock coming from the Prairies to Stillwater on the West Coast.

My parents, **James and Kate Lloyd**, were married in 1917 in the U.K. and had eight children: Albert, Archie, Billy, Andy, Ted, Belle, Roy, and Jean.

Ford Zilnic, our neighbour in Dropmore, Manitoba went out west and got a job with the Powell River pulp mill. Archie and Albert jumped the freight cars going west, and "rode the rods" to Vancouver. They got a job cutting shingle bolts for McNair Shingle Bolt Company in Stillwater. I came out in 1937 (11 years of age), with my mother and the other kids on the train, "riding the cushions". In 1939 Dad sold the farm. He came out with Billy and joined us in Stillwater.

There were baseball games every evening. We could play ping pong at Stillwater School and there was Old Time dancing at the Stillwater Hall with Mr. and Mrs. **Templeton**. There were shows in the Townsite at the Patricia Theatre.

The Stillwater "boys" built a third hall in 1949. **Reverend Max Warne** and my mother, **Kate Lloyd**, organized the building of the hall. The hall was used for Stillwater Logging Division public meetings, water board meetings, activity room for the school, and Christmas dinners for seniors in the community.

Men working on the boom and some of the guys working on the train lived at the Gordon Pasha Lake Hotel at Stillwater.

WWII

Bill Thompson Senior was Air Raid Officer and taught us how to put fires out. A few guys at the Stillwater powerhouse had rifles – just about shot each other! After Pearl Harbour, the Japanese were gone (employed in the shingle industry at Stillwater). Others were going into shipbuilding in Vancouver. Labour was a real premium. As kids, we got work in the summer months working the boom, assistant to the timber cruiser etc. At the end of the summer we were fired!

Albert, Archie, and Billy went into the Army; Andy and Belle into the Air Force, and I was in the Navy. After the war, Jean was in the Air Force. **Amazingly, five brothers and one sister survived the war and returned safely home to Stillwater.**

Looking Back with Ina Lloyd

Wonderful Memories of Stillwater (from 1925)

Ina Lloyd:

I arrived in Stillwater, in January 1925, with my parents Nat and Marion McNair. Jack Kelly and Wes Runnells met us at the dock.

*My father established the **Robert McNair Shingle Company** in 1924. He was superintendent of the operation. Over two hundred men were employed by the McNair Company. When he was up in Stillwater in the fall of 1924 he also arranged for our house to be built.*

After Brooks, Scanlon, and O'Brien left Stillwater in 1928, my father ran the railroad for seven years. Murray and Mel Kennedy worked as engineers on the engines.

*I attended the **Annie Bay School** from 1927-35. The school was named after Annie Frolander. Fred McRae had organized the school with Mrs. Annie Westerlund (Frolander). The school opened in 1926. It was not long before 40 students were enrolled and grades from 1-10 taught. In 1937 Annie Bay, Lang Bay, and Kelly Creek schools were closed and a modern school, Stillwater United, was opened with electricity and running water. Indoor plumbing was a source of wonder to the students.*

Bob Gela built right behind Stillwater United School. From there out going to Thunder Bay Road, mostly bachelors owned property.

People lived in the hotel, there were rooms upstairs. One time the Annie Bay School teacher lived in the hotel. Usually, the Powell River Company provided housing for the teachers. There was a store and post office in the hotel, near the front door. The store sold bread, cheese, flour, sugar, and can goods (no refrigeration). The ice cream came on Saturday nights on the Union Steamship; orders were taken in advance. We got our freight off the boat.

*The first **Stillwater Hall** was built in 1923 and burned down in 1925. After the hall was burned down, parties were held in people's homes and at the back of the hotel. In 1932 Stillwater had a new hall – it comprised of a bunkhouse. In 1949 Stillwater boys built a third hall. Max Warne and Kate Lloyd organized the building of the hall. In the year 2000 the hall was condemned and later demolished.*

Entertainment – a dance at Stillwater, alternating at Lang Bay. Men were working six days a week and socializing was done at the weekends.

Mr. Loubert and Golden Stanley owned their own land. There were about 25 houses in Stillwater (1930s).

A couple of times we'd walk over to the McRae property and see Catherine McRae. We walked everywhere – to Kelly Creek and Lang Bay.

Our house had a telephone, strictly for business. Our ring was three shorts and a long ring. Palliser's at Stillwater was one long ring. Messages from Vancouver were sent by telegram to the hotel. My parents never had a regular phone in the house.

Stillwater was a self-sufficient, bustling community in the late 1920s and 30s. We had church services there.

The Lloyd family led the influx of Prairie boys to Stillwater during the Depression years (Ina McNair married her prairie sweetheart Albert Lloyd in 1940). The Prairie boys travelled from the Prairies to Vancouver by hitching a ride on a train, then taking the Union boat to Stillwater with their last couple of dollars.

The young people in Stillwater had happy, carefree years during the Depression years. Rides on the Stillwater train were a favourite pastime, (as were) walking the boom sticks and diving into the water during the summer; bonfires on the beach near the hotel; singing around the fire; and dancing in the Stillwater hall with potluck suppers.

From 1935-37 I boarded in town (Townsite) to go to high school. I was picked up and brought home for the weekends.

Stillwater was a very special place to grow up in. The 1930s were hard times, but we enjoyed our teenage years.

Mrs. Palliser, McRae, and Phalen had cars in the 1930s. My father bought a car in 1930 when the powerhouse came in. As a special treat, my dad would take us and the McRaes to Willingdon Beach. We were asked, one time, to go to a corn roast at the Deighton farm at Myrtle Point – cars were stopping there but we didn't stop.

Stillwater was a lonely place in the 1940s with so many young men away in the services. I spent many summer days with Mrs. Molly Forrest, picking blackberries for "Jam for Britain". The berries were made into jam at Brooks School and sent overseas. All the Lloyd brothers came safely back after the war. Sadly, four Stillwater boys died overseas.

In 1945 a number of houses were torn down at Stillwater. Material from the houses, nails, and lumber were salvaged by area residents. The McNairs, Lees, and

Forrest families built their own homes with recycled materials on Scotch Fir Point Road. When the company left, the area became a dry sort and the population declined.

In the 1950s more people had cars and could drive into town. Woody Runnells and some of the younger fellows (including the Lloyd brothers) bought old cars.

The hotel was one of the last places to go – in the mid 1950s. The heart of the community went when the hotel closed down.

Almer McNair and my dad ran the store at Lang Bay for about two years. Same place as Lang Bay store is today. I bought my groceries from them. When my husband was logging at Lund, at Rassmussen Bay, I used to buy my groceries from Powell Stores in the Townsite.

The Union Steamship was direct to Vancouver. One could get logger-sized meals on board. They were first-class meals, silverware, and first-class service. In the 1930s some would take their sandwiches, as money was scarce.

When the ferry went through in the 1950s via Sechelt, one could drive a car to Vancouver or take the bus. In the early 1950s and 60s, the roads were not all paved. One time my sister was on the bus and it slid off the dirt road!

Ina Lloyd now lives in Westview (2007).

Looking Back with Maggie Poole

Powell River Pioneers – The Viertelhausen Family

Imagine leaving one of the largest cities in Europe at the beginning of the century to travel halfway around the globe to settle in a community that had only begun to emerge from the forest. The Viertelhausen family left a comfortable middle-class life in Rotterdam (Netherlands) to start a new life in Canada after Cornelia, the mother discovered that her husband had a secret mistress and a second family.

Cornelia's son, Joe, came first in 1907 and worked for the Minnesota Paper Company in Ontario before he came west to B.C., when rumours about a new paper mill reached him. He went to work for the Powell River Company as a carpenter's helper, then a surveyor, and finally into the machine shops after #1 and #2 paper machines were built.

The rest of the family, his sisters Julia and Jacoba along with his mother, followed Joe in May of 1908 and spent the winter in Québec before they travelled on to Powell River in 1910. (A third sister had married a tea planter and had travelled to the Dutch East Indies to take up the life of a plantation owner's wife).

Jacoba went to work as a postmistress at the first Powell River Post Office run by the Powell River Company. In 1912 she married Reginald Victor Stuart, a young Englishman who had worked as a scaler and bookkeeper for Canadian Puget Sound Lumber at Powell Lake. The photos from this time period show the happy couple and their families in front of the tents they were living and working in.

Shortly after their marriage, Reg was hired by H.R. MacMillan, the province's first Chief Forester and he became a forest ranger managing the Powell River/Howe Sound/Jervis Inlet area. He later became the Chief Forester and then the manager of the B.C. Loggers' Association. In 1941 he founded his own company, which came to be known as Forest Industrial Relations. As president, he negotiated the first industry-wide master collective agreement between management and forestry unions. Jacoba and Reg moved to Vancouver, but kept close connection to Powell River and their family.

Joe's second sister, Julia, had been educated in Rotterdam at a young ladies' needlework and cooking school. She was employed in Powell River by many of the small logging operations as a cook. A letter from the B.C. Iowa Company, dated 1921, recommends her as giving "satisfactory service - cooking for a crew of 16 men, showing economy and judgment in ordering supplies".

Julia married a local man, Joe Ursprung in 1911, but he eventually disappeared, leaving Julia to care for her small child. In 1916 she bought property at Lang Bay and built a small home for her and her mother to live in. The only access to the area was by boat, and the Union Steamship stopped regularly at the wharf in the bay. A trail from the wharf and the store led around the bay to the summer cabins and permanent homes of the locals.

Julia was a resourceful and independent pioneer woman. She grew a huge vegetable garden, kept chickens and goats, and worked as a cook to keep her family fed. After her sister Jacoba died, she became a second mother to her niece and nephews and they came every holiday by steamship from Vancouver.

In 1922 a huge forest fire swept through the district, burning from Myrtle Point to Stillwater. Most of the homes in the bay were destroyed. Julia and her family survived by wading out into the water and waiting for the fire to pass. Phil Stuart, Jacoba's and Reg's oldest son, remembered sitting on the beach, watching a sheet of flame sail through the air and ignite the trees on the western end of the beach. They were rescued by a tug from Myrtle Point camp.

The hardy family spent the rest of the summer in tents while their home was being rebuilt. Joe came and helped his sister, and eventually bought property from her and built his own house for his family next door.

Julia's property has remained in the family since that time. Three generations of children have spent wonderful summers on the beautiful sandy beach. Julia's old cabin was torn down to make way for new summer homes. Joe's house still stands, lovingly maintained by its current owners.

The old McQuarrie homestead, Padgett Road, Paradise Valley, Powell River; purchased by Vince and Josie Schulkowsky 1950.   Photo: Ann Bonkowski 2008
Insert: Mike Schulkowsky – farrier   Photo: Ruby Roscovich 2008

Powell River First Fifty Years: "Douglas Bay was named by Mrs. Isabel Kelly who had a farm in the bay in the early part of the century. She named it after a relative."
Walter Patrick cottages, Donkersley Road, Douglas Bay. Carvings by John D'Angio. Buildings demolished 2007-8. New house – Johnsons (Laura Johnson nee Patrick).   Photo: B.A. Lambert 2007

Douglas Bay property, Walter & Hannah Patrick (1920s) – end of the bay. The property was fenced for livestock. Purchased by the Munroes after WWII. Insert photo: Hannah Patrick and grandson Don 1931.
Photos: Laura Johnson

Douglas Bay summer cottages 1930s. Walter & Hannah Patrick owned land at Douglas Bay; their four children: Madge (MacGillivray), Nora (McQuarrie), Walter, and Syd either bought parcels of land from their parents or were given land as wedding gifts. Cottages – far distance to near: Donkersleys/Stanleys (D'Angios)/Cades (B. Black)/ Chesires (B. Smith)/Arnold & Nora McQuarrie (D. McQuarrie)/Syd Patrick (P. Black).
Far right: Mrs. Pritchard (Senior). Photo: Pritchard album

Douglas Bay summer cottages 1940s.
(L to R) (1) Pritchard house (previously owned by Madge MacGillivray (Patrick).   (2) Jack
Waugh/Hunters/Hollingshead/Stradoffs.   (3) Gladys Donkersley/Prices/Joe Borer/Oslines/Durlings – 1969,
original house moved to rear of property.   Photo: Pritchard collection

1940s skating pond, Lang's farm, Douglas Bay. Insert: Tom & Pearl Lang 1950s.
Previous owners: Kellys (1900s)/O'Connors/Williams/16 acre field sold to Lambert/Palmer/Gwilliams 1970s. Lot
purchased by Ed Melnyk 1970s.   Kelly Point owners: Langs/Walter Patrick (Junior)/Bill MacGillivray/
Pat Buhler (MacGillivray).   Photo: Pritchard collection

Anderson family, Irene Short's property, Lang Bay 1942.
Back Row (L to R) Gertrude Lusk/Shirley Lusk/Jim Anderson/Lloyd Anderson. Middle Row: Alina Aho/Irene Short
(Anderson). Front Row: Gloriette Aho/Shirley Anderson. Photo taken by Eleanor Anderson

Cooper summer home, Patrick Road, Douglas Bay 1942.
Back Row: (L to R) Mrs. McLeod/Gary McLeod/?/ Graeme Cooper/Russell M. Cooper. Front: Flora
Cooper/Gertrude Evans/Brenda Cooper/Myron McLeod (Note: Almer McNair bought property adjacent to Patrick
Road from Jack Wilson in 1950 – moved on 1958). Photo: Graeme Cooper

Looking Back with Bev Falconer (Carrick)

The Townsite – Then and Now

Jo Allman and I walked through the Townsite recently and, as old friends do, we reminisced. She and I first walked along these streets over seventy years ago. Of course, when we grew up here, it was not called the Townsite – it was Powell River, and it was the hub of the universe! Today Townsite people go to Westview for all their shopping, medical appointments, entertainment, and business dealings. In the early days they came from the other districts to the Townsite for these things – and to shop in the modern Company Store, a big department store on three levels. We did walk the beach trail twice a week for swimming lessons at Willingdon Beach, and very occasionally we took the bus to Westview to visit a friend. But aside from that, everything we needed or wanted was close by. There were few cars in town and we really didn't need one. Milk, eggs, vegetables, bread, meat, and newspapers were delivered to the door. The Company store would also deliver groceries. And when we went to Vancouver we took a taxi to the wharf. It would be convenient today to have our workplace and all the necessities of life so centralized. Just think how much money we could save on gas!

Starting at Brooks School, Jo and I walked along Marine Avenue – or Ocean View Avenue as it was called in the early years. Some sections of the sidewalk still have Ocean View Avenue imprinted in the cement. As we passed the old golf course we remembered how, as kids, we signed up for golf lessons in the summer and rode our sleighs down its snowy slopes in the winter – despite threats from the greens keeper. Now overgrown, the golf course is a popular place to pick blackberries and take dogs for a run. It is a great area to have, given the number of pets around now. Out of the 20 houses around my childhood home, I can think of just three dogs – and they were free to roam around – no need to walk a dog in those days. Our neighbour had an old black cocker spaniel, Rip. His favourite place to sleep was in the middle of Maple Avenue; the school bus, and the occasional car, had to drive around him because he wasn't going to budge!

Continuing our walk, we passed the two blocks of fine big homes just south of the tennis courts, "Bosses' Row". Only superintendents and managers of the Powell River Company, and Dr. Lyons, lived here. When the Company houses were sold many residents, including mill management, moved to Westview and "outsiders" (no longer necessarily mill workers) moved in. And then new owners throughout the Townsite made renovations which brought some individuality to homes that were formerly quite uniform.

There was another change too. The Townsite had a reputation of being rather exclusive and self-sufficient. It took time for newcomers to feel accepted into established social groups. Possibly this was due to our limited social contact with the outside world; at that time our only connection with Vancouver (or anywhere else) was by boat. Fortunately, people can change and now we are considered to be a very friendly, welcoming place. With these changes the community gradually lost the feel of a closed company town.

As we passed the tennis courts we thought of the days when a prevailing wind would carry fly ash from the mill. It covered the courts and made tennis balls black and also soiled laundry on clotheslines. That wind would also waft the strong fumes of sulphur to our nostrils. Thank goodness those two occurrences are things of the past.

Farther along we stood in front of the former Company Guest House. We thought of the gracious accommodation visiting Company executives were provided with in the early days of the Townsite. Their stay might even include a trip up Powell Lake to Rainbow Lodge. In later years, when time became a precious business commodity, attending meetings would be a matter of flying in and flying out. It was rather a sad loss of an institution and a slower way of life. We also remembered the magnificent gardens around the Guest House and the old Resident Manager's home in their glory days. Who could forget the high stone walls absolutely covered in purple, yellow, lavender, and white rock flowers. The garden crew had a greenhouse and nursery to supply these and other gardens, including Dwight Hall. The Company hired local UBC (University of British Columbia) students for the summer and some of them helped with the extra summer work in the gardens. Jo and I thought, with appreciation, of just how much the **Powell River Company** did to keep our **Townsite** a **model community**.

This Ocean View Avenue walk had been our Friday night route to the **Patricia Theatre**. We used to sit near the back row so we could watch everyone come in and see who had come with whom. The theatre was packed and we knew almost everyone. It was a great meeting place and was the thing to do in those pre-television days. The Patricia Theatre is still a popular place because Ann Nelson has been creative in order to compete with TV, videos, and DVDs. She offers foreign films and documentaries, stage acts, and speakers. On occasion when we were teenagers, if we had some babysitting money, we might get a soda or float after the show in **Josie Mitchell's Sweet Shoppe**. Also, on a special occasion, my mom would get me to ride my bike down to the Sweet Shoppe after supper to pick up a pint brick of ice cream for dessert. We lived at the other end of town, so I pedalled furiously to get home before it melted. Fridges were a rarity.

Walking along Maple Avenue for our return trip, we missed the old maple trees that formerly lined the street. They had seemed to embrace the houses and keep them in block families. But with the steady increase of car ownership after WWII, it became necessary to widen the streets. So in the 1960s, to accommodate more traffic, the trees were taken out. Also, people had to build their own garages as originally there were only a couple per block. People started getting fridges too, as metal now became available. It was no longer required to build warplanes and warships. When people acquired cars and fridges, their shopping habits changed. There was no need to phone a meat order in every day in the summer, or be home when the bread or vegetable truck came around. It wasn't necessary to get milk delivered every day to the porch where, in the winter the cat could lick the frozen cream as it expanded out of the bottle. Now a week's supply of groceries could be picked up with the car and be kept cool and sanitary in the fridge.

The Townsite has kept within its boundaries. The last of the original homes were completed around 1930. Then in 1946 a row of duplex homes were built on Willow Avenue for the returning servicemen. As the baby boomers started arriving thick and fast (27 on those two blocks) that area was well known as Stork's Alley, so well known in fact, that one couple received a letter addressed to them simply at "Stork's Alley, Powell River"! In recent years, four or five homes have been built on vacant lots on Marine Avenue. Also, there were three apartment buildings constructed on Maple Avenue. As we walked by them we couldn't help but think of the magnificent big pussy willow tree that was demolished to build the first apartment. Scores of children climbed that tree to get fat pussy willows. It was a rite of spring. Now the tree is gone and there are few children in the Townsite. Only in our memories we see the blocks filled with children playing marbles, jacks, "Run Sheep Run", Alarie, and skipping on the car-free streets.

We finished our walk where we began, at Brooks School, and realized what a centre of community activity it is with the restaurant, the Jazz/Dinner evening, Oyster Fest, live Metropolitan Opera videos, speakers, and concerts. I was curious to find out in what other ways newcomers to the Townsite meet and socialize now, and how they are getting a feel of community. During the 1940s the Red Cross and the Junior Red Cross kept us involved as we got together to knit, pick blackberries and make jam, have sales and raffles and all sorts of money-making projects for the war effort. There was also church involvement, and summer days at Willingdon Beach where an average of 600 people congregated daily. And Dwight Hall was our entertainment centre. Rooms downstairs housed the library, Scout, Guide, and Lodge meetings. Besides dances and plays upstairs, there were school Christmas concerts for the war effort held here, plus badminton, fall fairs, and music festivals – all punctuated by the loud clanking of the steam-heated registers. But life changes. So what are the new ways? Besides all the activities at Brooks, there are art shows and special events at the newly-decorated and charming Rodmay Hotel – and morning coffee at Ljubos. Some new residents tell of involvement with Ratepayer's meetings and volunteer work with the Heritage Society. I was talking to some new friends who were able to obtain the original plans of their Townsite house and are trying to keep their decorating true to those. They know many other couples who have also moved to the area for the lifestyle, have bought heritage homes and are making sensitive renovations. When they get together, a favourite topic of conversation is where they have found a door, window, or fitting authentic to the era. This common project gives a feeling of pride in their community and a sense of belonging.

The Townsite really was a model town. The Townsite Gang, a division of the mill, consisting of crews of all the tradesmen required (35 in total), kept the houses painted; sidewalks, roofs, and fences in good repair. Houses were painted every seven years. I remember when carpenters came to remove the old zinc drain boards and replaced them with "modern" varnished wood. The gardens, hedges, and lawns around public buildings were kept well manicured. This encouraged people to take pride in their own yards, as did the block garden contests.

After the homes were sold to the residents in 1955, many people made alterations. Other people moved to the districts to build their own homes, and a number of new owners used their purchase for a rental investment. After some years these rental houses, and many of the other homes that were no longer getting the TLC from the Townsite Gang, started to look very neglected and overgrown. Many of them still do. But now there are a lot of newcomers who are very interested in the heritage homes and are putting a lot of work into renovations. The **Townsite Heritage Society** is giving enthusiastic leadership. And dedicated individuals like Ann Nelson, Dr. Davis and many other volunteers are beautifying the downtown core of old buildings and gardens. Now there is a definite feeling that a charming new Townsite is emerging from the ashes.

Frank Haslam (centre) 100th birthday party 2004. Photo: B.A. Lambert
Left of centre: Joyce Lawler (daughter). Right of centre: Doug Lawler

Looking Back with Colin Palmer

Memories of Powell River 1965 – 2008

1965 – 1972

I arrived here in **1965** just after the building of the Kraft Mill was announced. Started as a teacher at Brooks and noticed a large influx of young teachers from all over the world. It seemed that every woman in town was pregnant as my wife Ann was constantly going to showers.

Many new houses and apartments were being built by contractors or homeowners. Joyce Avenue was a gravel road from Lytton Street to the south end of Joyce. Real estate companies were very busy and banks were giving 25-year mortgages for 6.25%.

Very small bus service, as most people used cars or trucks. Remember being stared at when we went for a walk.

Overseas messages sent by CN Telegraph office near where River City Coffee is now. Overseas phone calls had to be booked with time limits on them.

Only the south harbour existed with quite a large fishing fleet. Also, there was one long jetty with a large warehouse on the end.

Five most important people in town were the Mill Manager, the Mill Union President, the Judge, the Mayor, and the School Board Chair. The Regional District didn't exist until 1968.

Ferry and road trips to Vancouver were like the Monte Carlo Rally every Friday night and Sunday night.

The local passenger plane to Vancouver was a DC-3 (Dakota). A lot of people had their own aircraft.

First Nations sat at the back of the Patricia Theatre in a separate section.

There were significant pollution problems at the mill with few controls. Raw-coloured pulp and any waste went straight into the sea. Pentachlorophenols washed into sea from sawmill. Air pollution was so bad, cars had to pass through car washers specially built at mill parking exits – everyone thought this was normal.

Men and women couldn't sit together in a pub, and all drinkers had to sit down and be served. This resulted in many private drinking clubs or bars.

Garbage disposal was a landfill at Squatters Creek. The whole creek was eventually filled in. Community sewage ran through pipes into the sea at Grief Point, Willingdon Beach, and below the Townsite. Wildwood had an effective sewage lagoon. Recycling programs did not exist.

Powell River Anti-Pollution Association formed in 1969. Mainly in response to mill pollution and a proposal to build a bigger pipe at Grief Point to send all the community's sewage into the sea. It was supposed to go "away". Many alternatives proposed and acted upon for community and mill pollution control.

1972 – 1975

North harbour built and south harbour realigned. Decision made to keep airport where it is. The recreation complex was built. Two secondary sewage plants built. Powell River's first recycling operation supported by Council. Significant clean-up programs at the mill. Regional District government developed services in the Electoral Areas.

1975 – 1981

Major study was done in 1977 by local economic interests plus federal government to warn the community that industrial growth would be slowing down and hiring fewer people in the future. Gillies Bay iron mine closed down and MacMillan Bloedel predicted fewer machines and fewer workers in the future. There were probably about 3,000 workers in the mill at that time. Few people believed the report. Most new ideas were for big projects to replace a big industry. e.g.:
- a plywood plant   - a gas pipeline and fertilizer plant   - #12 paper machine
- a federal prison   - a Boeing aircraft plant at Black Point

1981 – 1987

Major layoff happened at mill – 250 workers who were all the youngest ones. A whole generation left Powell River permanently. 1986 Census showed a population drop of 7.5%. There has been nothing like it before or since. There was downsizing at Municipal Hall and a reduction in services. There was a major recession in B.C. and Canada. Interest rates were at 21% for loans and mortgages. Some people turned up at local banks and left their house keys on the counter – then left town.

Kathaumixw started in 1984. Powell River declared Blackberry Capital of Canada. Powell River declared Diving Capital of Canada. Powell River declared a Nuclear-Free Zone. Three-month Municipal Union strike.

1987 – 2008

During this period, mill work force reduced down to about 500. There were many early retirements. Kraft mill and sawmill shut down. Only three paper machines left. There was a succession of different owners.

The average age in Powell River was now 47. Only 120 children were in **all** kindergarten classes. Ten schools closed down in this period. **Total population now less than it was in 1983**.

Increase in number of small businesses and an influx of retirees from across Canada.

Powell River – The Decline of a One Industry Town

Barbara Lambert (Rathbone) 2009

"Looking Back, **I have witnessed, during the last four decades, dramatic changes in the economy of the Powell River area, from an affluent town with 2000+ workforce in the paper mill (early 1970s) to 350 in 2009**.

When I arrived as a teacher in 1968, I had great difficulty finding rental accommodation in Powell River. This is a story told over, and over again by people seeking jobs in this area from as far back as the 1920s. This is the reason people camped on Willingdon Beach in tents during the early twenties.

In 1969 #10 paper machine came online, over 2000 people were working for "Mac and Blo"." In the late 1960s the school system was bursting at the seams. Westview was continually expanding with more and more subdivisions.

It seemed that every household had two cars and a boat in the driveway. **In the early 1970s this town was rich. I was not to know that I was seeing the last of the "good times"**.

The Townsite continued to have a viable commercial centre in the late 1960s and early 1970s: the Overwaitea store, Bank of Montreal, Bank of Commerce, Powell River Credit Union, Rodmay pub and restaurant, Granada restaurant, pharmacy, hairdressing salon, coffee shop, bowling alley, and the historic Patricia Theatre. After Overwaitea moved to Westview in 1973 the Townsite commercial sector began to decline. There were still a few shops open in Cranberry, but the business area had fallen on "hard times" as **the majority of the business and services had moved to Westview**.

For six decades, from 1910 – 1970, this town had grown, and expanded, from a Company Town (1910 - 1955), to a Municipality which included the old Townsite and the surrounding villages and districts. **In the 1980s and 90s, everything was contracting in a one industry town.** Old-time families boasted three and four generations working in the Powell River mill – **now this was to end, as young people left town to find work elsewhere. Schools closed, houses became empty, and the town was full of old folks.**

In the new Millennium came a new economy with Powell River becoming an attractive retirement centre for newcomers from Vancouver and around the world. Just as the retired employees of the Powell River Company stayed to enjoy the beauty of the area and small town values (created by its semi-isolation), newcomers choose to live here for the same values plus the fact that housing prices were a bargain. Some children returned to find jobs in the health care and service industry. Home based computer jobs gave people the freedom to live in an isolated area. The Academy of Music and Vancouver Island University attracted professionals to locate in Powell River. Kathaumixw (from 1984) has brought tourists every two years to our community to enjoy a world class music festival.

Martin Rossander (2008):

"Looking Back: 2,500 employees reduced to 500 with promises of more reductions. **The income in the community has not kept pace with the reductions."**

Jack Banham (2008):

"Looking Back: Mill a disaster to what it used to be. Used to work at the mill as an apprentice at the weekends. Future of the mill – not that good. Present company buying all their chips. Sold electricity to some other outfit. Not making much newsprint – mainly specialty papers.

In the 1950s the Powell River Company was in its heyday."

Barbara Lambert:

Looking Back - We can enjoy Powell River's history by strolling around the old Townsite, largely preserved with its original building as a company town (with the exception of Riverside - demolished in the late 1950s). The historic Patricia Theatre continues to show movies and the re-furnished Rodmay Heritage Hotel is open for business – drop in for drinks at the McKinney Pub and Eatery (named after the first owner Andrew McKinney). See Dr. Henderson's house, recently purchased by the Townsite Heritage Society. Stop in at Cranberry and see many of the original buildings of a thriving shopping area from the early decades of the Twentieth Century. Take a walk on the Willingdon Beach Trail and imagine the cluster of tents and cabins near the beach in the early 1920s when "newcomers" were on a "wait list" for Townsite housing. Drop in at the Powell River Historical Museum & Archives and see the beautiful cedar baskets made by Sliammon First Nations. Conclude your tour by visiting Wildwood; drive past the Italian Hall and remember the young Italian men, 100 years ago, who built the foundations of the Powell River Company Townsite and mill.

The Powell River paper mill has brought great wealth to an isolated community on the B.C. coast. Its lasting legacy is Powell River – our town.

Nat McNair & Ina McNair – Stillwater pioneers. Back Row: Elaine Lloyd/Laurie Lloyd/Bob Millar
Front Row: Ina Lloyd (McNair)/Nat McNair/Lois Millar.   Photo: Ina Lloyd 1973

Viertelhausen family, living in a tent at Haslam Lake. Joe Viertelhausen worked for the Powell River Company.
Jacoba Stuart (Viertelhausen) was the first postmistress in the Townsite.
(L to R) Joe Viertelhausen/Cornelia Viertelhausen/Reg Stuart/Jacoba Stuart
Photo taken by Julia Ursprung (Viertelhausen) 1910

Stuart Lambert's 80th birthday – Lambert farmhouse, Paradise Valley 1994. Old-timers (L to R) Bob Vonarx/ Russell Lambert/Stuart Lambert/Oren Olson. Stuart was known as the "goat man" and Russell as the "egg man". Photo: B.A. Lambert

Open Air Market, Paradise Valley, Powell River, July 1, 2008. Clansman Pipe Band BR 164 performing at opening ceremonies. Centre (seated) – (L to R) Old friends - Ruby Roscovich/Barbara Ann Lambert. Photo: Ann Bonkowski

Information about the Editor

Barbara Ann Lambert

Barbara Ann Lambert was born in Yorkshire, England at the beginning of World War II. She lived with her parents, Ernest and Margaret Rathbone, and older sister, Joyce. She attended St. Oswald's Elementary School, Guiseley and Prince Henry's Grammar School, Otley, Yorkshire. In 1952 the family moved to Lancaster, Lancashire where relatives on both sides of the family lived.

After attending Lancaster Girls' Grammar School, Barbara trained as a teacher at Wentworth Castle Training College, near Barnsley, in Yorkshire. She completed her education at Liverpool University, England and the University of British Columbia (UBC), Canada. In 1975 Barbara received her Bachelor of Education degree in History and Special Education from UBC.

In 1966 Barbara immigrated to Canada. After accepting a teaching position in Powell River in 1968, Barbara met and later married Stuart Lambert. They have a daughter, Ann.

Barbara Lambert's teaching career covered 35 years in England, Germany and British Columbia, Canada. She retired in 1997 from the Powell River School District.

In 1998 Barbara self-published her first book on local history: *In Paradise: West Coast Short Stories, 1890 – 1960*.

In December 2000 Barbara self-published her second book: *Chalkdust & Outhouses: West Coast Schools, 1893 – 1950*.

In 2001 Stuart Lambert died at age 87. In memory of her husband, Barbara published in 2002, her third book through Trafford Publishing: *Rusty Nails & Ration Books: Great Depression & WWII Memories, 1929 – 1945*.

In 2005 Barbara published her first children's book through Trafford Publishing: *The Mystery of Billy-Goat Smith*.

In 2006 Barbara published her fifth book through Trafford Publishing: *Old-Time Stories: Billy-Goat Smith, Powell River Co. Xmas, Mr. Dippie & Others*.

BIBLIOGRAPHY

BOOKS

Berton, Pierre. *The Great Depression, 1929-39*. Toronto: McClelland & Stewart, 1990.

Boyer, Karen R. *An Economic Base Study of the Powell River Region*. Powell River, B.C.: Powell River Progress, 1977.

Broadfoot, Barry. *Ten Lost Years, 1929-1939: Memories of the Canadians Who Survived the Depression*. Toronto: Doubleday Canada, 1973.

Carlson, Linda. *Company Towns of the Pacific Northwest*. University of Washington Press, 2003.

Granatstein, J.L. *A Nation Forged in Fire: Canadians and the Second World War, 1939-45*. Toronto: Lester & Orpen Dennys, 1989.

Harbord, Heather. *Desolation Sound: A History*. Madeira Park, B.C.: Harbour Publishing, 2007.

Kennedy, Dorothy, and Randy Bouchard. *Sliammon Life, Sliammon Lands*. Vancouver: Talonbooks, 1983.

Lambert, Barbara Ann. *In Paradise: West Coast Short Stories, 1890-1960*. Nanaimo, B.C.: privately printed (Le Print Express), 1998.

Lambert, Barbara Ann. *Chalkdust & Outhouses: West Coast Schools, 1893-1950*. Friesens Printers, 2000.

Lambert, Barbara Ann. *Rusty Nails & Ration Books: Great Depression & WWII Memories, 1929-1945*. Victoria: Trafford Publishing, 2002.

Lambert, Barbara Ann. *The Mystery of Billy-Goat Smith* (children's book). Victoria: Trafford Publishing, 2005.

Lambert, Barbara Ann. *Old Time Stories: Billy-Goat Smith, Powell River Co. Xmas, Mr. Dippie & Others*. Victoria: Trafford Publishing, 2006.

Levez, Emma. *People of the White City: Stories from the Powell River Mill*. Powell River, B.C.: NorskeCanada, Powell River Division, 2002.

Marsh, James H., ed. *The Canadian Encyclopedia*. Edmonton: Hurtig Publishers Ltd., 1985.

Mobley, Carla. *Mysterious Powell Lake: A Collection of Historical Tales*. Hancock House, 1984.

Powell River's First 50 Years. Powell River, B.C.: *Powell River News*, 1960.

Southern, Karen and Peggy Bird. *Pulp, Paper and People: 75 Years of Powell River*. Powell River, B.C.: Powell River Heritage Research Association, 1988.

Thompson, Bill. *Once Upon A Stump*. Powell River, B.C.: Powell River Heritage Research Association, 1988.

Thompson, Bill. *Boats, Bucksaws and Blisters*. Powell River, B.C.: Powell River Heritage Research Association, 1990.

ARTICLES & PERIODICALS

"1912-1987 MacMillan Bloedel: 75 Years of Papermaking," *Powell River News*, April 10, 1987.

Powell River Digester, Powell River Company.

Powell River News & Town Crier, Glacier Ventures.

Frank and Johanna de Jong came to Canada on May 24, 1952 with their eight children: Joan, Mary, Gerry, John, Helena, Adrian, Nellie (carried by Frank), and three-month old Anna (in a bassinet on the plane). This photo was taken at Schipol Airport, Amsterdam, Holland. They travelled from Montreal to Vancouver by train; then by boat to the Powell River Company dock.

This photo of the ten de Jong siblings (Cathy and Frank Junior were born in Powell River) was taken in 2001 at Johanna de Jong's funeral in Powell River. Back row: (L to R): John, Frank (Junior), Adrian, Maria de Jong Front row: (L to R): Anna (Daly), Helena (O'Brien), Cathy (Francis), Gerry (Solowan), Joan (Bisson), Nellie (Holuboch). Photos: de Jong collection.

Index